AMERICA'S
SEWING BOOK

AMERICA'S SEWING BOOK

Sandra Ley

drawings by Olga Ley

CHARLES SCRIBNER'S SONS
NEW YORK

Dedication

This book is dedicated to the memory of my father, Willy Ley, who surprisingly, knew almost as much about sewing as he did about everything else.

Acknowledgements

I wish to thank the following people who helped make this book possible:

Olga Ley, my mother, whose endless patience makes everything possible.
Ruth Ramsay, who started me sewing in the first place.
All the manufacturers of fabrics, sewing machines and sewing notions who provided me with invaluable information and material.

Contents

AMERICA'S
SEWING BOOK

1

BASIC NEEDS

How many times have you spent days if not weeks or months shopping for the perfect dress (or blouse, or coat), and despite the fact that you know exactly what you want, not been able to find it?

Or perhaps you do find it at a price you don't want to pay. So then you settle for something you don't like as much, or simply give up and do without. How often do you find your child outgrowing an expensive new dress six months after you bought it?

It's usually on one of these occasions that you find yourself wishing you could make the garment yourself. This way you could have exactly what you want, made in the fabric and color that are just what you had in mind.

So you go into a fabric store or the sewing department of your favorite store. You are immediately faced with an overwhelming array of pattern books, fabrics, zippers, and threads, and you just don't know where to start.

Which pattern to use? And, if you do find a pattern you like, how do you know what size to buy? And what kind of fabric will work with that pattern? Does the garment have to be lined, or interlined, and if so, what with?

It usually at this point that the salespeople in the store prove to be no help at all. Over and over I have heard a saleswoman tell a bewildered customer "Just look in the pattern books." So you do—only to discover that pattern companies speak a language all their own; once again you simply don't know where to start.

Added to this is the fact that there has been a revolution in home sewing in the past few years, with the result that there are hundreds of new products on the market. Even the experienced sewer can become confused.

How often have you wished for new draperies or slipcovers, only to be put off by the prices and selection of fabrics available ready-made?

Have you ever found a ready-made dress that was exactly what you were looking for, only to find that it doesn't quite fit? Do you know why it doesn't fit, and is the alteration required minor or is it a major reconstruction job? With good professional dressmakers becoming harder and harder to find, the alternative is to learn to do it yourself.

Once you do start to learn to sew yourself, you will make a wonderful discovery. Sewing isn't just useful and economical, it's a marvelous form of creative self-expression. Every woman likes to be complimented on her clothes, but the satisfaction to be gained when you are complimented on something thought up and made yourself is hundredfold.

This book will teach you chapter by chapter exactly what you need to know to get started, even if you have never sewn before. It will show you how to look for patterns and how to find your correct size (*your* size, not a manufacturer's approximation of your size). It will teach you to become familiar with the ever-growing number of fabrics so you will be able to choose the perfect fabric for the garment you want to make. Then you will learn the proper way to lay out and cut the pattern, which is sometimes 50 percent of the job and is always essential to the look of the finished garment. After a first simple project you will move on to more detailed clothes and you will learn the professional tricks of both the couturier and the factory. Before you are finished you will be able to make a tailored coat or jacket—that's not really as formidable as it sounds!

You will learn to sew for children, learning in particular how to make clothes that grow with the child.

You will also learn enough about clothing construction to be able to tell if a ready-made garment fits you properly (not always a simple thing to do). If it doesn't fit, you will know whether the alterations required are worth the price of the article. A bargain is not a bargain if you have to practically remake it in order to be able to wear it.

Finally you will learn how to decorate your house or apartment at minimal cost with maximum results, using just fabric and your sewing machine and your new-found knowledge.

Before you can start any kind of sewing project, you will need to buy a number of tools. I have listed as essential the ones that you will need right away; the nonessential ones can be acquired later, after you decide how much sewing you are going to be doing. The initial expense may seem large, but these things will pay for themselves as soon as you discover the economy and pleasure of making your own clothes.

If you can, the best way to start is to set aside a place to keep everything together so that it is at hand when you need it. A separate sewing room is ideal, but in these days of small apartments and houses this is not always possible—a corner of a room will serve.

THE SEWING MACHINE

The first and most important piece of equipment you will need is a good sewing machine. Since a sewing machine is a major investment, shop around carefully before you decide which one to buy. There are many different types available, and the one you will need will depend on several factors. How much you want to spend? How much space do you have available? How much and what kind of sewing do you plan to do?

If price is a prime consideration, second-hand machines are available from reputable manufacturers, and many of them will rent a machine to you with an option to buy. This way you can use the machine and get used to it before you purchase it. Console models, which take up space, are usually heavier than portables and are more suitable for sewing heavy fabrics. Portable sewing machines can be kept in a closet and set up when you need to use them. They are suitable for most home sewing, and if you plan to sew only occasionally. A console model comes with a cabinet, into which the machine folds up, so that the cabinet becomes a decorative piece of furniture. When choosing a cabinet, select one for sewing comfort and utility rather than for decorative features alone. Shop around, ask questions, and try many different machines before you buy.

Modern sewing machines come in three categories. There are those that just do straight stitching, which is a straight line of stitches. These machines also sew forward and backward, and have an adjustable stitch length. Zigzag machines sew both in a side-to-side stitch and in a plain straight stitch. Automatic machines sew a large variety of decorative and embroidery stitches as well as straight stitch and zigzag.

Attachments can be bought for straight-stitch machines that will enable them to make zigzag stitches and buttonholes. The larger automatic machines have these stitches built into them.

Always buy from a reputable manufacturer who will give a guarantee and provide service when and if you need it. When you buy the machine, be sure that you understand how to operate it. Find out which attachments come with the machine and which are available if you want them later. The most important thing is to be comfortable with the operation of the machine, as a well-cared for machine will last you a long time.

Essential Attachments

If your machine does not come with the following attachments, or with them built into the machine, you will have to buy them separately.

Adjustable Zipper Foot—The zipper foot replaces the usual pressure foot and enables you to sew a straight stitch close to a raised edge. The foot can be adjusted to the right or left of the needle and is used for inserting most zippers.

Invisible Zipper Foot—This foot is used for inserting the new "invisible" zipper and is the only attachment not purchased from the sewing machine manufacturer. It is sold in the notions department along with the brand of zipper they are meant for. Made of plastic, it is used in place of the regular pressure foot to apply the invisible zipper. For more information about the invisible zipper foot, see page 191.

Seam Guide—The seam guide attaches to the bed of the machine, to the right of the needle, and is used to regulate the width of the seam as you stitch.

Buttonholer—The buttonholer is attached to the machine to make buttonholes. It comes with different templates for making different-size buttonholes. This attachment is not needed if your machine makes buttonholes automatically.

Needles—Machine needles come in different sizes for use with different-weight fabrics. Size 11 is the lightest, for use with lightweight fabrics; size 14 is the most often-used, for use with medium-weight fabrics;

size 16 is the heaviest, for use with heavyweight and pile fabrics. These sizes are also available in "ball point" needles, for use when sewing knits or synthetic fabrics. Special needles for sewing leather are available in the same sizes. Always have a few extra needles of different sizes on hand in case you break the one you are sewing with.

Bobbins—The size bobbin you need will be determined by the kind of machine you have. Have several on hand so that you can have a bobbin for every different color thread you are using. Always wind on an empty bobbin; never wind one color thread over a bobbin that is already partially wound with another color.

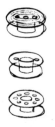

Tools—You will need a small screwdriver, a lint brush, and sewing machine oil if they do not come with your machine.

Nonessential Attachments

The need for the following attachments will depend on the kind of sewing you are doing. Some of them come with the machine, others will have to be purchased separately.

Hemming Foot—The hemming foot replaces the pressure foot and is used to turn a small hem as you sew. It can also be used to attach lace and ruffles. It is not used for sewing a skirt hem or similar hem, which is several inches deep.

General Purpose Throat Plate—The general purpose throat plate is used on zigzag machines when sewing in a zigzag stitch.

Binder Foot—The binder foot is used with a straight or zigzag stitch to apply bias binding to an unfinished edge.

Roller Foot—The roller foot replaces the pressure foot and is used when sewing slippery fabrics to prevent them from sliding.

Ruffler—The ruffler makes pleated or gathered ruffles automatically as you stitch.

Tucker—The tucker makes tucks in widths from ⅛ inch to 1 inch as you stitch.

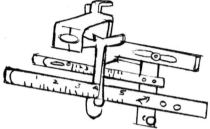

Edge Stitcher (for straight stitching only)—The edge stitcher is used for joining and inserting lace and making small tucks for the width of a pin to ¼-inch wide.

Gathering Foot—The gathering foot is used to gather the fabric along the row of stitching.

There are other attachments available for doing a variety of jobs. Be sure to ask when you buy your machine about all the attachments available for it.

Understanding Your Machine

Your most important guide in understanding your particular machine is the instruction manual that comes with the machine. Before you buy, be sure that all aspects of the machine are demonstrated to you and that you understand them fully.

How to Thread the Machine

To thread the machine you have to thread the needle and the bobbin case. To thread the needle, follow the instructions given with your machine, with the take-up lever at the highest point, threading from the spool, through the thread guide, between the needle-thread tension discs, through the thread guide, through the take-up lever, through the bottom thread guides, and through the needle. Not all machines thread the needle the same way. It can be done from left to right, from right to left, or from front to back. Follow the instructions given with your machine.

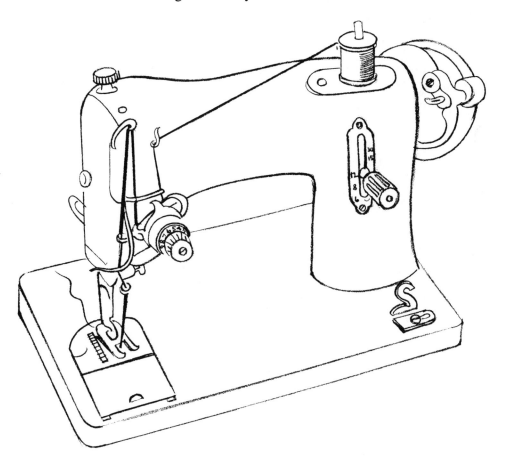

Bobbin cases thread in a clockwise or counterclockwise direction, depending on the machine. Be sure that you learn which direction is correct for your machine, because an improperly threaded bobbin will allow the thread to slip out of the threading notches, resulting in uneven stitches.

Once the needle and bobbin threads are in place, bring the bobbin thread up in the following manner. Close the throat plate over the bobbin, leaving a few inches of the bobbin thread extending out. Hold the needle thread in your left hand and turn the wheel of the machine with your right hand so that needle goes below the throat plate. Continue turning the wheel to raise the needle. The bobbin thread will be looped over the needle thread that you are holding in your left hand. Pull the looped thread out to straighten it and you are ready to sew.

How to Wind the Bobbin

Some of the newer machines wind the bobbin directly in the bobbin case, but most machines have a separate bobbin winder on the side or on top of the machine. Follow the instruction manual and always start with an empty bobbin, using the same type and color thread that you are using for the upper threading. Be sure that the bobbin winds the thread evenly, as an uneven bobbin will affect the stitching. If for some reason the bobbin does not wind evenly, call this to the attention of the sewing machine representative. It may require an adjustment that you cannot make yourself. Be sure not to wind the bobbin too full; most machines will stop the winding process when the bobbin is full.

Thread Tension

There are two thread tension controls on the machine, upper and lower. They control the needle and bobbin threads as they interlock, and the thread tension must be even or the stitches will not hold. Test the tension by sewing a straight line of stitching with a size 14 needle and the machine set for 10 stitches per inch. If the tension is correct, the loops will be even, as shown. If the bottom thread is in a straight line, as shown, the upper tension is too loose. If a straight line forms on the top, the upper tension is too tight.

The bobbin tension is usually set at the factory and very rarely needs adjusting. Most tension changes are made from the needle tension. To increase the top tension turn the tension wheel clockwise. To loosen the top tension, turn the tension wheel counterclockwise. If this does not correct the tension, you will have to adjust the bobbin tension. This is controlled by a small screw on the bobbin case or shuttle. To increase the tension turn the screw to the right; to loosen the tension, turn the screw to the left. Instructions for sewing with different fabrics will sometimes call for a change in the tension. Always make these changes with the needle tension.

How to Adjust the Pressure

The pressure dial or thumbscrew affects the amount of pressure that the pressure foot exerts on the fabric while sewing. If the pressure is not adjusted correctly, the fabric will not feed into the machine easily. If the pressure is too light, the fabric will slip and the seams will not be even. If the pressure is too heavy, it will affect the length of the stitch and mar the surface of the fabric. In general, the amount of pressure will be determined by the weight and thickness of the fabric. Lightweight fabrics require light pressure, medium-weight fabrics need medium pressure, and heavyweight fabrics, heavy pressure.

To test the pressure, stitch without any thread in the machine through two layers of fabric cut on the lengthwise grain of the fabric. To understand lengthwise grain, see page 128. If the seam edges remain even, the pressure is correct. If not, adjust the pressure until the fabric feeds evenly and smoothly without any marks.

To correct the pressure on a machine with a thumbscrew, turn the thumbscrew clockwise to increase the pressure; turn the thumbscrew counter-clockwise to decrease the pressure. To correct the pressure on a machine with a dial, follow the instructions in the manual to adjust the dial to the proper setting.

How to Regulate the Stitch Length

There are numbers on the stitch length regulator indicating the number of stitches per inch made by the machine. The length of the stitch needed will depend on the weight and surface of the fabric you are using. The average stitch length for most sewing is a setting of 10 or 12. You will want a shorter stitch for curved seams and lighter fabrics, say 15. You can judge the appropriate length by testing several lengths on a swatch of the fabric you are going to use before you start sewing. Whenever machine basting is called for set the regulator to 6 or 8. For backstitching, push the stitch regulator all the way up as far as it will go. For precise directions for setting the stitch regulator, refer to the instruction manual for your machine.

How to Clean and Lubricate the Machine

To keep your machine in perfect running order it must be cleaned and oiled at regular intervals. For general cleaning, use the little lint brush and regularly brush out all the areas of the machine that you can reach. This especially refers to the bobbin area. The instruction manual will tell you how to remove the bobbin case in order to brush out the lint that forms. Be sure to do this frequently, particularly if you use the machine often. The manual will also contain instructions for oiling the machine. If it does not, be sure to ask before you buy the machine where to oil it and how often. Always use sewing machine oil, which is sold in sewing machine stores and sewing notions departments. Some machines also require periodic lubricating with sewing machine motor lubricant. Instructions on how to do this will also be in the manual.

PRESSING

A large part of the time you spend making clothes will not be spent sewing, but ironing. That is, pressing the garment as you make it. Pressing while sewing is different from ordinary ironing. When you iron clothes, you slide the iron along the fabric. When you press as you sew, you must lift the iron and gently press down on the seam or section you are ironing. Do not allow the iron to slide along the garment, as this may distort the shape of the fabric.

It is essential that you press as you go along while sewing, or your clothes will not have the finished look that you want them to have. Also, it is difficult, if not impossible, to go from one step to the next without pressing.

You will need more than a good iron to do a professional job of pressing. Some tools will be necessary, others are nice to have to make the job easier. Most of the tools can be used to iron the clothes you already have to give them a professional pressing at home.

Essential Items

A Good Steam/Dry Iron—The easiest ones to work with are those that shoot a spray of steam or water that can be directed to a small area of the garment. The best modern irons have various temperature settings from "cool" for synthetics to "hot" for cotton and linens.

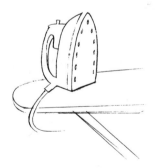

An Adjustable Ironing Board—The ironing board, which should be set up when you start to sew, must have a clean, padded cover.

Sleeve Board—The sleeve board, which looks like a little ironing board with two ironing surfaces, should be set up on top of the ironing board. It is used to press the seams of sleeves, short seams, and other small areas.

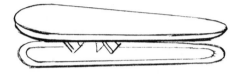

Tailor's Ham or Pressing Mitt—The tailor's ham is a firm cushion, and the pressing mitt is a softer, slightly smaller cushion roughly the shape of a mitten. Both are used for pressing darts and curved areas.

Pressing Cloths—You can buy pressing cloths ready-made for use with different kinds of fabrics, or you can prepare your own. Use cheesecloth for lightweight fabrics or heavy weight cotton or linen for heavier fabrics. Cut the material into foot squares and use them between the fabric and the iron to prevent the fabric from acquiring a shine because of direct contact with the iron.

Brown Wrapping Paper—Buy brown wrapping paper or use grocery bags and cut into pieces of different sizes. These will be used under seam allowances and pleats and darts to prevent ridges from showing on the right side of the fabric.

Nonessential

Seam Roll—The seam roll is a firm cylinder used to press seams open, preventing ridges from the edge of the seam allowances from forming.

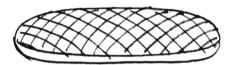

Tailor's Clapper—This is a wooden block used to press creases by pounding after the crease has been steamed.

Tailor's Board or Point Presser—These are both wooden boards with different surfaces and are used to press seams and points open.

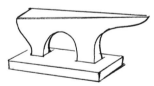

SCISSORS

You will need at least two pairs of scissors for convenience. Be sure that they are always kept sharp and try not to drop them, as they can be distorted by the shock and may not cut evenly. Always buy the best scissors you can afford, and use them to cut fabric only.

Essential

Bent-Handled Dressmaker's Shears—These are the scissors you will use to cut out the fabric. Get a 7- or 8-inch length and use them with the flat blade facing the underside of the fabric as you cut. Left-handed shears are available for those who prefer them.

Embroidery Scissors—These come in 4- and 5-inch lengths and are used for cutting the ends of the threads as you sew, for cutting out buttonholes, and for cutting basting and seams when you have to remove stitches.

Nonessential

Trimming Scissors—These come in a 6-inch length and are used for trimming seams and trimming other small areas.

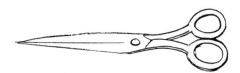

Pinking or Scalloping Shears—Pinking and scalloping shears are used for finishing seams by making a zigzag or scalloped edge. *Never* use them for cutting out the fabric; they are only for use on finished seams.

MEASURING DEVICES

Essential

Tape Measure—You must have a flexible (not steel or wood) one, 60 inches long. Choose one that will not tear or stretch.

Ruler—Rulers are used to alter patterns and to lay the pattern out on the fabric. Choose a see-through plastic one or a steel, draftsmen's ruler 12 inches long.

Yardstick—Choose one made of metal or varnished wood so that there will be no rough edges to catch the fabric.

Nonessential

6-Inch Sewing or Knitting Gauge—These come with a moveable indicator and are used to measure short lengths, such as hems.

Skirt (Hem) Marker—A skirt marker with powdered chalk and a bulb will allow you to mark the hem of a dress or skirt without any help.

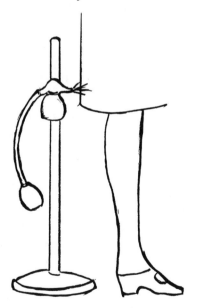

FABRIC MARKERS

Essential

Dressmaker's Carbon Paper, Also Called Tracing Paper—This is used to mark most kinds of fabrics. Choose a package that has paper in several different colors.

Tracing Wheel—It comes with or without teeth and is used with the dressmaker's carbon paper to mark the fabric.

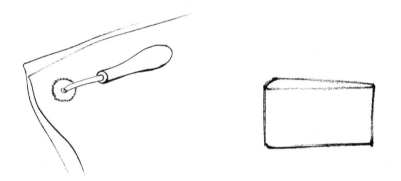

Tailor's Chalk or Chalk Pencil—Both are used to mark fabric that will not show carbon paper markings. Choose either tailor's chalk, which comes in small squares, or a chalk pencil, which can be sharpened to a fine point.

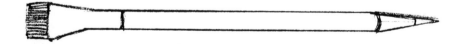

Black and White Embroidery Thread—The thread is used to make tailor's tacks on woolens and other thick fabrics.

GENERAL NOTIONS

Essential

Pins—You must have nonrust dressmaker's pins, and if you are working with knits, "ball point" pins. Some pins come with glass heads and are very easy to use, but they are more expensive than the regular ones.

Thread—The kind of thread you need will depend on the kind of fabric you are using. Choose a color that looks slightly darker on the spool than the fabric color.

Mercerized Cotton—for use on cotton and linen fabrics.

Cotton-Covered Polyester Thread—for general use and specifically for use with knits and synthetics.

Polyester Thread—for use on synthetic fabrics.

Silk Thread—for use with silks and wools and for tailoring.

Silk Buttonhole Twist—A very heavy silk thread that is used for decorative topstitching, buttonholes, and sewing on buttons.

Basting Thread—A cotton thread, usually black or white, used for basting and making tailor's tacks. This thread is not strong enough for regular sewing.

Hand Sewing Needles—Buy a package with an assortment of sizes and use the ones you find most comfortable.

Seam Binding—This is used to finish hems on dresses and skirts. Usually you will use the ribbon kind, but it is available in stretch lace for a decorative finish, mostly on knit fabrics. Bias seam binding is also available for use on flared hems and for facings.

Zippers—There are several different kinds of zippers available. See Chapter 4 for instructions on making your selection. The length of the zipper needed is determined by the pattern.

Transparent Tape—Use it to alter a pattern and to repair any tears in the pattern that may occur.

Pin Cushion—Pin cushions are available in a multitude of shapes and sizes, but the most useful are those with a plastic band that strap to your wrist.

Nonessential

Beeswax—Beeswax comes in a holder with grooves, and the sewing thread is passed through the grooves to strengthen the thread. It is used for hand sewing.

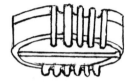

Loop Turner—This is a long wire with a little hook on one end that is used for turning bias loops. For more information, see page 258.

Needle Threader—This is very useful if you have trouble seeing the eye of the needle to thread it. It can be used both for hand sewing needles and for sewing machine needles.

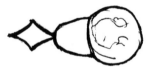

Tweezers—Ordinary cosmetic tweezers are very handy for removing basting stitches and tailor's tacks.

Adjustable Dress Dummy—A dress dummy that can be changed to fit you and other members of your family is very useful. With a dress dummy you can see how the garment will look as you progress, and you will be able to make adjustments that are difficult to make on yourself without help.

2

UNDERSTANDING PATTERNS, MEASUREMENTS and ALTERATIONS

BASIC PATTERN INFORMATION

When you take the pattern out of the envelope, in most cases you will discover that you have pieces for only half of a garment (half of the bodice front and back, one sleeve, and so forth). This is because the garment is cut out with the pattern pinned to the folded fabric, thus giving both sides of the garments as you cut.

Pieces are included for all the views shown on the pattern envelope. Sometimes two pieces will be incorporated into one, such as a long sleeve that will have a line showing where to cut the pattern piece in order to get a short sleeve. In pattern catalogues the patterns are arranged according to size categories, with a few exceptions. These exceptions are clothing types, such as evening clothes and separates. If you handle them carefully, tissue-paper patterns can be used over and over. Very often you will find a particular style that suits you, and you will want to make it in several different fabrics. You can preserve the life of such a pattern by transferring the shape of the pieces and all the markings on the pattern to heavy brown paper, or for more permanency, to a nonwoven interfacing.

How to "Read" a Pattern, How to Tell an "Easy" Pattern

The drawing or photograph on the front of the pattern envelope (and in the catalogue, or pattern book) can be a help in selecting your pattern if you know what to look for and don't let the quality of the drawing, which is usually bad, influence you. You are usually offered two views of the pattern One is a warm-weather version (sleeveless, or short-sleeved), the other is a cold-weather version (long sleeves, high collar). Almost invariably you will find that the details are interchangeable within the same pattern. If, for example, you like the neckline shown on the long-sleeved version but want to use the short sleeves shown, you will have no problems as long as you are

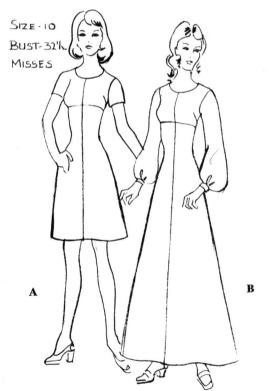

Size-10
Bust-32'½
Misses

A   B

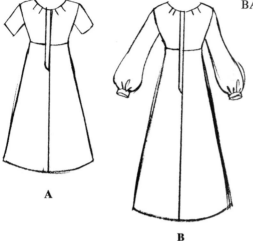

A

B

working with just one pattern. The drawings will usually show a printed fabric and a solid-color version. From these sketches you can get a good idea of the scale of the print that will look best with this particular style.

These sketches also indicate the current fashion accessories that the designer had in mind to be worn with the garment; you can follow these or not, depending on your taste. Don't let them influence your choice of pattern. On occasion they attempt to show color coordination when it comes to separates, but don't let the colors shown influence you. If the pattern is shown in green and you don't like green, don't dismiss the pattern if you like the style. Remember you are creating the garment and the choice of color or print is entirely up to you.

In addition to the color drawings or photographs on the front of the envelope, there are on the back small, line drawings, usually of the back of the garment. I have found that these drawings very often tell you as much, if not more, about what the finished garment will look like as the artist's conceptions on the front, which can be misleading. These little line drawings give a good idea of how full or flared or straight a skirt or a sleeve is. They show you whether the garment has a zipper up the back, or in the case of skirts and pants, if the zipper is on the side or in the back. In any case, whenever you look at drawings of patterns, the first thing to look at is the seams. Is there one dart on the front of the dress, or two? This will affect the fit of the dress. The more darts, the closer the fit. Look at the sleeves. Are they smooth-fitting, set in, or are they puffed at the top of the shoulders? Does the dress have raglan sleeves, or are they more complicated, with underarm gussets? Learn to look for details as well as for the overall silhouette. Look at the line drawings to see what the back of the garment is like. If the skirt is pleated in front, do the pleats continue in the back? If they do, you will have a fuller skirt than if it is pleated only in the front. The pattern size measurements are also printed on the back of the pattern envelope. For an explanation of these measurements, see page 46.

Once you have learned to look for these details, you will be able to tell how difficult the garment is to make. In starting out, you want to look for simple styles with a minimum of pattern pieces, and a minimum of darts, tucks, pleats, and other details that will be difficult for the beginner. All the pattern companies now have sections in their catalogues devoted to "easy" patterns. They are called "Quickies" or "Jiffy," or something similar, and to begin with you might want to pick most of your styles from these sections. But there is no reason to restrict yourself to these patterns as long as you know how to select an "easy" pattern from any section in the catalogue.

How to Understand and Use the Pattern Primer

With every pattern you buy, you will find inside the envelope, in addition to the actual pattern pieces, the pattern "primer." This is the instruction sheet for cutting out and sewing the garment. The primers vary in layout from company to company, but they all contain the same information. It is very important that you use these instruction sheets as guides in your sewing, as they have been designed to show you the best and fastest way to construct the garment they are made for. Even the most advanced dressmaker is advised to refer to them, and for beginners they are absolutely essential. The front of the instruction sheet includes the following information:

1. Drawings of the front and back views of the garments included in the envelope.
2. Drawings of the pattern pieces, which tell you what the pieces are and which view they are for.

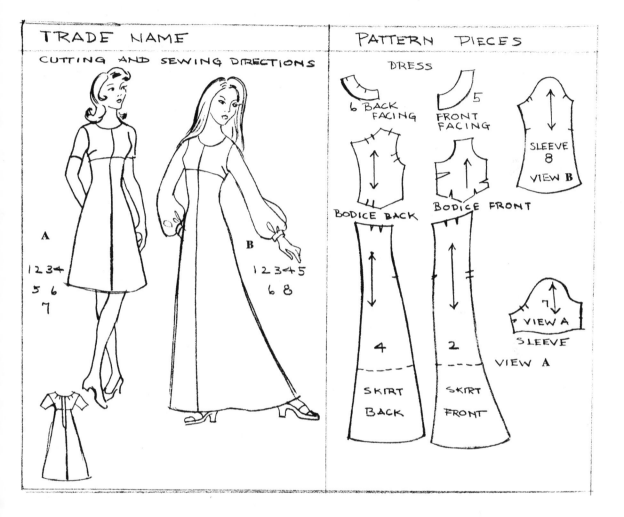

3. Basic cutting and sewing instructions, which are given in further detail in this book, but they will give you a quick review as you go along.

4. Actual cutting layouts for the different views, given for the varying widths of fabrics shown on the outside of the envelope. This also includes layouts for any linings and interfacings.

To use these layouts, find the one for the pattern view you are making, the width of the fabric you are using, and the size you are making. Circle it with a heavy pencil and follow it carefully, using the pattern pieces needed,

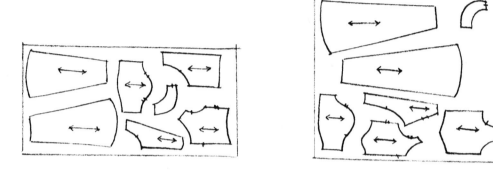

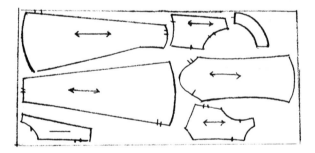

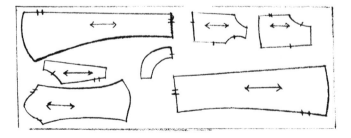

checking that you pin the pattern piece to the double or single thickness of fabric as indicated on the layout. Be sure that you check for any special cutting notes.

The back of the instruction sheet is devoted to the actual sewing instructions. They are given step by step, with very clear drawings of each step and special close-up drawings for any complicated details. There are written instructions accompanying the drawings, and it is very important that you follow them in the order given. Before you start to sew your garment, study the drawings and read the instructions that apply to the view you are making. Also study the pattern pieces so that you understand how they will fit together. Do not attempt to skip over the instructions or to do anything out of the order given. As I said before, these instructions have been carefully worked out by experts and when followed exactly they will show you how to best make your garment in the shortest length of time.

If there are terms used in the pattern primer that you do not understand, refer to this book for a full explanation. The pattern primer is your most important guide to creating a professionally finished garment.

How to Mark Your Fabric from the Pattern

All printed patterns have markings which are very important in constructing the garment. The most common markings are

The Cutting Line—the heavy outside line of the pattern. It is also found within a pattern piece to be cut off for a different style, for example, a short skirt within a longer skirt. This line is also indicated by a small pair of scissors drawn on the line. Always cut the fabric in the direction the scissors point.

The Seam Line—the broken line usually ⅝ inch from the cutting line. This is the line along which the garment will actually be sewn.

Darts—broken lines forming long triangles. Sometimes there is a solid line in the center, along which the dart will be folded.

The Fold Line—a long unbroken line along which the garment will be folded.

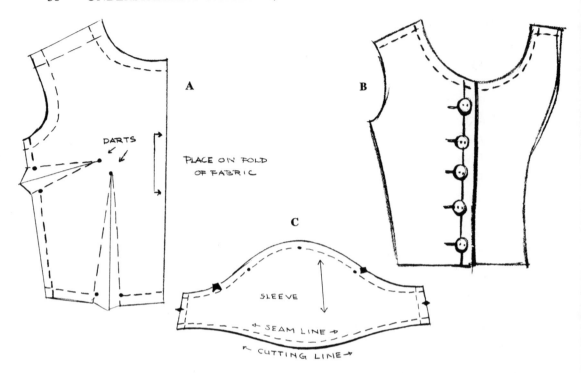

The Roll Line—an unbroken line which indicates where the garment will be softly rolled.

Buttonholes and Buttons—circular markings which show the exact size of the button to be used. These circles are cut by a horizontal or vertical line which shows the exact length of the buttonhole.

Large and Small Circles, Triangles, and Squares—markings used for joining different sections. They are usually used where easing or gathering of the fabric is required.

Notches—small black triangles sticking out from the cutting line. They are used to match seams and are numbered in the order the seams will be matched.

Gathering and Easing Lines—the easing line is a single broken line with arrows and small circles; the gathering line is a double line with arrows and small circles. These lines indicate where the fabric is to be eased or gathered.

Grain Lines—long unbroken lines with arrows at both ends. They are placed in the center of the pattern piece, which will be placed on the lengthwise grain of the fabric when cutting.

Lines for the Fold of the Fabric—solid lines which form brackets. They indicate that the edge of the pattern is to be placed on the fold of the fabric.

Adjustment Lines—double lines running crosswise on the pattern. They indicate where to lengthen or shorten on the pattern piece (not on the fabric).

Zipper Line—drawing of a zipper, indicating where the zipper will be placed.

Hemline—solid crosswise line which indicates the finished edge of the garment. This line can be raised or lowered to alter the length of the garment.

In order to construct your garment, most of these markings will have to be transferred to the fabric after the pieces of the garment have been cut out, and before the tissue pattern has been removed from the fabric. Usually the markings will be made on the wrong side of the fabric, but certain markings such as buttonholes and pocket placements will have to be made on the right side of the fabric. There are several methods of marking—what you use will depend on the fabric you are working with and the purpose of the marking.

Dressmaker's Tracing Wheel and Dressmaker's Carbon Paper (Also Called Tracing Paper)

Dressmaker's carbon paper, which is paper with one colored or white waxy side, can be used to mark most firm fabrics. It is not suitable for sheer fabrics or rough-surfaced woolens. The color of the paper used will depend on the color of the fabric. The carbon paper comes in several colors in one envelope, so you can test the various colors on a scrap of your fabric. For most fabric colors, you will probably find that white or yellow will be right, but don't use these light colors on a very dark fabric. In general, never use a sharply contrasting color unless you test it on a scrap of the fabric first, and steam iron or wash it to be sure the mark will come out.

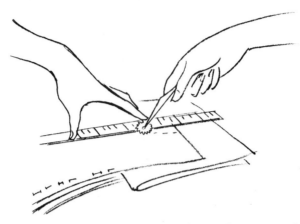

To mark two layers of fabric at one time, place one piece of carbon, waxy side up, under the bottom layer of the fabric and slip a second piece of carbon, waxy side down, between the pattern piece and the top layer of the fabric. Remove just enough pins from the pattern tissue to allow the carbon paper to fit. To mark straight lines (for darts, fold lines, and so forth), use a ruler to guide the wheel. To mark one layer of fabric, place one piece of carbon with the waxy side facing the wrong side of the fabric. To mark darts, make a crosswise line at the starting point of the dart, and then mark the stitching lines and the fold line down the center of the dart.

It is not necessary to mark all the seam lines, but for a beginner it is a help to mark extremely curved seams and areas with a pointed or right-angle turn, such as the points of a collar. Cut the carbon paper into smaller pieces for greater convenience in marking small areas, such as buttonholes. The same piece of dressmaker's carbon paper can be used several times.

Tailor's Tacks

Tailor's tacks can be used to mark all kinds of fabrics, but they are essential for use on heavy wools, tweeds with a nap, and sheer or delicate fabrics where dressmaker's carbon paper marks would show on the finished garment. You can use any kind of thread, but I prefer embroidery thread in a contrasting color, which will stay in the fabric longer and will show more clearly.

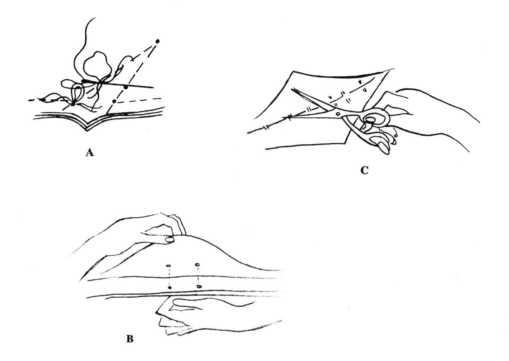

Use a long, double thread without a knot at the end. Thread the needle and take a small stitch through the pattern piece and through one or two layers of fabric, depending on how many layers you are marking. Take another stitch through the first, leaving a one-inch loop. Continue in this way. marking the important points, such as the bold dots on darts, or at even spaces along straight or curved lines.

Gently remove the pattern piece away from the fabric so that the thread mark tears through the pattern and is left undisturbed on the fabric. You can repair the pattern with a small piece of cellophane tape. If you are working with a pattern that has been made of heavy paper or fabric, cut a small hole where the markings will fall before making the tailor's tacks. Cut the loops and carefully separate the two layers, making sure that you do not pull the threads out of the fabric. Cut the threads between the layers, thus leaving tufts of thread in both pieces of the fabric. Do not leave the marked pieces lying around too long as the threads are likely to work themselves out, leaving you with an unmarked piece of a garment. When you have finished the construction, pull the marking threads out with a pair of tweezers.

Pins and Tailor's Chalk or Chalk Pencil

Tailor's chalk or a chalk pencil can be used to mark all fabrics, but test a scrap of the fabric first to be sure that the chalk mark will show up. Chalk marks are not permanent and can be brushed off after you have finished construction.

Mark with pins by sticking one pin down through the bold marking on the pattern, penetrating the pattern and both layers of the fabric. Then stick another pin up through the same marking from the underside of the fabric. When all the pin markings have been made, upon the pattern from the fabric and carefully remove the pattern. Tearing through the tissue, and be sure to leave the marking pins undisturbed on the fabric. Mark over the pins with chalk on the wrong side of both pieces of the fabric. When marking darts or continuous lines, connect the markings by ruling a straight line with chalk. Once all the chalk markings have been completed, remove the pins.

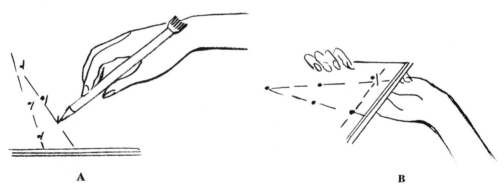

A   B

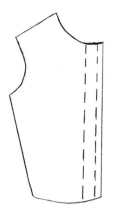

Marking by Basting

Marking by basting is used to transfer the markings to the right side of the fabric. Once the markings have been made on the wrong side of the fabric, using one of the above methods, baste over them, by machine or by hand, through a single layer of fabric. These basting stitches will be removed after the garment is completed.

How to Take Measurements to Determine Pattern Size

Pattern sizes are divided into categories according to figure types. These categories are based on figure proportions and are labeled "Misses," "Juniors," and so forth. They are not determined by age groups but by figure shapes. Your pattern size will probably not be the same as your ready-to-wear size but will likely fall into the same category. Your pattern size is determined by your measurements. All patterns are cut to allow ease in the fit of the finished garment. That is to say, a size 34 bust will not measure exactly 34 inches but will allow a few inches more so that the garment will fit comfortably. The amount of ease allowed will also depend on the style of the garment.

The standard ease allowed is usually as follows:

Bust—3 to 4 inches for a fitted bodice; 5 to 6 inches for a loose bodice; 1½ to 2 inches for patterns made for knit fabrics only.

Hips—2 to 2½ inches for a straight skirt.

Front Waist Length—¼ inch.

Back Width—½ to 1 inch.

Upper Arm—1 to 2 inches for a fitted sleeve.

The first thing to do to determine your pattern size is to take your measurements, and in order to do this you will need the following: a soft, non-stretchable tape measure, a piece of yarn long enough to go around your waist, and the help of a friend.

Take the measurements in this order and write them down in the form of a chart.

Bust—measure around the fullest part with the tape held firmly.

Waistline—measure at the thinnest part of your middle and then tie the yarn around your waist and leave it there until you have finished measuring.

Hips—measure around the fullest part.

Back Waist Length—measure from the first vertebra at the back of your neck to the yarn tied around your waist. (Your friend will have to take this measurement for you.)

Shoulder to the Fullest Point of the Bust—measure from the middle of the shoulder to the point of the bust.

Front Waist Length—measure from the middle of the shoulder over the fullest point of the bust to the yarn tied around your waist.

Front Width—measure from armhole to armhole 3 inches below the base of the neck.

Back Width—measure from armhole to armhole about 4½ inches below the base of the neck.

MISSES'

Misses' patterns are designed for a well proportioned, and developed figure; about 5'5" to 5'6" without shoes.

Size	6	8	10	12	14	16	18	20
Bust	30½	31½	32½	34	36	38	40	42
Waist	22	23	24	25½	27	29	31	33
Hip	32½	33½	34½	36	38	40	42	44
Back Waist Length	15½	15¾	16	16¼	16½	16¾	17	17¼

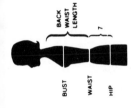

About 5'2 to 5'4

MISS PETITE

This new size range is designed for the shorter Miss figure; about 5'2" to 5'4" without shoes.

Size	6mp	8mp	10mp	12mp	14mp	16mp	18mp
Bust	30½	31½	32½	34	36	38	40
Waist	22½	23½	24½	26	27½	29½	31½
Hip	32½	33½	34½	36	38	40	42
Back Waist Length	14½	14¾	15	15¼	15½	15¾	16

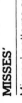

About 5'2 to 5'4

JUNIOR

Junior patterns are designed for a well proportioned, shorter waisted figure; about 5'4" to 5'5" without shoes.

Size	5	7	9	11	13	15
Bust	30	31	32	33½	35	37
Waist	21½	22½	23½	24½	26	28
Hip	32	33	34	35½	37	39
Back Waist Length	15	15¼	15½	15¾	16	16¼

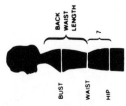

About 5'4 to 5'5

JUNIOR PETITE

Junior Petite patterns are designed for a well proportioned, petite figure; about 5' to 5'1" without shoes.

Size	3jp	5jp	7jp	9jp	11jp	13jp
Bust	30½	31	32	33	34	35
Waist	22	22½	23½	24½	25½	26¼
Hip	31½	32	33	34	35	36
Back Waist Length	14	14¼	14½	14¾	15	15¼

About 5'1 to 5'3

YOUNG JUNIOR/TEEN

This size range is designed for the developing pre-teen and teen figures; about 5'1" to 5'3" without shoes.

Size	5/6	7/8	9/10	11/12	13/14	15/16
Bust	28	29	30½	32	33½	35
Waist	22	23	24	25	26	27
Hip	31	32	33½	35	36½	38
Back Waist Length	13½	14	14½	15	15⅜	15¾

About 5'5 to 5'6

WOMEN'S

Women's patterns are designed for the larger, more fully mature figure; about 5'5" to 5'6" without shoes.

Size	38	40	42	44	46	48	50
Bust	42	44	46	48	50	52	54
Waist	34	36	38	40½	43	45½	48
Hip	44	46	48	50	52	54	56
Back Waist Length	17¼	17⅜	17½	17⅝	17¾	17⅞	18

HALF SIZE

Half size patterns are for a fully developed figure with a short backwaist length. Waist and hip are larger in proportion to bust than other figure types; about 5'2" to 5'3" without shoes.

Size	10½	12½	14½	16½	18½	20½	22½	24½
Bust	33	35	37	39	41	43	45	47
Waist	26	28	30	32	34	36½	39	41½
Hip	35	37	39	41	43	45½	48	50½
Back Waist Length	15	15¼	15½	15¾	15⅞	16	16⅛	16¼

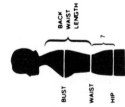

About 5'2 to 5'3

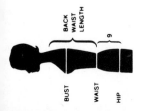

Courtesy of Butterick Patterns

Sleeve Width—measure around the upper arm at the underarm seam.
Sleeve Length—measure from shoulder to elbow, then from elbow to wrist.
Height—measure without shoes.

Your figure type is determined by your bust, waist, and hip measurements, your height and the back waist length measurement. Check the charts
given and find the size that is closest to your measurements. [Write down
the measurements from the chart in a column next to the chart you have
already made with your own measurements.] Your pattern size when buying
dress, blouse, jacket, and coat patterns is determined by your bust measurement within your figure type. The pattern size for pants is determined by
your hip measurement, for skirts, by your waist measurement. The exception
to this is if your hips are two inches larger than the pattern measurement
for your waist size. In that case, buy the size nearest your hip measurement.
You will then have to alter the waist.

Once you have found the size closest to your measurements, compare
the two sets of measurements. Any discrepancies will indicate whether you will
have to alter your patterns to get a perfect fit. All alterations will be made
on the pattern pieces before you ever begin to cut your fabric.

How to Make a Muslin Shell and How to Alter Patterns

If you discover that major alterations will be necessary, or if you have
any particular figure problems (such as very wide shoulders, or one hip higher
than the other), it would be advisable to make a basic muslin shell before you
start cutting into expensive fabric. The muslin shell is an unfinished shell of
a dress that will show you exactly how the pattern will fit. It is usually only
necessary to make one muslin shell, as corrections made on it can be transferred to all the patterns you use. The only time you might want to make an
additional shell is if there is a great change in your measurements, or if you
want to make a complicated pattern in very expensive fabric.

To make the shell, purchase a "basic fitting pattern" in the size closest
to your measurements. All pattern companies make these patterns; they are
listed in the index at the back of the large pattern catalogues. Pick a dress
style with set-in sleeves and a waistline seam. The shell can be made out of

unbleached muslin, or you can use a firm cotton, such as broadcloth or ging-ham. Just don't spend too much money on this fabric as it will never be a finished dress. The "basic" pattern, like any other pattern you buy, comes with a primer with detailed sewing instructions for making the dress shell, which with the aid of this book, you should be able to follow without any difficulty.

To make any of the following adjustments, mark the corrections as shown on the muslin, then carefully take the muslin apart and transfer the corrections to the pattern. Once you have made the alterations on the basic pattern, you will have a guide for altering all the patterns you use in the future. Tools needed to make pattern alterations:

1. A large flat even surface, either a large table, a cutting board, or the floor.

2. Tissue paper—to lay under the pattern when increasing or changing the pattern.

3. Pins.

4. Cellophane tape—to tape the pattern to the tissue paper or to itself wherever necessary.

5. A ruler, preferably see-through.

6. Tailor's chalk or a chalk pencil—to mark corrections on the muslin.

7. A black felt-tip pen or heavy black pencil—to transfer the corrections to the pattern.

Before you start altering the pattern, you will have to know where the adjustments will be necessary. To do this, you will have to measure the pattern pieces and compare the measurements with your own.

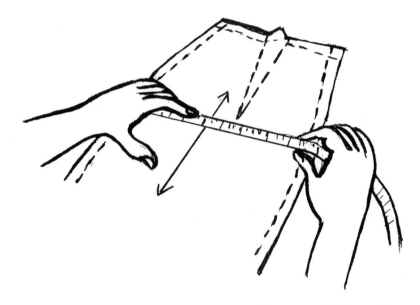

To measure the pattern pieces, unfold them carefully and iron them flat with a dry iron. Measure as shown between the seam lines, not from the edges of the patterns. Remember that the following measurements allow for ease, so take these measurements from the pattern chart rather than from the actual pattern pieces: bust, waist, hips, and back waist length. Otherwise, measure the pattern pieces and write down in the third column on your chart where you have not already filled in the pattern measurements. Measure the pattern the same way you measured yourself: for sleeve length, front width, back width, and so forth.

Very often when you alter a pattern, the original cutting and seam lines and other details will have to be redrawn. I have indicated these changes clearly in the following drawings.

There are a few rules to remember when making flat alterations of patterns. All grain lines must be kept straight. Any change made on the front of the garment which affects the seam lines will have to be made on the back and on any facings which will be attached to those pieces.

Whenever you have to make the muslin larger, cut the muslin, allowing the spread of the garment to take place, and then pin or baste strips of fabric under the opening so that the muslin can then be taken apart and measured.

To lengthen or widen the pattern piece, use the tissue paper taped under the pattern.

To make a piece shorter or smaller, take tucks in the pattern piece. These tucks will be *half* of the amount to be removed (to take in ½ inch, the tuck will measure ¼ inch, for example).

When making a piece wider or narrower and you have half of the pattern, divide the amount of the adjustment to be made into quarters and add or remove one-fourth in the front and back of the pattern (to add 1 inch to the complete garment, add ¼ inch to the sides of the front and back). If you need the alteration only in the front or the back, add or remove one-half of the amount required.

The basic alterations are lengthening and shortening. For the bodice, how much you lengthen or shorten is determined by the difference between the back waist length measurement of the pattern and your own back waist length measurement. The same method of comparing your measurement to the pattern measurement will apply when changing the length of skirts, sleeves, or pants' legs.

In most cases, your pattern will have a line for lengthening and shortening printed crosswise on the bodice and sleeve sections. If these lines are not printed on the bodice pieces, draw a crosswise line one inch above the marking for the natural waistline. It is at these crosswise lines that you will make your adjustment.

To lengthen the bodice, sleeve, or skirt—first cut out a piece of tissue paper the width of the pattern piece and about two inches longer. Cut the pattern along the lengthening line and using cellophane tape, tape the bottom half of the pattern to the tissue paper. Line up the top half of the pattern with the grain line and tape it to the tissue paper carefully, allowing the increase to form out of the tissue paper. Measure the increase at both ends of the pattern and in the center to make sure it is even. See illustration.

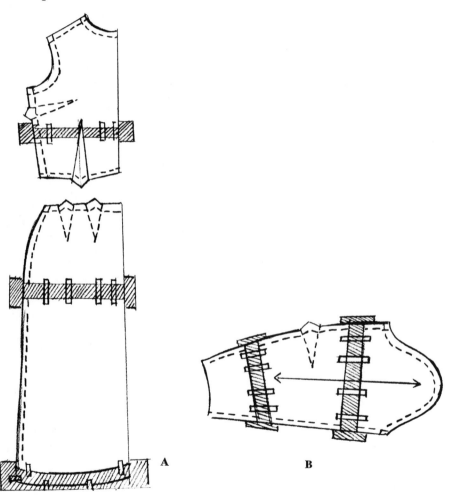

A   B

To shorten the bodice, sleeve, or skirt—fold along the same lengthening and shortening line, remembering to take into the fold *half* of the amount to be taken in. Make sure the grain line is kept straight. Tape the tuck to the pattern, measuring all along the line to make sure it is even. See illustration.

The second most common alterations are those that change the width of the garment.

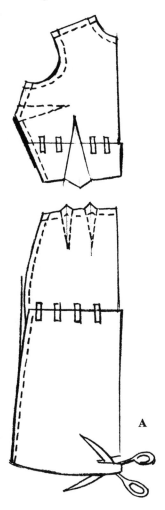

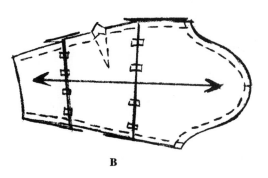

A

B

To reduce the waist and hips—if the alteration is to take in less than one inch in the total circumference measurement, draw a new seam line and cutting line at the side seams of the pattern. If you are making this adjustment in a dress, mark one-fourth of the amount to be taken in at the bust, and continue drawing the line down to the hem of the garment.

If the alteration is to take in more than one inch, how you make your alteration will depend on the style of the garment. For a fitted dress with a waistline seam, cut the pattern as shown and take a tuck one-quarter of the total measurement. You may have to clip the seam allowance to make the pattern lie flat.

For a princess-style dress, draw new seam and cutting lines, dividing the total measurement by the number of seams.

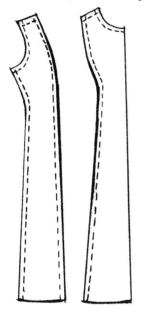

To take in the waist without affecting the bust or hips—mark one-quarter of the total waist measurement desired at the waist only, redrawing the cutting and seam lines so that they taper in from the original bustline and taper back out just above the hip line.

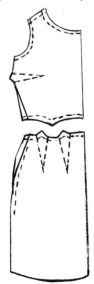

To increase the waist and hips—if the alteration is less than one inch, add one-quarter of the total measurement to the sides of the pattern, starting at the bust, and continue drawing new seam and cutting lines to the hem.

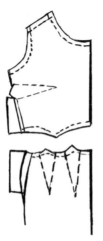

For alterations more than one inch, cut the pattern as shown and spread one-quarter of the amount required, using a piece of tissue paper underneath the pattern, and tape the pattern to the paper. A small pleat will form at the seam allowance and hem, just tape it flat.

For a princess-style dress, divide the amount to be let out by the number of seams and alter each as shown, redrawing the seam and cutting lines.

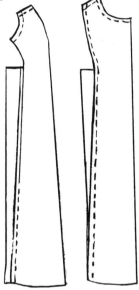

To increase the hips without increasing the waist—if the alteration to be made is two inches or less, mark one-quarter of the amount on the sides of the pattern at the hip line. Draw new seam and cutting lines, tapering from the waist to the hem.

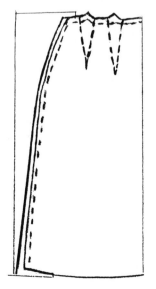

If the alteration is more than two inches, for skirts, cut the pattern from top to bottom parallel with the grain line and increase by one-quarter of the total measurement. Then tape the pattern pieces to the tissue paper. If you have to let out a large amount, it will be necessary to add a dart on each piece near the side seam. If you have added less, simply taper along the side to the original waist measurement.

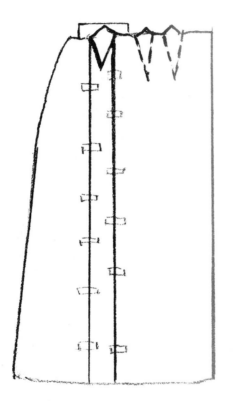

For A-line dress styles, cut the pattern to the hip line and across to the side of the pattern. Spread the pattern pieces one-quarter of the total measurement and tape them to the tissue. Redraw the seam and cutting lines, tapering from the bust.

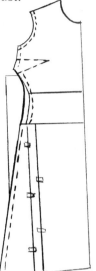

For a princess-style dress, divide the amount of the alteration by the number of seams and redraw the seam and cutting lines, tapering from the waist.

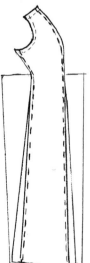

ALTERATIONS MADE FROM THE MUSLIN— BODICE ADJUSTMENTS

The Length of the Bust Dart

The bust dart must always point to the fullest point of the bust without actually touching it. The underarm bust dart should end ½ inch from the fullest point. Front darts (those starting at the waistline or at the side of the waist) should end ½ to 1 inch away from the fullest point. It doesn't matter exactly what the measurement of the dart is, as long as the fabric of the bodice fits smoothly over the bust.

To Shorten the Dart   Sew the muslin exactly as marked on the pattern and try it on. If the dart (or darts, if there is a front dart) is too long, it will pinch the fabric over the bust. To correct it, mark the correct position for the dart on the muslin. Transfer the marking to the pattern and redraw the dart as shown.

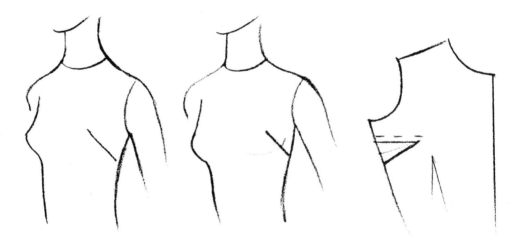

To Lengthen the Dart   If the dart is too short, there will be too much loose fabric over the bust. To lengthen, mark the correct position on the muslin, transfer the marking to the pattern, and redraw the dart or darts as shown.

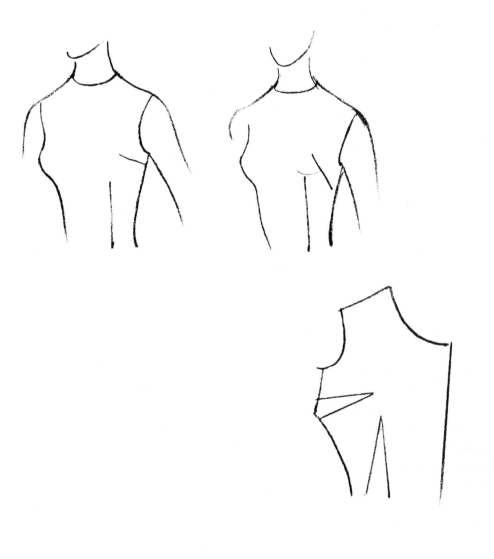

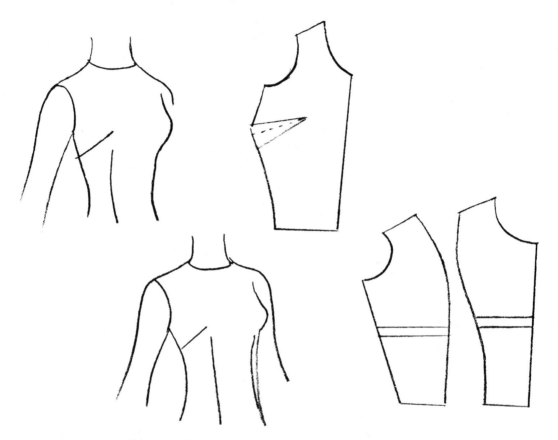

Raising the Bust Dart

Indications: The bust dart falls below the fullest part of the bust.

To alter all bust darts, mark on the muslin where the dart should fall and redraw the dart or darts to point to the mark.

For patterns with princess styling, place the altered pattern under the one to be altered and using the first pattern as a guide, take a tuck above the armhole notch one-half of the amount to be raised and tape it to itself. Cut through the pattern below the bust and add the amount you removed before. This will keep the length of the entire bodice correct. Redraw the seam and cutting lines at the armhole below the notches.

Lowering the Bust Dart

Indications: The bust dart is above the fullest part of the bust.

To alter all bust darts, mark the fullest part of the bust on the muslin and redraw the dart or darts to point to the mark.

For patterns with princess styling, place the altered pattern under the one to be altered and using the first pattern as a guide, cut through the armhole notch. Spread the pattern the amount to be lowered. Below the bust, take a tuck one-half of the amount you have just lowered and tape. Redraw the seam and cutting lines at the armhole below the notches.

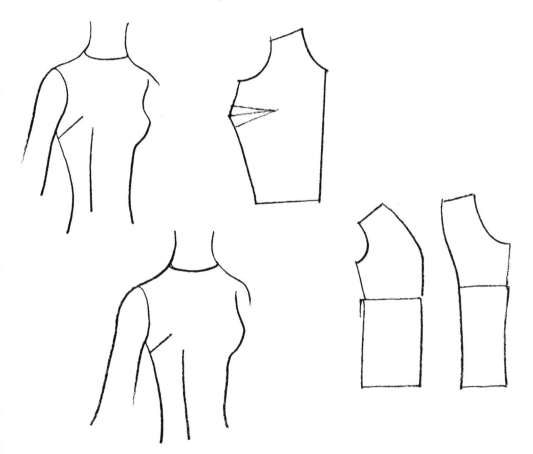

Narrow Shoulders

Indications: The dress is too loose through the shoulders.

Mark the amount to be taken in on the muslin.

Cut the pattern from the center of the shoulder to the armhole notches. Lap one-quarter of the total amount to be taken in and tape. Redraw the seam and cutting lines at the shoulders.

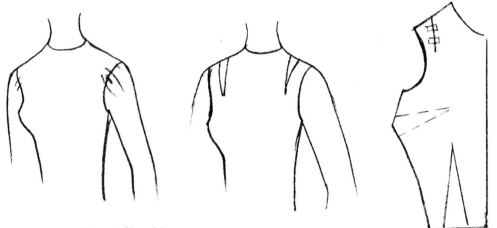

Broad Shoulders

Indications: The dress pulls and wrinkles across the back of the shoulders.

Cut the muslin and allow it to spread in order to determine the amount needed to be let out.

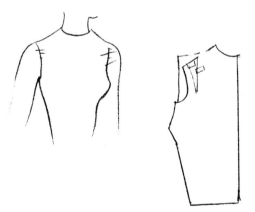

Cut the pattern from the center of the shoulder down and across to the armhole notches. Spread one-quarter of the amount to be let out. Redraw the seam and cutting lines at the shoulders.

Sloping Shoulders

Indications: There is too much fabric in the front and back of the armhole.

On the muslin, pin and measure the excess amount of fabric from the seam line at the shoulder to determine the amount to be removed.

Cut the pattern from the armhole toward, but not reaching, the center. Lap and tape the amount to be removed, tapering toward the neckline. Redraw the armhole below the notches, lowering the armhole the same amount you just removed.

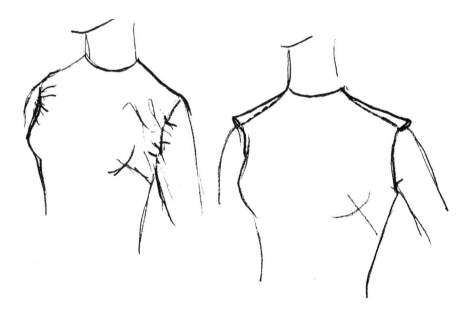

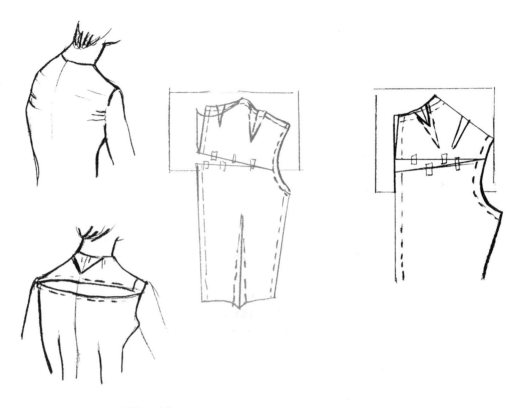

Round Shoulders

Indications: The dress pulls across the back of the shoulders and there is too much fabric at the back of the armholes.

Cut the muslin across the back between the armhole seams. Allow the dress to spread in order to determine the amount needed to be added.

To alter a bodice with a neckline dart—cut the pattern in a straight line below the dart to the armhole seam. Spread apart from the amount needed and tape to the tissue paper. Redraw the seam and cutting lines at the neck edge of the shoulder seam, adding the same amount added at the center back. Redraw the neckline dart, making it the same width, but shorter. Draw a new dart at the shoulder as wide as the amount added to the shoulder seam.

To alter a bodice with a shoulder dart—cut the pattern in a straight line below the dart to the armhole seam. Spread apart the required amount and tape to the tissue. Redraw the seam and cutting lines from the lower cut edge to the center back neckline. Draw a new neckline dart as wide as the amount added to the neckline. Shorten the shoulder dart.

Very Straight Back

Indications: The back of the dress wrinkles above the shoulder blades.

On the muslin, pin out the wrinkles to determine the amount to be taken in.

Cut the pattern in a straight line below the neck or shoulder darts, lap the edge the amount to be taken in, and tape to itself. Redraw the back seam and cutting line to straighten the back. Make the neckline dart (if there is one) shorter, or take it out completely, depending on the amount taken in.

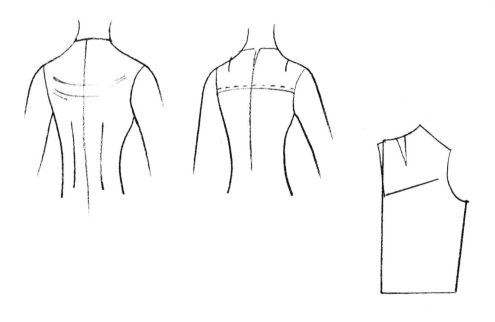

Small Bust

Indications: Wrinkles form over the bust.

Pin the wrinkles out of the muslin to determine the amount to be taken in.

For a fitted bodice with bust darts, redraw the darts to make them smaller. Redraw the seam and cutting lines as shown.

For a princess-style dress, place the altered pattern under the one to be altered and using the first pattern as a guide, take a tuck at the bust one-half of the amount to be taken in.

Remake the fitted style and make the princess style in muslin to be sure of the fit before you cut into expensive fabric.

Full Bust

Indications: The dress is too tight across the fullest part of the bust, and when you move, it is too tight across the back.

For a fitted style, cut the muslin as shown in order to determine the amount to be let out.

Make the same cuts up the front through the bustline and crosswise through the bust dart to the center front on the pattern, allowing the pattern to spread until it matches the corrected muslin. Redraw the darts; make them deeper and correct their length so that they fall properly. Redraw the seam and cutting lines.

For a princess style, place the altered pattern under the new pattern as a guide, [make the same cuts in the princess pattern,] and spread the pattern until you have the correct adjustment. Redraw the seam and cutting lines.

Remake the fitted style and make the princess style in muslin to be sure of the fit before you cut into expensive fabric.

Flat or Hollow Chest

Indications: The dress wrinkles below the neckline and above the bustline.

Pin a tuck across the chest above the bust to determine the amount to be taken in.

Take a tuck in the pattern across the chest, taking in one-half of the amount and tapering toward the armhole. Tape it to itself. Redraw the center front line to straighten.

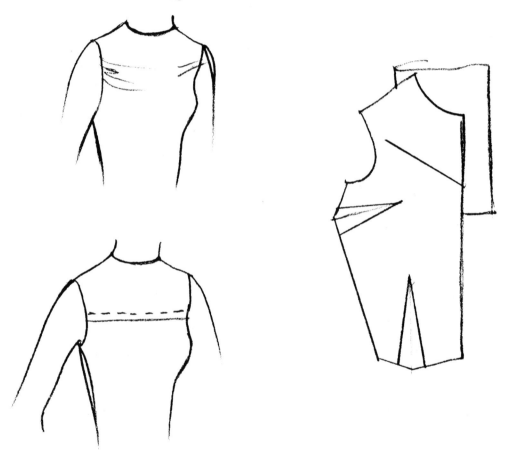

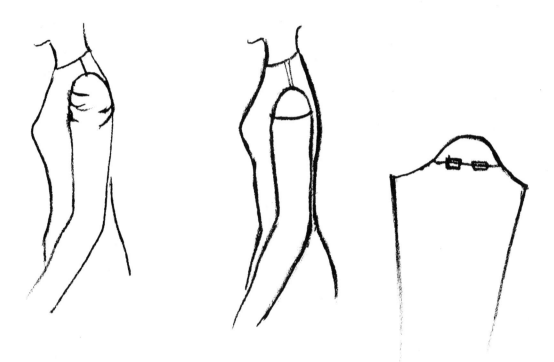

SLEEVE ADJUSTMENTS

Sleeve Cap Too Full

Indications: The sleeve cap wrinkles, or in the case of fabrics like permanent-press, which do not ease well, it is difficult to fit the sleeve into the armhole.

Pin out the extra fabric on the muslin to determine the amount to be taken in.

Take a crosswise tuck in the sleeve cap on the pattern to take in the amount measured on the muslin. Redraw the seam and cutting lines at the top of the sleeve cap.

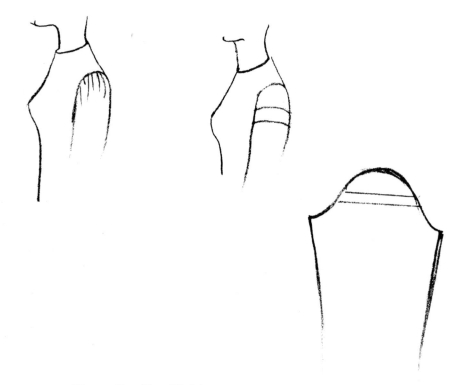

Sleeve Cap Too Tight

Indications: The sleeve cap wrinkles and pulls.

To determine the amount to be let out, cut the muslin crosswise across the sleeve cap and spread until the sleeve cap fits comfortably.

Cut the pattern crosswise at the sleeve cap and spread the amount determined by the corrected muslin. Tape to the tissue paper and redraw the seam and cutting lines at the top of the sleeve cap.

Large Arm

Indications: The sleeve wrinkles and pulls.

Cut the muslin down the center of the sleeve, tapering toward the shoulder. Allow the sleeve to spread to the width required, and then pin.

For set-in sleeves, cut the pattern from the center of the sleeve cap as shown, spread the amount required, and tape. Small darts will form on both sides of the slit; tape them down. Redraw the top of the sleeve cap, adding the amount removed by the darts. Redraw the grain line down the center of the sleeve.

For raglan and kimono sleeves, add the same amount as shown.

Be sure to make any of these corrected sleeves in muslin before cutting into expensive fabric.

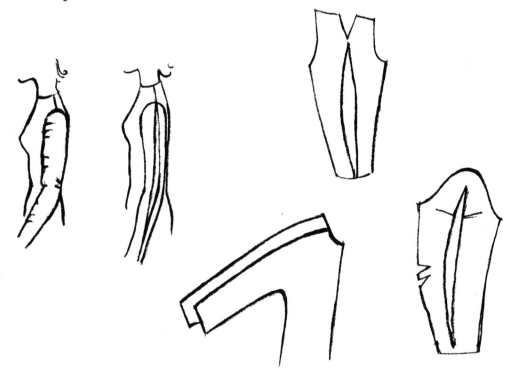

Thin Arm

Indications: The sleeve is too big and droops.

Pin out the fullness on the muslin to determine the amount to be taken in.

Take a lengthwise tuck in the pattern that is one-half of the width to be taken in. Be sure that you do not take too much in at the wrist because the hand won't be able to slip through the sleeve. Taper if necessary.

For raglan and kimono sleeves, take in the same amount as shown.

Be sure to make any of these corrected sleeves in muslin before you cut into expensive fabric.

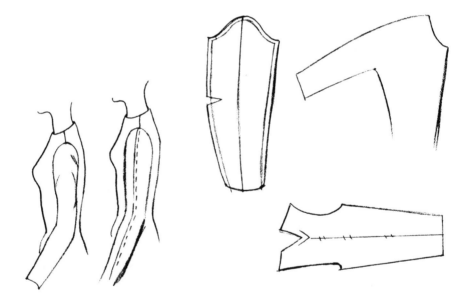

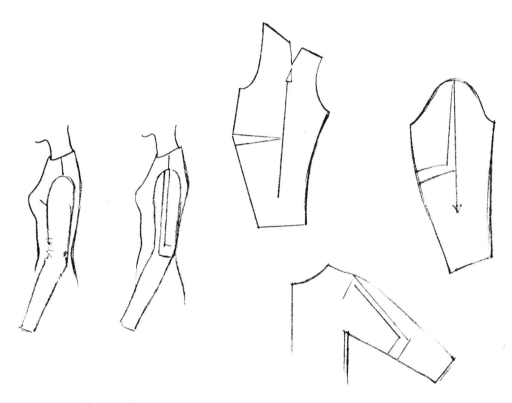

Large Elbow

Indications: The sleeve is too tight at the elbow.

On the muslin, cut the stitches between the seam-line notches at the elbow. Then cut the sleeve between the darts across to the grain-line marking; then cut up to the sleeve cap edge. Allow the sleeve to spread, and then pin. Make an extra dart at the elbow.

Cut the sleeve pattern in the same way and make the adjustment as on the muslin. Draw in the extra dart.

For raglan and kimono sleeves, make the same alterations as shown.

Be sure to make any of these corrected sleeves in muslin before you cut into expensive fabric.

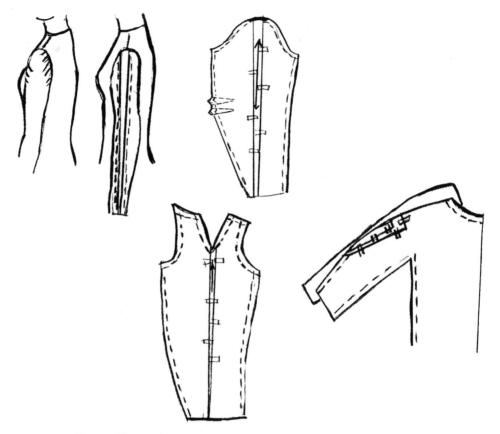

Large Upper Arm

Indications: The armhole is too tight and the sleeve is too tight above the elbow.

On the muslin, cut the stitches in the sleeve cap between the notches. Cut the sleeve along the lengthwise grain marking and allow the sleeve to spread.

Cut the sleeve pattern the same way and make the adjustment, keeping the amount of spread equal distances from the new grain line formed in the center of the sleeve. On the front and back of the dress pattern, add one-half of the amount added to the sleeve. Redraw the seam and cutting lines, tapering to the waist.

For raglan and kimono sleeves, add the same amount as shown.

Be sure to make any of these corrected sleeves in muslin before you cut into expensive fabric.

Very Large Upper Arm

Indications: The alteration for Large Upper Arm is not sufficient.

Cut the muslin lengthwise along the grain line and allow it to spread to determine the amount to be let out.

Cut the pattern parallel to the grain line as shown. Spread, forming darts at each side of the new grain line as shown. Tape, and add the amount to the top of the sleeve cap as shown.

Make the corrected sleeve in muslin to be sure of the fit before cutting into expensive fabric.

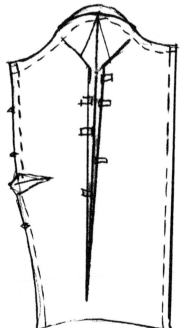

SKIRT ADJUSTMENTS

One Hip Higher or Larger Than the Other

Indications: The skirt is too tight and pulls at one side of the hips, and the hem of the skirt is uneven.

For a dress with a waistline seam, cut the stitching on the shorter side from the waist to the darts. Pin the darts to fit. You will have to make a paper pattern of the left side of the skirt, front and back, out of tissue paper. Transfer the adjustment to the side of the pattern that needs it. Redraw the darts, the seam lines, and cutting lines as shown.

To adjust an A-line dress, cut the stitching from the shorter side up the side seam. Allow the edges to spread until the grain and hem are straight. Pin the back dart to fit.

Make a tissue-paper pattern for the left side of the dress, front and back, and transfer the adjustment to the side required as shown.

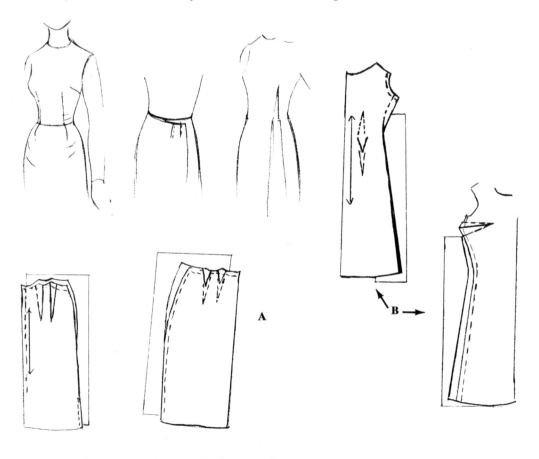

A

B →

Small Buttocks

Indications: The back of the skirt wrinkles below the darts.

For a dress with a waistline seam, cut the stitches at the back waist and pin out the wrinkles to determine how much to take out. Make the darts shorter.

Transfer the adjustment to the pattern, forming a tuck down the back and taking in one-quarter of the total amount as shown. Redraw the waist seam and cutting lines, removing the amount necessary. Redraw the darts, making them shorter.

For an A-line dress, remove the zipper below the back at the shoulder blades and pin out the wrinkles at the center back and side seams. Pin the darts to make them shorter and narrower.

Transfer the adjustments to the pattern, redrawing the seam lines, cutting lines, and darts as shown.

Large Buttocks

Indications: The dress wrinkles between the waist and hips, and the side seams are distorted. The hem of the skirt hangs shorter in the back.

For a dress with a waistline seam, cut the stitching at the waist seam and open the darts. Make the darts shorter and add to the side seams.

Transfer the adjustments to the pattern, redrawing the waist and side seam lines, cutting lines, and darts as shown.

For an A-line dress, open the side seams and zipper seams below the shoulder blades. Allow each seam to spread equally.

Transfer the amount of the adjustment to the pattern, redrawing the seam and cutting lines at the side seams and center back.

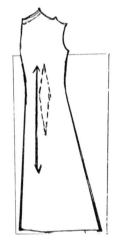

Large Waistline

Indications: The dress is too tight at the waist.

Open the seams at the waist, and if necessary, the darts. Let out the waist the same amount at both sides of the dress. If that is enough, leave the darts alone. If not, pin the darts less deeply, dividing the amount needed by the number of darts plus the seams. For example, if there are two darts in the front and two darts in the back, and three seams (two side seams and center back), the total amount is divided by seven.

Transfer the adjustments to the pattern by redrawing the darts, the side seams and center back seam, and the cutting lines, tapering the lines as shown.

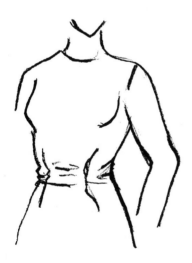
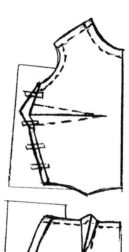

Small Waistline

Indications: The dress is too large at the waist.

Cut the stitches of the seams at the waist, and if necessary, the darts. Take in both sides of the dress equally, and if that is enough, leave the darts alone. If not, pin the darts more deeply, dividing the amount needed by the number of darts plus the seems.

Transfer the adjustment to the pattern and redraw the darts, the side seams and center back seam, and the cutting lines, tapering the lines as shown.

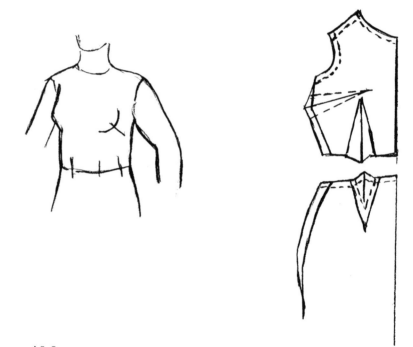

Large Abdomen

Indications: The skirt pulls at the abdomen which causes wrinkles and the hem to rise in the front.

For a dress with a waistline seam, cut the stitches at the front waist seam and front skirt darts. Allow the skirt front to drop until the hem is even. Pin the skirt to fabric placed behind the muslin and repin the darts to fit. If the waist has become smaller, add to the side seams.

Transfer all adjustments to the pattern, redrawing the seam and cutting lines at the waist. Redraw the darts.

To correct an A-line dress, cut the muslin up the front sides to the bustline as shown. Spread, forming an equal increase on each side.

Transfer the adjustments to the pattern by cutting the pattern and spreading it to match the corrected muslin. Cut through the bust dart to make the pattern lie flat and allow it to overlap where necessary.

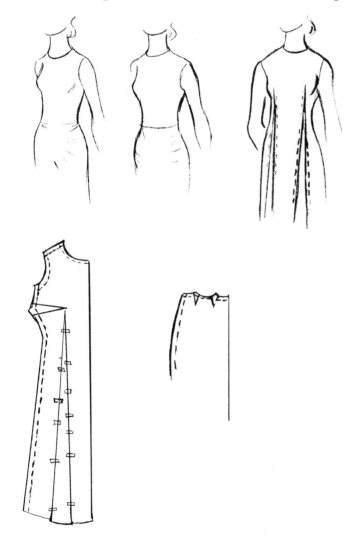

PANTS

Pants in all styles and lengths have become a very important part of every woman's wardrobe. They are not difficult to make, but getting a perfect fit is essential to the finished appearance. Because of this, it will be necessary to take new set of measurements. Unless your measurements match those of the pattern exactly, you will have to make a muslin pants shell to help you get the fit exactly right. All the alterations will have to be made on the flat pattern, as you cannot make major changes after the fabric has been cut.

First, you will have to take that new set of measurements. Start by tying a piece of yarn around your waist and leave it there until you have finished. Make another chart listing the following measurements, with yours in one column and those of the pattern closest to yours in the next column. Buy a classic pants pattern (not hip huggers) in the size closest to your waist measurement, unless your hip measurement is much larger than that given with your waist size. In that case, buy the pattern according to your hip measurement and take in the waistline.

The following ease is allowed in pants patterns:

Hips—2 inches

Thigh—2½ inches

Crotch Depth—½ inch for 35-inch hips or less; ¾ inch for 35- to 38-inch hips; 1 inch for 38-inch hips or over.

Remember to take the ease into consideration when measuring the pattern pieces.

Measurements for Pants

Waist—measure around the yarn tied around your waist. The tape should be held as tightly as you would comfortably wear a waistband.

Hips—Measure around the fullest part, roughly 7 to 9 inches down from the waist.

Thigh—measure at the fullest part of the thigh.

Knee—measure around the knee with the knee straight.

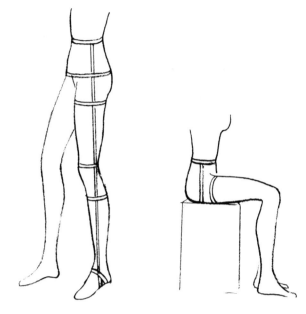

Calf—measure at the fullest part of the calf.

Instep—measure from the heel over the instep with the foot relaxed.

Side Length—measure at the side from the waist to the desired length of the pants.

Crotch Length—sit on a flat chair or bench and measure from the waist to the chair, holding the tape straight from the hip to the chair.

Take out the front and back pieces of your pants' pattern and iron them flat. If there is no crotch line printed on the pattern as shown, using a ruler, draw one at the widest part of the crotch. Measure from the waist within the seam allowance to the crotch line. Compare this measurement to your crotch length measurement, allowing for the ease as given. If the pattern measurement is different from your own, you will have to alter the pattern by either lengthening or shortening.

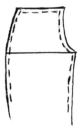

How to Make the Crotch Length Shorter

Folding along the adjustment lines on the pattern, take a tuck one-half of the amount needed. Fasten it to itself with transparent tape. Redraw the seam and cutting lines at the side of the pattern as shown.

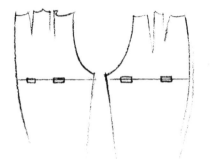

How to Make the Crotch Length Longer

Cut the pattern along the adjustment lines and tape the bottom of the pattern to a piece of tissue paper, and keeping the grain lines straight, spread for the amount needed. Tape the top half of the pattern to the tissue paper.

Measure the thigh width of the pattern by drawing a crosswise line on the pattern at the same place where you took your thigh measurement. Measure within the seam allowances and add the front and back measurements together. If the total is different from yours with 2½ inches for ease, you will have to either make the pattern wider or make it narrower, depending on whether your measurement is larger or smaller than the pattern.

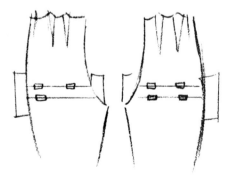

How to Make the Pants' Leg Wider

Place tissue paper under the pattern and redraw the seam and cutting lines at the side seams of the pants, allowing one-quarter of the amount to be widened at each seam. Taper toward the hem as shown.

How to Make the Pants' Leg Narrower

Redraw the seam and cutting lines at the side seams of the pants, taking in one-quarter of the amount to be taken in at each seam. Taper toward the hem as shown.

Measure the length of the adjusted pants along the outside seam from the waist within the seam allowance to the hem. Compare to your side measurement. If the pants are either too short or too long, they will have to be altered.

How To Shorten the Leg

Draw crosswise adjustment lines on the leg above the hemline in the same place on the front and back. Take a tuck, folding along the line, and take in one-half of the amount needed in the same way that the crotch was shortened. If the pants must be made even shorter, cut off at the hemline.

How to Lengthen the Leg

Draw crosswise adjustment lines on the leg above the hemline in the same place on the front and back. Cut along the line and tape the bottom to tissue paper. Keeping the grain line straight, spread the pattern the amount required and tape the top of the pattern to the tissue paper in the same way that the crotch was lengthened. If the pants must be made even longer, add to the hemline.

If the waistline is either too small or too large, you will have to alter the pattern at the waist.

How to Make the Waistline Smaller

Subtract your waist measurement from the pattern's to determine how much you have to take in. Redraw the side and center seam lines and cutting lines, taking in one-eighth of the amount required. Take in the same amount on the pattern for the waistband or the facing.

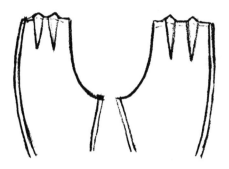

How to Make the Waistline Larger

The difference between your waistline measurement and the pattern's will determine how much you have to let out. With tissue paper behind the pattern pieces, redraw the side and center seam lines and cutting lines, letting out one-eighth of the amount required. Add the same amount to the waistband or the facing pieces.

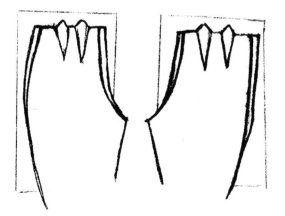

Since you have chosen the pants' pattern according to your hip measurement, no alteration at the hip should be necessary.

You will only need to take the knee, calf, and instep measurements into consideration if you are making very tight-fitting pants. If there is any difference between your measurements and those of the pattern, alter the leg seams as necessary.

Now that you have made all the flat pattern alterations, you are ready to make the pants' muslin shell to make sure that no further alterations will be necessary. Like the dress muslin shell, it can be made out of either unbleached muslin or a cotton fabric. In this case a fairly heavy cotton, such as denim or cotton hopsacking, would be suitable. Sew all the seams, following the instructions for construction given on the pattern primer. Be sure to make a waistband and baste it to the pants. Try the pants on and check for the following fitting points.

Make sure that the waist and hips fit comfortably, if not, check your pattern alterations and change where necessary. Make sure the crotch length is comfortable when you stand and sit.

If there is pulling across the front and/or back at the crotch, you will have to let out the crotch inner seams. If there are wrinkles or folds at this point, you will have to take in the crotch inner seams.

How to Make the Crotch Inner Seam Wider

On the muslin, cut the stitches at the crotch to determine how much will have to be added.

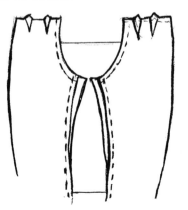

Redraw the seam and cutting lines at the inner crotch as shown, adding one-quarter of the amount needed, tapering the lines toward the leg seam.

How to Make the Crotch Inner Seam Narrower

Pin the muslin at the crotch to determine how much to take in.

Redraw the seam and cutting lines at the inner crotch as shown, removing one-quarter of the amount needed, tapering the lines toward the leg seam.

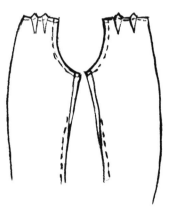

You may still have to make further alterations if you find that you have any of the following figure problems.

Large Buttocks

Indications: The pants are too tight across the buttocks and the side seams are distorted.

Cut the stitches holding the waistband at the back and open the darts. Let the back of the pants fall until the side seams straighten out. Add fabric to the back of the pants and inner leg seams until the pants hang straight. Pin the darts to fit. Add to the side seams if the waistline has become too small.

Transfer the adjustment to the pattern by redrawing the seam and cutting lines at the waistline and those of the inner leg at the crotch. Redraw the darts and the seam and cutting lines at the sides if necessary.

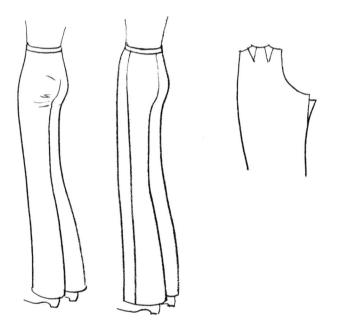

Flat Buttocks

Indications: The pants wrinkle and there is too much fabric at the back of the pants.

Pin the back of the pants to determine how much to take in.

At the adjustment line on the back of the pants' pattern, make a tuck, tapering with the widest point at the center seam. The depth of the tuck at the widest point should be half of the amount to be removed, tapering to nothing just before you get to the outer leg seam. See illustration. Redraw the seam and cutting lines at the inside of the crotch.

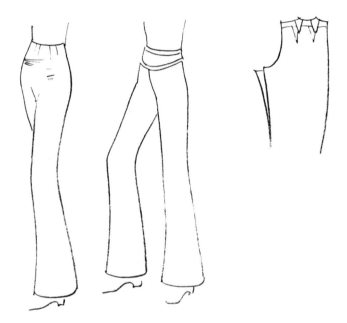

Large Abdomen

Indications: The pants are too tight and pull across the abdomen, and the side seams are distorted.

Cut the stitches holding the front of the pants to the waistband and open the darts. Let the front of the pants fall until the side seams straighten. Add fabric to the front of the pants and to the inner leg seams until the pants hang straight. Pin the darts to fit.

Transfer the adjustments to the pattern by redrawing the seam and cutting lines at the waistline and those of the inner leg at the crotch. Redraw the darts.

Protruding Hips

Indications: The fabric pulls and strains at the hip bones in front.

Cut the stitches that hold the front of the pants to the waistband and open the darts. Repin the darts to fit.

Transfer the adjustment to the pattern by redrawing the darts, shortening or widening them where necessary. If the waistline has become smaller, add to the side seams by redrawing the seam and cutting lines, adding one-quarter of the amount needed at each seam.

All of this may seem like an awful lot of work just to get a perfect-fitting pair of pants. But remember, that is something that most women cannot have unless they just happen to be a perfect ready-made size, or unless they can afford to have their pants custom-made. Take your corrected pants' pattern and make it permanent by transferring it to heavy paper or to non-woven interfacing. You will then have a guide for making all styles of pants—shorts, jumpsuits, knickers, and whatever else fashion comes up with—that will fit you perfectly every time.

CHAPTER

UNDERSTANDING FABRICS

Once you have selected the pattern, the next decision is crucial to the success of your sewing. How can you know which fabric is suitable for the style you have selected? Even though you may never have sewn before, you already know part of the answer from having bought and worn clothes. You already know, for example, that you cannot make a filmy blouse out of a heavy, stiff fabric like denim. While common sense plays a part in your selection, you will have to know something about the composition and weave of fabrics before you can make really knowledgeable decisions about what fabric to choose.

NATURAL FIBERS

The natural fibers are derived from plant or animal sources. These fibers are woven and knitted into different kinds of fabrics and finished in various ways, but they always maintain their original properties.

Wool

The wool fiber comes from the fleece of sheep. Sometimes hair or fur from other animals, such as camels and goats, is used or incorporated into fabrics classified as wool. Due to its natural crimp, the wool fiber spins into yarns and has a great amount of elasticity and resiliency. When wool is woven or knitted into fabric, it has very good shape-retaining abilities and tailors well.

The Wool Products Labeling Act requires that wool fibers be classified and also that they be properly labeled. The categories for wool are as follows:

Virgin Wool—This is wool that has never been used before, nor has it been reclaimed for making yarn or fabric. It comes in different qualities and weights.

Pure Wool or 100 Percent Wool—This wool is composed wholly of new wool that is being used for the first time in the complete manufacture of a wool product. The product may also contain 5 percent of another fiber as surface ornamentation and still qualify as 100 percent wool under the Wool Labeling Act.

Wool Product—This applies to any product or portion of a product that contains or purports to contain, or is in any way represented as containing wool, reused wool, or reprocessed wool.

Reprocessed Wool—This is wool that has been manufactured into a woven or felted state for the first time, and then is reduced to fiber for reuse without ever having been worn or utilized by the consumer. This wool may include clothing manufacturing clippings of unused new materials or mill ends accumulated during the manufacturing process.

Reused Wool—This is wool that has been returned to a fibrous state after having been spun, woven, knitted, or felted into a product that has ben used by the consumer. It is usually blended with new wool fibers.

Woolen fabrics are suitable for many different kinds of garments, depending on the weight and weave of the fabric.

Clothes made of 100 percent wool, or blends, or combinations of other fibers with wool usually have to be dry-cleaned unless the manufacturer's instructions call for washing. For hand washing, use a mild soap or a special wool soap and cool water. Soak for a few minutes. Block the garment and allow it to dry on a flat surface. For machine washing, use mild suds and cool water at a gentle agitation setting for two minutes. Interrupt the cycle for ten minutes and let the garment soak, then complete the wash cycle. Do not use a machine dryer. Block the garment on a flat surface and allow it to dry.

Press on the wrong side with a steam iron or a damp pressing cloth.

Linen

Linen fiber is made from the stems of the flax plant. It is the oldest fiber known to mankind. There are Egyptian wall paintings that date back to 2000 B.C. which show the manufacture of linen. Flax is woven into a fabric that is very strong and that has natural luster. Due to the stiffness of the fibers, linen fabrics tend to break along creases and edges. Linen fabrics have a tendency to wrinkle, but this shortcoming can be corrected with finishes which make it crease-resistant. It may shrink unless it is preshrunk.

Linen fibers are made into fabrics which are used to make blouses, dresses, pants, skirts, and suits.

If a garment made of linen has not been preshrunk, it has to be dry-cleaned—otherwise linen washes well. Hand wash in hot water and hang on a rust-proof hanger to dry. Machine wash in hot water at a regular setting for five to eight minutes. Machine dry at a regular temperature setting and remove while it is still damp enough to iron. Iron at a high setting.

Silk

Silk is made from the cocoon of the silkworm. The cocoon is unreeled into a fiber which forms a continuous filament, the only natural fiber that does this. The filament is then turned into fine threads, which make the silk yarn. It is woven or knitted into a fabric which is very resilient and lustrous. The fabrics are generally light in weight and very strong. Silk is available in a great number of different weaves and weights which are used to make blouses, dresses, skirts, pants, and suits. Silk is also used for making sewing thread.

Most silk fabrics have to be dry-cleaned. If the fabric is labeled "washable," hand wash in a mild soap or a detergent in lukewarm water. To dry, hang on a rust-proof hanger, away from direct light. Machine wash in a mild soap or a detergent in lukewarm water for three minutes at a mild agitation setting. Machine dry at a low temperature setting for a few minutes and hang to finish drying. Iron on the wrong side while still damp, using a low temperature setting. Use a thin pressing cloth to avoid water-spotting.

Cotton

Cotton is made from the protective seed fibers of the cotton plant. Cotton is much stronger wet than dry and therefore stands up well to repeated washings. Fabrics made from cotton are very absorbent and durable. Cotton fibers are made into 100 percent cotton fabrics or are blended or combined to make a vast number of fabrics with different textures, weaves, and weights. These fabrics are used for making blouses, dresses, skirts, pants, sportswear, suits, and children's clothes. Cotton is also used to make sewing thread.

Cotton fabrics are washable. Hand wash in hot water and allow to dry on a rust-proof hanger. Machine wash in hot water at a regular speed setting for ten minutes. Use a chlorine bleach unless the label says not to. Machine dry at a regular setting and press with a hot iron while the garment is still damp.

SYNTHETIC FIBERS

Synthetic, or man-made, fibers were first developed in the middle of the nineteenth century. The first commercially produced synthetic was rayon, in 1910. Synthetics are produced from natural substances, such as cellulose (of plant origin) or protein (of animal origin), or are produced entirely from chemical origins. Synthetic fibers are sold under the different manufacturers' brand names and are made into fabrics which may have names of their own. New synthetic fibers and fabrics are being introduced every day, and the best way to be aware of them is to follow the textile advertising in magazines and to explore new fabrics as they come into the stores.

Most fabrics made of synthetics are easy-care and washable, but this varies with the individual fabric, so always be sure to check when you buy your fabric. If the fabric does not have a label that gives the cleaning instructions, ask the salesperson, and if she doesn't know, insist on finding out from the buyer, as it is essential to the success of your sewing projects that you know how to care for your clothes.

Acetate

Fabrics made from acetate fibers are luxurious and have a silklike appearance. They have excellent drapability and the ability to retain crispness. These fibers are used in such fabrics as jersey, taffeta, satin, faille, lace, brocade, crepe, and tricot. They are also used in blends with other synthetic fibers. These fabrics are suitable for blouses, dresses, lingerie, and linings.

They are usually dry-cleaned unless the label indicates that they are washable. If that is so, they should be hand laundered in lukewarm water or machine washed in warm or cold water, using a mild agitation setting. Machine dry at a cool setting or hang the garment to dry on a rust-proof hanger, away from direct heat. Iron while damp with a steam iron at the lowest setting. Do not use acetone or other organic solvents, such as nail-polish remover or perfumes containing such solvents, as they will affect the fabric adversely.

Trademarks and Manufacturers
Acele—E. I. du Pont de Nemours & Company, Inc.
Avicolor—FMC Corporation, American Viscose Division
Avisco—FMC Corporation, American Viscose Division
Celanese—Celanese Fiber Company
Celaperm—Celanese Fiber Company
Celara—Celanese Fiber Company
Chromspun—Eastman Kodak Company
Estron—Eastman Kodak Company

Acrylic

Fabrics of acrylic fibers are generally of light, fluffy constructions. The fabrics are warm and lightweight and hold their shape well.

Acrylic fibers are found in knits, fleece fabrics, pile fabrics, and sheers. They are also used in blends with other man-made fibers. These fabrics are suitable for skirts, pants, dresses, suits, and sports clothes.

Acrylic fabrics may be dry-cleaned or hand laundered, depending on the manufacturer's instructions. Hand wash in warm water with a soap or a detergent. Rinse in warm water with a fabric softener. For machine washing, use warm water and a mild agitation setting. Add a fabric softener to the final rinse. Machine dry at the lowest temperature setting, or hang on a rust-proof hanger to dry. Iron with a moderately warm iron. Never use a hot iron.

Trademarks and Manufacturers
Acrilan—Monsanto Company
Creslan—American Cyanamid Company
Orlon—E. I. du Pont de Nemours & Company, Inc.
Zefkrome—Dow Badische Company
Zefran—Dow Badische Company

Metallic Yarns

Fibers of gold, silver, and other colors with a metallic finish are blended with other fibers to give the fabric a decorative feature.

Metallic-yarn novelty fabrics are used for blouses, dresses, and dressy pants suits.

Depending on the manufacturer's instructions, these fabrics can be dry-cleaned or hand laundered. Hand wash in lukewarm water and iron at the lowest setting.

Trademarks and Manufacturers
Lurex—Dow Badische Company
Mylar—E. I. du Pont de Nemours & Company, Inc.

Modacrylic

Modacrylic yarns are used for making fake furs and deep-pile fleece fabrics, which are suitable for coats, coat linings, and trims.

Most fake furs should be dry-cleaned, using a fur-cleaning process. For washable fabrics, machine wash in warm water and add a fabric softener to the rinse. Use a dryer at a low temperature setting and remove the garment when the tumbling has stopped. Iron only at the lowest setting if absolutely necessary.

Trademarks and Manufacturers
Dynel—Union Carbide Corporatoin
Verel—Eastman Kodak Company

Nylon

Nylon is smooth, resilient, and lustrous. It comes in a great many different fabric textures and weaves. Nylon is very often used in blends with other fibers.

The fabrics made from nylon are used for blouses, dresses, skirts, pants, suits, and lingerie.

Trademarks and Manufacturers
Antron—E. I. du Pont de Nemours & Company, Inc.
Caprolan—Allied Chemical Corporation
Cedilla—Celanese Fiber Company
Celanese—Celanese Fiber Company
Chemstrand—Monsanto Company
Blue C—Monsanto Company
Enkalure—American Enka Corporation
Quiana—E. I. du Pont de Nemours & Company, Inc.
Touch—Allied Chemical Corporation

Olefin

Wool-like in texture, olefin is very light in weight and is quick-drying. Olefin fibers are used alone and in blends to make textured fabrics, fake furs, and deep-pile fabrics. The textured fabrics are suitable for skirts, pants, dresses, suits, and coats. The fake furs and deep-pile fabrics are used for coats, jackets, coat linings, and trims.

Machine wash in lukewarm water and add a fabric softener to the rinses. Machine dry only at a very low temperature setting. Do not iron fabrics of 100 percent olefin.

Trademarks and Manufacturers
Hurculon—Hercules Incorporated
Marvess—Phillips Fibers Corporation

Polyester

Polyester is available in different weights and textures. It is used for making knits, permanent-press fabrics, and sewing thread, is also used in blends with other fibers. These fabrics are suitable for blouses, dresses, pants, skirts, suits, and lingerie.

Polyesters are either hand or machine washable. Hand wash in warm water with a fabric softener added to the final rinse. Let the garment dry on a rust-proof hanger. Machine wash in warm water and add a fabric softener to the rinse. Machine dry at a low temperature setting and remove as soon as the tumbling cycle has stopped. Use a moderately warm iron for pressing.

Trademarks and Manufacturers
Avlin—FMC Corporation, American Viscose Division
Blue C—Monsanto Company
Dacron—E. I. du Pont de Nemours & Company, Inc.
Encron—American Enka Corporation
Fortrel—Celanese Fibers Company
Kodel—Eastman Kodak Company
Quintess—Phillips Fibers Corporation
Trevira—Hystron Fibers Incorporated
Vycron—Beaunit Corporation

Rayon

Rayon is made in different textures and weights and is very often blended with other fibers. It is used to make a variety of fabrics which are used to make blouses, dresses, skirts, pants, suits, coats, lingerie, and linings.

Fabrics made with rayon usually have to be dry-cleaned, but follow the fabric manufacturer's instructions. If the fabric is washable, wash by hand in lukewarm water with a mild soap or a detergent. Allow the garment to dry on a rust-proof hanger. Iron on the wrong side while the garment is damp, using a moderate setting.

Trademarks and Manufacturers

Avisco—FMC Corporation, American Viscose Division
Avril—FMC Corporation, American Viscose Division
Bemberg—Beaunit Corporation
Coloray—Courtalds North America, Incorporated
Cupioni—Beaunit Corporation
Englo—American Enka Corporation
Enka—American Enka Corporation
Enkrome—American Enka Corporation
Zantrel—American Enka Corporation

Spandex

Spandex is stretchy, supple, light in weight and is used in stretchable fabrics. The fabrics are used for making bathing suits, ski pants, sportswear, foundation garments, and elastic banding.

Hand or machine wash in lukewarm water; do not use chlorine bleach. Rinse completely and allow the garment to drip dry. Use a low temperature setting for machine drying. Iron only at low temperatures.

Trademarks and Manufacturers

Lycra—E. I. du Pont de Nemours & Company, Inc.
Vyrene—UniRoyal Fiber and Textile

Triacetate

Triacetate fibers are wrinkle- and shrink-resistant, and when made into fabric, will hold pleats well. It is used in fabrics such as flannel, sharkskin, taffeta, and tricot. These fabrics are suitable for blouses, dresses, skirts, pants, and sportswear.

Pleated garments should be hand washed in warm water and hung to drip dry. Other garments can be machine washed and dried. Iron at a high temperature setting. Do not use acetone.

Trademarks and Manufacturers
Arnel—Celanese Corporation

YARNS

Once the fibers have been formed, they are spun into yarn, and the nature of the yarn influences the character of the finished fabric. The yarn is made from the staple, or filament, of the fiber. Natural fibers (except silk) come in short lengths, which form the staple. Silk and synthetics form long filaments, although synthetics are sometimes cut into shorter staples to imitate natural fibers. Both natural and synthetic fibers are used alone or in blends to form the yarn.

The original yarn is in the form of a "single," which is then twisted to produce a "ply yarn." The amount of twist affects the strength and character

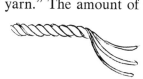

of the fabric. Novelty yarns are made in several ways. A single or ply yarn can be varied in thickness and in the amount of twist to form a "slub" yarn. They can also be made of various colors and fibers. Novelty ply yarns are

formed by having different types of singles twisted into one yarn, these making bouclé and ratiné yarns, which have very distinctive textures. Synthetic yarns can be heat-set to form textured yarns such as looped, coiled, or crimped yarns. It is textured yarns such as these which are used to make synthetic stretch fabrics.

Once the fiber has been turned into yarn, it has to be made into fabric. There are different ways of doing this, the most common of which is weaving. All woven fabrics are made with the yarn threaded lengthwise (the warp) and with the crosswise yarn (the woof, weft, or filling) woven over and under and back and forth. This process forms the woven fabric with its outside edges forming the "selvages," which are more tightly woven than the rest of the fabric. The number of threads on the weaving loom determines the different textures and effects available in woven fabrics.

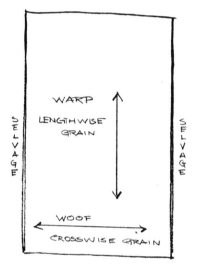

WEAVES

Plain Weave

The most common of the weaves used is the plain weave. The fabric is formed by the yarn in the weft direction alternately passing over and under

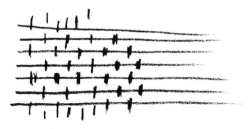

each yarn in the warp direction. The same construction is used with double or multiple threads to form a basket weave. Basket-woven fabrics are softer and are not as strong as plain-woven fabrics of the same weight threads.

Twill Weave

The twill weave is formed with the threads more closely woven. The warp and filler threads are interlaced and form a diagonal ridge, usually running from the lower left to the upper right of the fabric. Typical examples are gabardine and denim. Herringbone is also formed by twill weaving, with the diagonal ridges forming a chevron design.

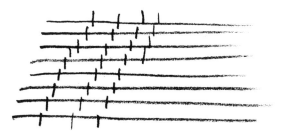

Satin Weave

Satin weave is formed by having the warp threads pass over several filler threads before being caught, thus creating "floats." These floats are parallel to each other and create the smooth appearance of satin and cotton satin.

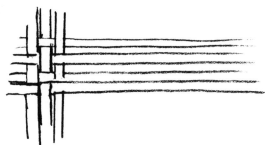

Leno Weave

The leno weave produces an open, lacy fabric. A typical example is marquisette, which is used for casement curtain fabrics.

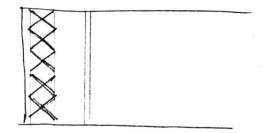

Dobby Weave

Dobby weaves produce effects such as birds-eye piqué and other small, geometric patterns repeated throughout the fabric.

Jacquard Weave

Jacquard weaves are made on a special loom and produce intricate designs woven into the fabric. Typical examples are damasks, tapestries, and brocades.

KNITS

Knitted fabrics have undergone a revolution in the last few years. Originally available only in the single knit (machine made to resemble the "stockinette" stitch of hand knitting), knits are now to be had in a great variety of weights, textures, and patterns. Knits are produced by machines with needles that form a series of interlocking loops with one or more yarns at the same time. Because of the looped construction, knits are more flexible and stretchy than woven fabrics.

Single Knits

These are made with a single set of needles and produce a fabric with a right ("knit") side and a wrong ("purl") side like hand knitting. The most typical example is jersey. Single knits are often made in circular or tubular form, but nowadays most circular knits are cut apart before they reach the store.

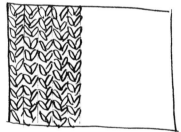

Double Knits

Double knits are produced by machines that have two sets of needles that form an interlock stitch, which gives a double thickness to the fabric. In a plain double knit, both sides of the fabric are similar, but not identical. They are also available in many different textures and patterns.

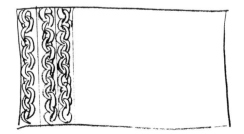

Tricot

Tricot is made on a warp knitting machine that produces a run-resistant, lightweight fabric which is used largely for lingerie and as backing for bonded fabrics.

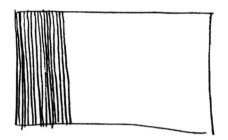

OTHER FABRICS

Nonwoven fabrics are made by matting the fibers together, using either a heat or a chemical process. This produces a fabric which will not unravel, run, or curl when it is cut, and it can be cut in any direction.

Felt

Felt is a nonwoven fabric made largely of wool or fur fibers and is produced by matting the fibers under heat, steam, and pressure. It comes in a great variety of weights, but is not as strong as a woven or a knitted fabric.

Synthetic Nonwovens

Synthetic nonwoven fabrics are made of synthetic fibers (nylon and rayon, or polyester) that are held in place by chemical bonding agents. They are available in different weights and are suitable for use with different fabrics. These fabrics are used for interfacings.

Pile Fabrics

Pile fabrics are woven with a third yarn which forms loops that stand up tightly on the surface of the fabric. For most pile fabrics these loops are cut, forming a plushy surface which usually has a nap running in one direction. Examples of these cut-loop fabrics are velvet, velveteen, and corduroy. Terry cloth is made in the same way, with the loops left uncut.

Blended Fabrics

To make blended fabrics, two or more fibers are blended into the yarn before spinning, before the yarn is made into fabric.

Combination Fabrics

In making combination fabrics, yarns of different fibers are combined in the weaving process.

Laminated Fabrics

To make laminated fabrics, a foam backing is heat-set permanently to another fabric to produce a fabric with a warm interfacing built right in.

Bonded Fabrics

Bonded fabrics are produced by joining one layer of fabric to another by heat-setting with an adhesive or urethane foam. Most bonded fabrics are composed of a face fabric and a backing, usually acetate tricot, which forms a built-in lining. When buying bonded fabrics, it is very important to make sure that the surface fabric has not been pulled off-grain.

BASIC FABRIC DICTIONARY

The following fabrics are made of natural fibers, although almost all of these different weaves are now available in synthetics, or blends, or combinations of synthetic and natural fibers. This does not change the weight or the suitability of the fabrics for the types of garment listed.

Wool

Lightweight
Challis—Challis is woven, very soft, and lightweight. It has a smooth

surface and is usually printed, often in classic "peasant" florals. Challis is suitable for blouses, dresses, full, flowing pants, and full skirts.

Crepe—Crepe has a pebbly, grainy surface, with a very dry hand. This refers to the general feel, drape & texture of the fabric. It comes in very light to heavy weights. Light to medium crepes are suitable for blouses, dresses, lightweight jackets, and dressy pants outfits. The heavier weights are suitable for jackets and lightweight coats.

Jersey—Jersey is a single-thread knit fabric with a right and wrong side, like the knit and purl of hand knitting. It is a very soft fabric. Jersey is suitable for blouses, dresses, soft, simple suits, and loose, flowing pants.

Medium Weight

Broadcloth—Woolen broadcloth is tightly woven, with a nap running in one direction. It is fairly firm and is especially suitable for tailoring. It is used for skirts, pants, tailored dresses, and suits.

Double Knits—Double knits are knitted with two interlocking threads, so that both sides of the fabric are similar. They are available in solid colors and with patterns knitted into the fabric. They are firm but soft and very easy to work with. Double knits are suitable for dresses, skirts, pants, suits, jumpsuits, and lightweight coats.

Flannel—Wool flannel is soft, and slightly napped with a plain or twilled (obvious diagonal rib), dull surface. It is suitable for skirts, pants, tailored dresses, suits, and lightweight coats.

Gabardine—Gabardine is tightly woven and firm, with a twilled surface. It has a slightly firm hand. It is suitable for skirts, pants, tailored dresses, suits, and lightweight coats.

Tweed—Tweed is woven, fairly rough in texture, and usually has different colors woven into the fabric. Tweed is available in medium to heavy weights. It is suitable for skirts, pants, and tailored dresses in medium weights, and for suits and coats in the heavier weights.

Worsted—Worsted fabrics are tightly woven, with a firm surface and a crisp hand. Worsted yarns have undergone a larger number of processes than regular woolen yarns and are therefore smoother and stronger.

The yarns are more even and are subjected to greater twisting. They are easy to tailor and wear longer than other woolens. Worsteds are suitable for skirts, pants, tailored dresses, suits, and coats.

Heavyweight

Chinchilla Cloth—Chinchilla cloth is a very heavy wool with a spongy texture and a nubby surface. It is sometimes used for simple skirts and suits, but is most often used for coats.

Coating—Coating is a broad term referring to any woolen heavy enough for warm coats. It is also suitable for simple jackets or suits, and skirts and pants.

Melton—Melton is heavyweight and has a smooth surface. It is short napped and very thick. It is used for heavy jackets and coats.

Ottoman—Ottoman has a cross-corded surface similar to faille, but with larger ribs. It is suitable for skirts, tailored dresses, suits, and coats.

Linen

Lightweight

Sheer—Sheer and lightweight linen is plain-woven, with a slight sheen that all linen has due to the natural luster of the fiber. Sheer linen is suitable for blouses and summer dresses.

Medium Weight

Dress Weight—Dress-weight linen is also plain-woven, and can be had in solid colors and prints and with embroidery. It is suitable for blouses and dresses.

Heavyweight

Suiting Weight—Suiting-weight linen is like dress-weight linen, but heavier. It is suitable for skirts, pants, tailored dresses, suits, and summer-weight coats.

Tweed Linen—Tweed linen is woven and usually is multicolored like wool tweed. It also comes in patterns like hound's-tooth. It is suitable for skirts, pants, tailored dresses, suits, and summer-weight coats.

Cotton

Lightweight

Dotted Swiss—Dotted swiss is crisp and sheer, made of either voile or lawn, with soft yarns forming small dots on the right side of the fabric. It usually comes in solid colors with white dots, but it is also available in other color combinations. It is used for blouses, summer dresses, and sportswear.

Lawn—Lawn is a very lightweight firm cotton with a crisp hand. It is usually printed, often in florals, and is suitable for blouses, summer dresses, and full skirts.

Organdy—Organdy is sheer, with a very crisp finish. It is usually used for blouses and summer evening dresses. It is very often used as a trim (collar, cuffs,) for a dress or a blouse made of another fabric.

Voile—Voile is sheer, usually printed, with a medium to crisp hand. It is suitable for blouses and dresses and is very often used for summer evening dresses.

Medium Weight

Broadcloth—Cotton broadcloth has small crosswise ribs and a firm texture. It comes in solid colors and prints and is suitable for sportswear, blouses, and dresses.

Cotton Piqué—Cotton piqué is a firm cotton which has raised cords that give different, patterned effects. Most popular in white, it also comes in solid colors and prints. It is suitable for blouses, dresses, summer suits, sportswear, and as a trim for use with other fabrics.

Cotton Satin, Also Called Sateen—Cotton satin is woven in a satin weave, giving the fabric a definite sheen. It comes in both solid colors and prints. It has a fairly crisp hand and is suitable for blouses, dresses, and skirts.

Gingham—Gingham is woven, usually in checks, but also in stripes and plaids. It is firm-textured. The most usual combination is a check of white with another color. It is suitable for blouses, dresses, skirts, pants, and sportswear.

Poplin—Poplin is similar to cotton broadcloth, but it has slightly heavier ribs and a crisper texture. It is available in solid colors and prints and is suitable for sportswear, skirts, dresses, and lightweight suits.

Seersucker—Seersucker has crinkled stripes woven in the lengthwise direction, usually a solid color alternate with a white stripe. It also comes in solid colors, prints and plaids. The stripes come from very narrow to half-inch widths. It is suitable for blouses, sportswear, skirts, dresses, and lightweight summer suits.

Velveteen—Velveteen is a cotton fabric with a closely woven, cut pile running in one direction, which resembles velvet. It is available in solid color and prints. It is used for dresses, skirts, pants, suits, and coats.

Heavyweight

Corduroy—Corduroy has a cut pile, and therefore a nap running in one direction. It comes with wales (ribs) from very narrow (pinwale) to very wide. It also comes without any wale when it resembles velveteen, and with novelty cords and ribs. It is suitable for sportswear, pants, skirts, tailored dresses, suits, and coats.

Cotton Knit—Cotton knits come in light to medium weights and can be single-thread like jersey, or double knit. It is very soft, and in the double knits, very stable and easy to handle. It is usually printed, but also comes in solid colors. It is suitable for blouses, T-shirts, and dresses —and in double knits, for skirts, pants, and suits.

Denim—Denim is a twill-woven, medium- to heavyweight cotton. It usually comes in solid color warp with white weft, but it is also avaliable in stripes, plaids, and prints. Most often used for making jeans, it tends to fade and soften with repeated washings. It is used for making pants, skirts, sportswear, and casual suits.

Duck—Duck is plain-woven and very durable. It is made in different weights and is often called *canvas*. It is suitable for skirts, pants, and sportswear.

Terry Cloth—Terry cloth has a looped pile on one or both sides, and can be either knitted or woven. This is the fabric that bath towels are made of, and it is best used for bathrobes, beach wraps, and sports dresses.

Silk

Lightweight

Chiffon—Chiffon is transparent, usually extremely soft, and plain woven. Available in both solid colors and prints, it is difficult to handle and therefore not recommended for a beginning sewer. It is used for soft blouses and soft, usually evening, dresses.

China Silk—China silk is plain-woven and very soft, with a sheen to the surface. It is usually used for linings, but can also be used for blouses.

Organza—Organza is sheer, with a crisp finish like organdy. It is suitable for blouses and evening dresses. It is also used as an interfacing for some fabrics.

Silk Jersey—Silk jersey is a knitted jersey which is very soft and delicate, and drapes beautifully. It is available in solid colors and prints and is suitable for blouses and dresses.

Medium Weight

Brocade—Brocade is jacquard-woven. Usually metallic thread is woven into the design, which has an embossed, interwoven effect. The background of the fabric is twill, or satin, or a combination of weaves, making it light to medium to heavy weight. It is used for evening blouses, dresses, and in the heavier weights, suits, and coats.

Crepe—Silk crepe has a pebbly, grainy surface like wool crepe and comes in different weights from light to medium. It is suitable for blouses, dresses, and dressy pants outfits.

Faille—Faille has crosswise ribs and a slight gloss. It is soft and is used for blouses, dresses, and dressy pants outfits.

Peau de Soie—Peau de Soie (French for "skin of silk") is a satin-weave silk with a grainy surface. It comes in both single and double face and is used to make blouses, dresses, and loose, flowing pants.

Satin—Satin is a very smooth fabric in a satin weave, with an almost shiny surface. It can be combined with other weaves. It is suitable for evening clothes: blouses, dresses, suits, and coats.

Shantung—Shantung is a plain-weave silk with heavier weft threads, which create an irregular surface. It is suitable for dresses, blouses, and suits.

Silk Tweed—Silk tweed is a woven fabric, usually multicolored, and with an appearance similar to wool tweed. It has a firm, but soft hand and comes in medium to heavy weights. In medium weights, it is suitable for blouses and dresses; in the heavier weights, it is suitable for tailored dresses, skirts, suits, and summer-weight coats.

Surah—Surah is a twill-woven silk. It is available in prints, stripes, and plaids. It is used to make blouses and dresses.

LININGS, UNDERLININGS AND INTERFACINGS

Very few clothes are made with a single layer of fabric. Most of the clothes you make will call for at least one form of a second layer of fabric to be incorporated into the construction of the garment. These fabrics are inside the finished garment, and except for coat and jacket linings, they never show on the outside. These hidden fabrics take three forms: linings, underlinings, and interfacings. The purpose of the underneath layers of fabric is to add body and strength to the fiinished garment. Some styles will call for one of the three methods of adding this extra body, other styles will call for two, or all three. How many you use will depend entirely on the individual garment you are making, but before you start sewing, you must know the function of each method and how it is different from the other two.

The selection of the fabric used for linings, underlinings, and interfacings is as important as the choice of the outer fabric. The fabrics must be compatible. If your outer fabric is washable, the underneath fabric must also be washable, or the garment will be ruined the first time you wash it. If the outer fabric is permanent-press, any lining or underlining must also have a permanent-press finish. The weights of the different fabrics must also be compatible. If the lining, underlining, or interfacing is too heavy, the garment will not hang correctly; if it is too light or flimsy, it will not be strong enough to serve the purpose of giving body to the garment. You must also choose these fabrics so that they will be durable enough to last the life of the garment.

Nothing is more irritating than a garment in which the lining or underlining has unraveled or torn before the outer fabric has worn out.

Linings

Linings are used to finish the inside of a garment, and in the case of coats, jackets, and vests, they will show when the garment is worn. They are cut from special lining pattern pieces given with the pattern, or they can be cut from the same pattern pieces as the outside of the garment, but in both cases they are constructed separately and are sewn into the garment by hand or machine. Linings give body to the garment, and can be used in conjunction with underlinings and/or interfacing. Linings also help reduce wrinkles and prevent clinging in the finished garment. Your pattern will call for the use of a lining when the designer feels that one is necessary. If your pattern does not provide lining pieces and you feel that you want to line the garment, as you might for straight or A-line skirts or jackets made of a rough outer fabric, use the same pattern pieces used to cut out the garment, eliminating collars, facings, waistbands, trims, and so forth. For detailed instructions on making linings, see Chapter 5 and Chapter 6.

Fabrics Used for Linings

Brocade—A jacquard-woven fabric, made of silk or synthetics; it is heavyweight for linings. It is used for lining evening coats and fur coats. Dry-cleanable.

China Silk—A very lightweight silk, it is used as a lining for soft fabrics. Dry-cleanable.

Crepe—Crepe comes in two weights for lining, light and heavy. The lightweights are used for lining knits and jersey. Dry-cleanable and washable. The heavy weights are used for lining jackets and coats. Dry-cleanable.

Fake Fur—Fake furs are used for lining jackets and coats. Dry-cleanable.

Organza—Organza is used for lining medium-weight fabrics. Dry-cleanable.

Satin—Satin linings with or without fleece backing are used for lining heavy jackets and coats. Dry-cleanable.

Taffeta—Taffeta is used for lining heavy fabrics and leathers. Dry-cleanable.

Fabrics manufactured specifically for linings

Armo—made by Armo Company, it is a medium-weight lamb's wool that is used as an interlining for jackets and coats. Dry-cleanable.

Bataan Batiste—Made by Ascot Textile Corporation, it is light in weight and is used to line lightweight cottons. Washable.

Butterfly—made by Stacy Fabrics Corporation, it is a lightweight poly-ester, silklike fabric that is used to line lightweight fabrics. Washable and dry-cleanable.

Ciao—made by Armo Company, it is a 100 percent polyester crepon fabric that is used to line all weights of fabrics. Washable.

Earl Glo—Made by N. Erlanger, Blumgart and Company, Inc., it is available in several forms: (a) acetate sheath, which is lightweight and is used for all weights of fabrics. Hand washable. (b) acetate faille taffeta, crepe-back satin, rayon twill, and acetate satin are used for lining medium-weight vests, jackets, and coats. Dry-cleanable.

Empress Satin—Made by Ascot Textiles Corporation, it is available in two forms: (a) Plain Finish, which is used for jackets and coats. Dry-cleanable. (b) Season-All, which is metal-insulated and combines inter-lining and lining for use in jackets and coats. Dry-cleanable.

Intimate—Made by Ascot Textiles Corporation, it is a lightweight lining for use with lightweight fabrics. Washable.

Intimate Quilted—Made by Ascot Textiles Corporation, it is a quilted lining that combines interlining and lining for jackets and coats. Dry-cleanable.

Keynote Plus—Made by Fabricators, it is for use with permanent-press fabrics. Washable.

Love-Life—Made by Fabricators, it is available in two weights: soft, for use with all weights of fabrics; crisp, for use with medium- and heavy-weight fabrics. Washable.

Marvelaire Polyester—Made by N. Erlanger, Blumgart and Company,

Inc., it is a lightweight fabric for use with all weights of fabrics and permanent-press fabrics. Washable.

Milium—Made by Dearing Milliken, it combines interlining and lining for use in jackets and coats. Dry-cleanable.

Pellon All-Bias Fleece—made by Pellon Corporation, it is a nonwoven polyester fleece that is used for interlining jackets and coats. Washable and dry-cleanable.

Polee—Made by Ascot Textile Corporation, it is lightweight, for use with all weights of fabrics and permanent-press fabrics. Washable.

Saja—Made by Hayden Textile Incorporated, it is medium weight, for use with medium-weight fabrics. Washable and dry-cleanable.

SiBonne—Made by Armo Company, it is a silklike rayon that is used for lining all weights of fabrics. Washable.

Interlinings

An interlining is a layer of fabric that is put between the lining and the outer fabric of a coat or jacket to add warmth. It is cut from the lining pattern pieces and is sewn in with the lining. Interlining fabrics are fluffy or fleecy, usually made of lamb's wool. For details on constructing interlinings, see Chapter 6.

Underlinings

Underlinings, or as they are sometimes called, backings, are used to give the garment more shape and support. They are cut out of the same pattern pieces as the outside of the garment. The underlining and the outer fabric are basted together and are handled as one piece of fabric during the garment construction. When you use an underlining, all the pattern markings are made on the underlining, thus avoiding marking the outer fabric. Except for knits, most of the fabrics you use can be underlined. All loosely woven fabrics should be underlined. In working with blouses or dresses, you can underline the body of the garment without underlining the sleeves. For straight skirts that you don't want to line, you can underline just the back of the skirt to prevent it from "sitting out." When a garment is underlined, the

LININGS, UNDERLININGS AND INTERFACINGS 119

hems, facings, and interfacings are sewn to the underlining only, so that no
stitches show on the outside. The weight of the underlining fabric will depend
on the effect you want to create. If you want to add a lot of body for a
sculptured look, choose a fairly crisp underlining. For soft fabrics and
designs with a fluid line, choose an underlining that is lighter and softer than
the outer fabric. When you go to buy the underlining fabric, take the outer
fabric with you. Put the two fabrics together and handle them as if they were
one layer. Make sure that the two fabrics feel compatible, and that they drape
well together. Always choose an underlining fabric that is close-woven, as a
fabric in which the threads separate easily will not wear well. For instructions
on constructing underlinings, see Chapter 5.

Fabrics Used for Underlinings

Batiste—A very lightweight cotton, it is used with lightweight and soft
fabrics. It is washable when preshrunk.

China Silk—A very lightweight silk, it is used for underlining soft fabrics. Dry-cleanable.

Marquisette—A lightweight mesh, it is used to add body to sheers. It is
washable when preshrunk.

Muslin—A lightweight, woven cotton fabric, it is used as underlining
for dresses and suits. It is washable when preshrunk.

Organdy—It is used for adding stiffness to light- and medium-weight
fabrics. It comes in silk, which is dry-cleanable, and in cotton, which is
washable when preshrunk.

Organza—It is used as an underlining for all weights of fabrics. The
silk is dry-cleanable; the cotton is washable when preshrunk.

Taffeta—It is used when crispness in the silhouette of the garment is
wanted. Dry-cleanable.

Fabrics Manufactured Specifically for Underlinings

About Face—Made by Hayden Textile Incorporated, it is available in
two weights: medium-soft, for use with all weights of fabrics where a
soft finish is wanted; crisp, for use with all weights of fabrics where a
firm finish is wanted. Washable and dry-cleanable.

About Face Basic Liner—Made by Hayden Textile Corporation, it is used for underlining light- and medium-weight fabrics. Washable and dry-cleanable.

Bataan Batiste—made by Ascot Textile Corporation, it is used for underlining lightweight cotton fabrics. Washable.

Earl Glo Acetate Sheath—made by N. Erlanger, Blumgart and Company, Inc., it is used for underlining all but sheer fabric weights. Washable.

Interlon Bias—made by Stacy Fabrics Corporation, it is a nonwoven with "give," for use where soft shaping is wanted. Washable.

Intimate—made by Ascot Textile Corporation, it is used for very lightweight fabrics. Washable.

Love-Life—made by Fabricators, it comes in soft and crisp weights and is used with all weights of fabrics. Washable.

Marvelaire—made by N. Erlanger, Blumgart and Company, Inc., it is used for all weights of fabrics. Washable.

Pellon All-Bias—made by Pellon Corporation, it is a nonwoven underlining available in featherweight and lightweight and is used to underline all weights of fabrics. Do not use for pants or for areas of the garment that will receive stress, such as the sleeves. Washable and dry-cleanable.

Saja—made by Hayden Textile Incorporated, it comes in two weights: medium-soft, for use with all weights of fabrics where softness is wanted; and crisp, for use where firmness is wanted. Washable, dry-cleanable.

SiBonne—made by Armo Company, it comes in soft-weight, for use with all weights of fabrics where softness is wanted, and crisp, for use where a little more firmness is wanted. Washable and dry-cleanable.

Siri—made by Armo Company, it comes in four weights, ranging from super-soft to crisp, for all weights of fabrics. Use the appropriate weight for the amount of firmness wanted. Washable and dry-cleanable.

Solo—Made by Fabricators, it comes in three weights: soft, for use with all fabric weights; medium, for use with knits and linens; firm, for use with loose-weave fabrics. Washable.

Taffeta Supreme—Made by Ascot Textile Corporation, it is used with heavyweight fabrics. Washable.

Touche—Made by Ascot Textile Corporation, it comes in two finishes: soft, for use with medium-weight fabrics where softness is wanted, and crisp, for use with medium-weight fabrics where more firmness is wanted. Washable.

Tritessa—Made by Ascot Textile Corporation, it comes in two finishes: soft, for use with medium-weight fabrics where softness is wanted; crisp, for use with medium-weight fabrics where more firmness is wanted. Washable and dry-cleanable.

Undercurrent—Made by Stacy Fabrics Corporation, it comes in two finishes: soft, for use with all weights of fabrics where softness is wanted; medium, for use with all weights of fabrics when more firmness is wanted. Washable and dry-cleanable.

Veriform—Made by Stacy Fabrics Corporation, it comes in two finishes: soft, for use where soft shaping is wanted; crisp, for use where firmer shaping is wanted. Washable and dry-cleanable.

Veri-Super—Made by Stacy Fabrics Corporation, it comes in two finishes: soft, for use with medium-weight fabrics where softness is wanted; crisp, for use with medium-weight fabrics where more firmness is wanted. Washable, dry-cleanable.

Whisper—Made by Ascot Textile Corporation, it is used for underlining medium-weight fabrics. Washable.

Interfacing

Interfacing is used to give strong support to collars, lapels, cuffs, buttonholes, and other small areas where firmness and shaping are required. The pattern will tell you where interfacing is called for and will provide you with special pattern pieces to cut out. Interfacing is always used under buttonhole areas. Interfacing fabrics are available in woven, nonwoven, and iron-on forms. The fabrics come in many different weights, and the one you need will depend on the fabric and the style of the garment you are making. The heavier the outer fabric, the heavier the interfacing will have to be. A simple, flat collar will call for a lighter weight interfacing than a stand-up collar, which will need a heavier weight.

Take the outer fabric with you when buying interfacing, and handle the two fabrics together as one to determine the final effect. Some styles will call for more than one weight of interfacing in the same garment. It doesn't matter whether you use a woven or a nonwoven interfacing as long as the weight is suitable for the shaping job it has to do. Iron-on interfacings come both woven and nonwoven, and will adhere to the outer fabric when pressed with a hot iron. When using an iron-on interfacing for large areas, such as the facing of a dress or jacket, the interfacing should be ironed on to the facing rather than the body of the garment. Always test a small piece of iron-on interfacing on a swatch of the fabric of you are using, to make sure that the resulting bind is not too stiff.

For detailed instructions on using interfacing, see Chapter 5.

Nonwoven Interfacing

Nonwoven interfacing is a nonwoven fabric which has synthetic fibers that are held in place by chemical bonding agents. This fabric is very similar in feeling to felt. These interfacings are available in regular and in "all-bias" constructions. Regular nonwovens are made of straight fibers and have no "give." They are used to give strong support for backing small areas, such as scoop and V-necklines, waistbands, and tabs. They are available in several weights, but for today's softer styles, the lighter weights are most suitable. "All-bias" nonwovens are made of crimped fibers and have a bias-like "give" in all directions. They come in different weights, ranging from very light to fleece weight. They can be used as interfacings for collars, facings, and lapels, and as underlinings in areas that do not receive too much stress, such as the body of jackets, coats, and vests. The fleece weight can be used to underline a coat, thus making a warm interlining unnecessary.

Fusibles

Fusibles are new to the sewing market. They are not fabrics but a web of polymerized synthetic fibers which are used to adhere two layers of fabric together. They come in either the web alone, or with a backing paper, which is peeled off during the application of the fusible. They can be used for applying interfacing and for hems, facings, collars, belts, trims, and appliqués.

They can be used to eliminate a great deal of hand sewing, but be sure to pre-test them on swatch of the fabric you are using. Always be sure to follow the manufacturer's instructions exactly when applying them.

Fabrics Manufactured Specifically for Interfacing

About Face Basic Liner—Made by Hayden Textiles Incorporated, it is used for shaping light- and medium-weight fabrics. Washable.

Armo Hair Canvas—Made by Armo Company, it is used to interface the collars and lapels of tailored garments. Armo hair canvas is marketed under the following names:

   Fino—for use with medium- to heavyweight wools. Dry-cleanable.

   Finolight—for use with lightweight to medium-weight woolens and for heavyweight synthetic blends. Dry-cleanable.

   Acro—for use as an interfacing and an underlining with lightweight fabrics. Washable.

   P-17—for use with medium-weight wools and wool blends. Dry-cleanable.

   P-20—for use with heavyweight wools. Dry-cleanable.

   P-26—for use with medium-weight wools. Dry-cleanable.

   P-27—for use in small areas and as shaping for heavyweight fabrics. Dry-cleanable.

Armo Press—Made by Armo Company, it is for use with permanent-press fabrics. Washable.

Ascot—Made by Ascot Textile Corporation, it comes in both regular and permanent-press and is made in the following forms: woven, in light to heavy weights, for use with the corresponding weight fabric; non-woven, in light and medium weights, for use with the corresponding weight fabrics; iron-on woven and iron-on nonwoven, for use where an iron-on facing is wanted.

Ascot All-Bias—Nonwoven interfacing with the soft "give" that all-bias nonwovens possess. For use where soft shaping is wanted. All Ascot interfacings are washable and dry-cleanable.

Bravo Canvas—Made by Stacy Fabrics Corporation, it is for use where hair canvas is wanted. Dry-cleanable.

Bravo-Set—Made by Stacy Fabrics Corporation, it is for use with light- and medium-weight wools. Washable and dry-cleanable.

Earlaire of Reemay—Made by N. Erlanger, Blumgart and Company, Inc., it is nonwoven and available in light and medium weights, for use with the corresponding weight fabric. Washable and dry-cleanable.

Face Flex—Made by Hayden Textile Incorporated, it comes in two forms: iron-on woven, for use where an iron-on interfacing is wanted; iron-on nonwoven, for use in small areas. Washable and dry-cleanable.

Face Form—Made by Hayden Textile Incorporated, it comes in two forms: iron-on nonwoven, for use in small areas; woven, for use with medium- to heavyweight fabrics. Washable, dry-cleanable.

Facelon—Made by Hayden Textile Incorporated, it comes in two forms: nonwoven, in three weights from light to heavy, for use with corresponding fabric weights; nonwoven bias in lightweight, for use where lightweight interfacing is wanted. Washable, dry-cleanable.

Hymo Canvas—Made by Stacy Fabrics Corporation, it is a hair canvas available for regular and heavy shaping. Dry-cleanable.

Interlon—Made by Stacy Fabrics Corporation, it is available in two forms: nonwoven, in three weights from light to heavy, for use with corresponding weight fabrics; durable press, for use with durable-press fabrics. Washable and dry-cleanable.

Kyron—Made by J. P. Stevens and Company, Inc., it is nonwoven and available in three weights from light to heavy, for use with corresponding weight fabrics. Dry-cleanable.

Pellon—Made by Pellon Corporation, it is available in two forms: regular, which is nonwoven and available in three weights from light to heavy, for use with corresponding weight fabrics; all-bias, available in featherweight and lightweight, for use with lightweight fabrics and knits. Washable and dry-cleanable.

Pelomite Detail—Made by Pellon Corporation, it is a medium-weight, iron-on nonwoven, for use in small areas. Washable and dry-cleanable.

Prima Canvas—Made by Hayden Textile Incorporated, it is a hair canvas, for use with medium- and heavyweight wools. Dry-cleanable.

Sta Shape—Made by Stacy Fabrics Corporation, it comes in three forms: lightweight canvas, for use with light- and medium-weight fabrics (dry-cleanable); hair canvas, for use with medium- to heavyweight fabrics (dry-cleanable); durable press, for use with durable-press fabrics (washable and dry-cleanable).

Shape-Flex Iron-on—Made by Stacy Fabrics Corporation, it is available in three forms: all purpose, for use with cottons and washable fabrics and not recommended for use with synthetic fabrics (Dry-cleanable); nonwoven, for use in small areas where a heavy stiffening is wanted (washable and dry-cleanable).

Suit Shape—Made by Stacy Fabrics Corporation, is used in tailoring for knits and woven fabrics. Washable and dry-cleanable.

Thermolam Multi-purpose Fleece—Made by Stacy Fabrics Corporation, it is a lamb's wool that is used as an interfacing when soft shaping is wanted for small areas. Washable and dry-cleanable.

Worsted Canvas—Made by Stacy Fabrics Corporation, it is a very fine quality hair canvas in light- and medium-weights for use with luxury wools. Dry-cleanable.

Fusibles (See Page 122)

Stitch Witchery—Made by Stacy Fabrics Corporation.
Wonder Under—Made by Pellon Corporation.
Suit Shape—Made by Stacy Fabrics Corporation.

HOW TO CHOOSE THE PROPER FABRIC TO GO WITH YOUR PATTERN

Next to a well-fitting pattern, the most important aspect of sewing professional-looking clothes is the selection of the fabric. The choice of fabrics available to the modern home sewer appears to be almost infinite. This is really only a first impression, because once you get to know fabrics, what they are made of and how they are to work with, you will quickly be able to decide which is the perfect fabric for the type and style of garment you want to make.

One of the best ways to get to know fabrics is to haunt the fabric stores and the fabric departments of your favorite department stores. Look at the fabrics, read the labels, and most important, handle them and get to know the names of the ones that appeal to you most. Very often a fabric will inspire you to look for a special pattern, instead of the other way around, but most of the time you will start your sewing project by buying the pattern first.

The back of the pattern envelope lists a number of fabrics that are most suitable for that style. The pattern also tells you the type of "hand" the fabric should have. "Hand" refers to the texture, drape, and general feel of the fabric. The pattern may call for "soft" or "crisp" fabrics, and as long as you choose fabrics with the qualities specified, you will choose correctly. When choosing prints, plaids, or checks, keep in mind the scale of the pattern in relation to the style of the garment and your own size and proportion. Do not choose a large print if the style of the garment you are making is very complicated, or if it calls for a number of small pieces. If the pattern envelope says that obvious diagonal fabrics are not suitable, don't use them; you won't like the results. Just remember, the larger, or more complicated the surface of the fabric, the simpler the style of your garment should be.

If you want to use a fabric that is not listed in the fabric suggestions for your pattern, note the characteristics and weight of the fabrics that are listed, and if the fabric you want to use is similar, go ahead. One important note, if the pattern calls for "knits only," don't attempt to make the garment in a woven fabric. The pattern has been made with only enough ease for knit fabrics, which have more give than woven ones.

HOW TO DETERMINE HOW MUCH FABRIC TO BUY

Now that you have selected your pattern and the fabric you want to use, you have to know how much fabric to buy. Fabric is sold by the yard, or fraction of a yard, but it is equally important to know the width of the fabric. Linens are usually 36 inches wide, cottons 36 to 45 inches wide, silks 36 to 45 inches wide, woolens 54 to 60 inches wide, and most synthetics 39 to 45 inches wide. But these widths vary, so be sure that when you find out the price of the fabric, you also find out the width. In most cases, you can determine how much fabric to buy when you know the width of the fabric. Consult the chart on the back of the pattern envelope; it will give the amount of fabric needed for the pattern view, the size, and the width of the fabric.

Explanation of "With Nap" and "Without Nap"

The amount of fabric needed is determined by the layout used when cutting out the pattern pieces. For most fabrics, it doesn't matter whether the pattern pieces all face the same direction when you lay them out, but for some fabrics it matters a great deal. These are fabrics with a design, nap, or weave which looks different if held in the two lengthwise directions. If this is the case, the pattern will have to be laid out with the tops of all the pieces facing the same direction.

Fabrics with design features to be considered are prints with the print running in one direction, border prints, and plaids with the design running in one direction. Some prints and plaids will also require matching, which will mean that you will need a little more yardage; you will find more about matching and border prints in Chapter 5.

Some fabrics have the nap running in one direction, such as corduroy, velvet, and velveteen. You can have the nap running either up or down in the finished garment, but you must make sure that all the pieces in one garment are facing in the same direction.

Some fabrics have a weave that causes the light to reflect differently, depending on how the fabric is held. These fabrics include: twill weaves such as gabardine, whipcord, and twill, and satin weaves such as satin and cotton satin. Wool flannel also falls into this category.

The chart on the back of the pattern will say "w/without nap" when a layout provides for all the pieces to face in one direction, and "without nap" when it does not. This does not mean that you can't use one of these special fabrics if you want to; it just means that you will have to design a special layout yourself. In order to do this, you will have to have more fabric than is called for on the pattern. One of the best ways to figure out how much fabric you will need is to fold a tablecloth to the width of the fabric you want to use, lay out the pattern with all the pieces facing on one direction, and measure the amount of fabric taken up by the pattern. This is also a good method to use when you want to use a fabric whose width is not given on the envelope.

PREPARATION OF THE FABRIC FOR CUTTING

Although most modern fabrics are ready for cutting when you buy them, there are certain steps that you will have to take before you can lay the pattern out on the fabric and actually cut it. These steps, which are vital to the success of the final results, apply to woven fabrics, and they must be followed for lining and underlining fabrics as well.

The Grain of the Fabric

The lengthwise (warp) and crosswise (weft) yarns of the woven fabric form the grain of the fabric. The lengthwise threads are called the lengthwise grain, or the straight of the goods. The crosswise threads are called the crosswise grain. For the fabric to be ready for cutting, these threads must be at perfect right angles to each other. If they are not, if the fabric has been stretched or distorted on the bolt, it is considered to be off-grain. If the garment is cut with the fabric in this condition, it will not hang straight, and it will never fit correctly. Some fabrics, such as those with permanent-press or wash-and-wear finishes and bonded fabrics cannot be corrected if they are off-grain, as the finishes have locked the threads in that position permanently. For this reason, it is important that you learn to recognize whether a fabric is on-grain. Examine any fabric you want to buy very carefully to

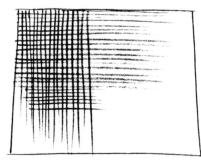 

be sure that it has not been pulled off-grain in either of the two ways illustrated. If you do get a piece of fabric that is slightly off-grain, and it doesn't have any of the permanent finishes mentioned, it can be corrected.

Most fabrics are sold with the right side of the fabric folded to the outside on the bolt. Some, however, come with the right side folded in. With prints and most other fabrics, it is easy to see which way they are folded. Some woolens, such as tweed, are identical either way, in which case determine the side you want to have facing out on the finished garment and work with it accordingly. If you are not sure by just looking which is the right side, ask the salesperson when you buy the fabric.

How to Tell If the Grain Is True

In order to be sure that the fabric is on-grain, you will have to make the two crosswise edges thread-perfect. The closer-woven lengthwise edges of the fabric are called the selvages. They cannot be pulled off-grain and will be used to help correct the grain if it needs to be straightened. To make the fabric thread-perfect, clip one of the selvages near the edge of the fabric and carefully pull a thread along the crosswise grain of the fabric. Cut along the pulled thread, carefully pulling it an inch or two at a time as you go along.

If the thread breaks, continue cutting along the line it left until you can pick it up again. When you have cut until you reach the other selvage, you have made the fabric thread-perfect. Repeat the process with the other edge of the fabric.

Some fabrics can be made thread-perfect by clipping the selvage and carefully tearing along the crosswise grain, but this will not work with all fabrics—for example, linen—and is not recommended unless you cannot straighten the fabric by pulling the thread.

With pile or napped fabrics, clip at the selvage and unravel the threads until you get one that is the entire width of the fabric.

Once the fabric has been made thread-perfect, fold it in half lengthwise, with the crosswise edges and the selvages even. If the grain is true, the crosswise edges will match and no further work is needed to straighten it. If the crosswise edges are uneven, the fabric is off-grain and needs to be straightened.

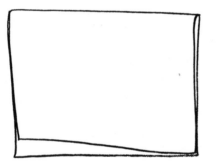

How to Straighten the Grain

If the fabric is off-grain and has been preshrunk, you can straighten the grain with a steam iron. (If the fabric needs to be preshrunk and has to have the grain straightened as well, it can be done in one operation, which will be described after the following paragraph.)

To straighten the grain by ironing, pin the thread-perfect crosswise edges together, with the fabric folded in half lengthwise. Then pin along the selvages, making sure that they match. Keep the fabric on a flat surface and be sure that all the edges match. Wrinkles will form. The more the fabric is off-grain, the more wrinkles you will have. Dampen the underneath layer of the fabric, and with a steam iron, press the fabric along the lengthwise grain. If it still remains off-grain, press along the crosswise grain, and repeat both pressing operations until the grain straightens. Do not press the center fold of the fabric, as the cutting layout may not call for it, and it might be difficult to remove.

How to Straighten the Grain and Preshrink at the Same Time

If you have purchased a washable fabric that has not been preshrunk, or if you are not sure, it is advisable to follow this procedure whether the fabric is off-grain or not.

Pin or baste the selvages and crosswise edges that have been made thread-perfect and fold the fabric in pleats about ten inches wide. Place the fabric in hot to warm water and let it soak for several hours at least. It is even better to leave it overnight. Take the fabric out of the water and gently squeeze as much water out as possible. Lay the fabric out to dry flat on a sheet and straighten the grain by gently smoothing and pulling the fabric with your hands. Repeat the smoothing while the fabric is drying. When it is dry, steam press it along the lengthwise grain as described before.

Most domestic woolens have been preshrunk, but if you have a piece that you are not sure about, it will have to be preshrunk. It is best to have all dry-cleanable fabrics preshrunk professionally by a dry-cleaner. If you want to do it yourself, make the crosswise ends thread-perfect and fold and baste the edges together as described for washable fabrics. Get some old sheets the length of the piece of fabric, but fold them so that they are a few inches wider than the fabric. Get the sheets thoroughly wet, lay the fabric out flat, and place a wet sheet over it. Fold the sheet and the fabric together in wide folds, starting at the outer edges and folding toward the middle. Wrap another wet sheet around the fabric, and either place it in a plastic bag or wrap it with plastic sheeting, such as you get from the dry-cleaner. Leave it in the plastic for several hours. Remove the plastic and spread the fabric out to let it dry flat. If the grain needs straightening, smooth it as it dries.

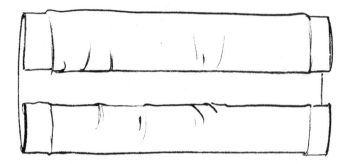

Halfway through the drying process, turn the fabric over so that the underside gets a chance to dry and smooth out any wrinkles where necessary. Use a steam iron to press along the lengthwise grain when the fabric is dry.

True Bias

The true bias of woven fabrics is formed in grain-perfect fabric when the fabric is folded with the crosswise threads running in the same direction as the lengthwise threads. Some patterns will call for pieces of the garment to be cut on the bias. Cutting on the bias gives the most stretchability that a woven fabric will allow, but it is not often done, as bias-cut garments are not as strong as those cut on the lengthwise grain.

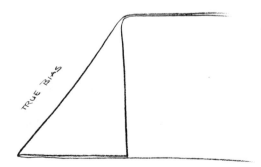

FIRST PROJECT—
A SIMPLE
TWO-PIECE
SKIRT

Now that you have read the first three chapters, you are ready to start your first sewing project: a simple two-piece skirt. The project will teach you a number of basic techniques that you will use for all your sewing, and when you are finished, you will have a skirt that will be an important addition to your wardrobe.

First of all, you will have to know what to buy. Start by looking for a pattern of a two-piece skirt without a center front seam or back seam, and with a waistband. You now know your pattern size and if any alteration will be necessary. If you do need to alter the pattern, refer back to Chapter 2 to make sure that you know how to make any adjustments. It doesn't matter which pattern company's pattern you buy, as long as you find one for a simple skirt with two side seams, no center seams and a waistband. For this first project, ignore any pockets or other trimmings; you will get to these later.

Once you have your pattern, you will have to buy the fabric. For this

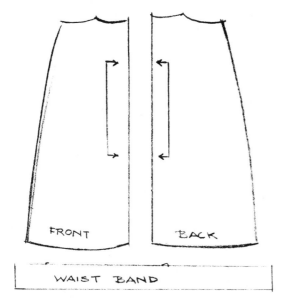

skirt, I suggest a light- to medium-weight wool, such as a lightweight tweed, or for a summer skirt, a cotton duck or poplin. Pick a solid color (no checks or plaids), preferably in a light to medium color, as it is sometimes difficult to see what you are doing when working with really dark colors like navy or black. These dark colors will pose no problem when you are more experienced. The back of the pattern envelope will tell you how much fabric you need to buy. At the same time, buy a lining fabric in a matching color (or as close to the color as you can get). If no measurement for lining is given on the pattern envelope, use the same measurement given for the outside of the skirt, following the amount given for the width of the lining fabric. A light-weight rayon lining is best for woolen and a lightweight cotton, such as batiste, is best for a cotton skirt.

You will also need notions—a 7-inch nylon coil zipper, thread, and seam binding—all in a matching color. It is always best to buy everything at the same time to avoid the frustration of setting everything up and then discovering that you are missing one important item that will prevent you from proceeding with your work. For this skirt, you will also need a small piece (⅓ of a yard) of woven or nonwoven interfacing for the waistband.

It is now time to prepare your fabric and cut out the skirt. Straighten the crosswise edges and grain of both the outer fabric and the lining (refer to Chapter 3). This last is important, because if the lining fabric is cut off-grain, your skirt will not hang properly. Also be sure to preshrink all cotton and lining fabrics, and be sure to find out whether any woolen fabric you have has been preshrunk. If not, you will have to preshrink it yourself (refer to Chapter 3).

Remove the pattern pieces that you will use for the skirt—the skirt front and back, and the waistband—and press them flat with a dry iron.

Following the layout given on the pattern primer for the width of your fabric, pin the pattern to the outside fabric. Do this by pinning the center of the skirt to the fold of the fabric first, and then pin the rest of the pattern within the cutting lines, placing the pins about two to three inches apart. It is not necessary to trim the margins of the pattern pieces before you pin; they will fall away as you cut. There is one exception to this. I have found that when you pin a piece on the fold of this fabric (in this case, the front and the back of the skirt), it helps to trim the pattern to the fold line to make it easier to pin the pattern flush to the fold of the fabric.

Now cut the fabric, following the cutting lines on the pattern, being

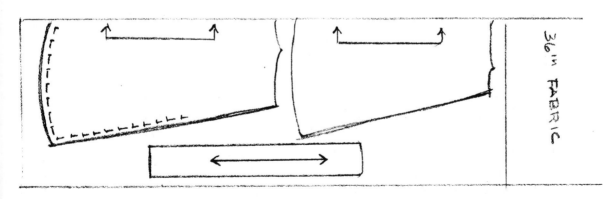

sure to cut all notches outward. With tailor's tacks or tailor's chalk on wool and dressmaker's carbon paper on other fabrics, mark all the darts and the line for the zipper. Refer to Chapter 2 for marking instructions.

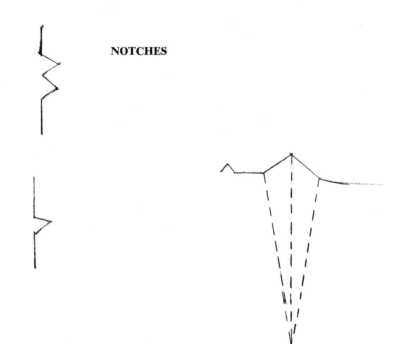

NOTCHES

Using the same pattern pieces that you used for the front and back of the skirt, but not the waistband, pin to the lining fabric, again being sure that the center front and the center back of the skirt are pinned to the fold of the fabric. Cut out the front and back pieces of the lining. Also cut a strip of interfacing, on the lengthwise grain if you are using a woven interfacing, the same length as the waistband, but half as wide. Mark the darts on the lining with dressmaker's carbon paper and unpin the pattern pieces from the lining and the waistband. Now you are ready to start sewing.

The first step in sewing the skirt is to stay-stitch the curved edges of the two main pieces so that they do not stretch out during construction. Stay-stitching is a row of regular machine stitching that is made through one layer of fabric sewn ⅛ inch inside the seam line, or to put it another way, ½ inch from the edge of the fabric. Some patterns will call for stay-stitching to be made closer to the edge, but for this skirt, ½ inch is correct. Stay-stitch in the direction of the arrows.

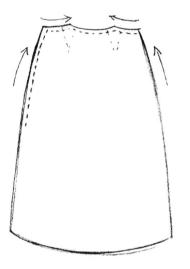

You are now ready to sew the darts. In all machine sewing, unless otherwise called for, place the fabric with the right sides of the fabric (the outside of the garment) facing each other. Start by stitching about half an inch, put the machine in reverse, and backtrack over the first few stitches. Then put the lever back into forward and stitch over the previous stitches. To start the darts, fold the fabric along the fold line of the marking and place a pin through the stitching line so that it comes out through the stitching line on the other side. Place a couple of pins at right angles to the stitching line and remove the pin that is sticking through the stitching line. Start

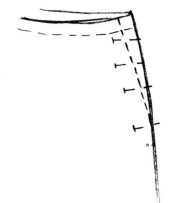

stitching along the stitching lines. Sew in a straight line until you get to the point of the dart, running the stitches off the fabric. Then, lifting the pressure foot, gently pull the fabric away from the needle, leaving a few inches of thread. Cut the two threads and carefully tie them in a knot. Continue to

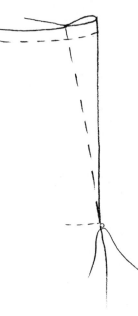

make the remaining darts in the same manner. Press the darts over a tailor's ham or pressing mitt with all the darts facing the center of the skirt.

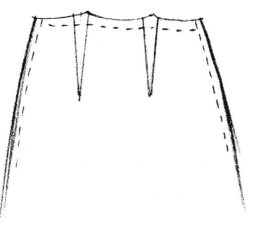

Take the front of the skirt with the wrong side facing you, and right sides together, pin to the back of the skirt on the right-hand side with the pins at right angles as shown. Pinning in this way will enable you to sew

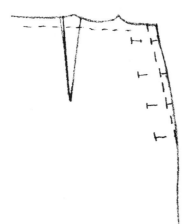

over the pins without damaging the needle of the machine. With the machine set for the longest stitch, machine baste just along side of the seam line. Press the seam open. Turn the skirt over, and leaving an opening the length of the zipper plus one inch, pin and baste in the same way. Press the seam open and you are ready to try the skirt on for the initial fitting.

You have already made any major fitting adjustments in the pattern before you cut the skirt out. The only changes you can make now are minor ones. Try on the skirt right-side out, with your slip and any other undergarments you would normally wear. Pin the zipper opening closed in a ⅝ inch seam.

Check that the waistline is comfortable without pulling or straining. If it is a little too tight, cut the basting stitches and repin in the right-hand seam (the one without the zipper opening) until the fit feels right. If the skirt is too loose at the waist, pin as much as is needed to make the skirt feel comfortable. The side seams should hang straight down at right angles to the floor, and the whole skirt should have enough ease to be comfortable without being too loose. Once you have made any corrections, you are ready to stitch the seams permanently.

Adjust the machine back to regular stitch length (between 10 and 13 stitches per inch) and sew on the stitching line (right next to the basting), allowing for any corrections in fitting you want to make. On the left side, where the zipper is to be inserted, baste (readjusting the stitch length on the machine) from the top of the skirt to the marking for the bottom of the zipper. This opening should be the length of the zipper plus one inch. Set the machine for the regular stitch again, backtrack once or twice just below the opening, and continue sewing the rest of the seam in the usual manner. Press all the seams open.

Take the regular pressure foot off your machine and replace it with the zipper foot, with the foot adjusted to the right of the needle. Turn the skirt wrong-side out and place it on the machine with the top of the skirt facing you and the seam for the zipper nearest the needle. Pull out the right-hand seam allowance under the zipper foot. Open the zipper and place it face down on the seam with the bottom of the zipper at the bottom of the basting stitches. Put the rest of the skirt and the left seam allowance to the left of the needle. (See sketch.) The top stop of the zipper should be one inch from the top of the skirt seam. The zipper coil (teeth) should be on the seam line. Pin at right angles along the right-hand zipper tape, adjust the machine to baste, and stitch along the zipper tape from the bottom to the top, following the guideline on the tape. Remove the pins as you sew.

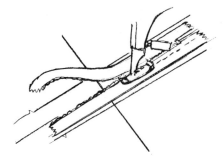

Close the zipper and turn it face up, thus folding the seam allowance where the tape is basted to it. Adjust the zipper foot to the left of the needle and change the machine to the regular length stitch. Smooth the seam allowance to the left of the zipper coil, and starting at the bottom, stitch through the fold and the zipper tape.

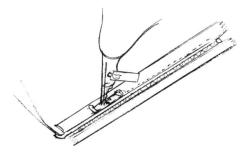

Still with the skirt wrong-side up, spread it out with the zipper face down over the unattached seam allowance (left hand). Smooth the zipper so that it is perfectly flat. A small pleat will form at the bottom of the zipper. Pin, again with the pins at right angles to the needle. Starting with the needle at the seam allowance, stitch, turning at right angles along the guide line on the zipper tape, and stitch to the top of the skirt. You have sewn through the

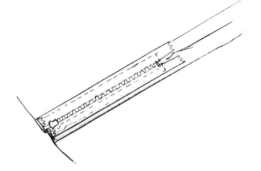

zipper tape, the seams allowance, and the front of the skirt. At the bottom of the zipper, pull the top thread through to the wrong side of the skirt and knot the ends of the thread. Carefully remove the basting stitches and press the zipper on the wrong side.

Make the darts on the lining the same way as you did for the outside of the skirt. With the wrong side of the front of the lining facing you, stitch the right-hand seam. Turn the entire lining over and stitch the left seam below the zipper opening. In stitching the lining, be sure that you allow for any fitting changes you made on the skirt. Press the darts toward the centers and press the seams open. With the *wrong* sides facing, pin the lining to the skirt at the waistline, folding back the seam allowances to expose the zipper on the inside. Machine baste the lining to the skirt. Slip-stitch the lining to

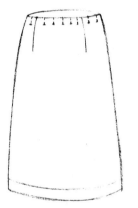

the zipper tape on the inside. See the section called Hand Sewing in Chapter 5 for instructions on how to slip-stitch.

Machine baste the interfacing to the wrong side of the long, unnotched edge of the waistband. Press under the seam allowance along the unnotched edge. With the right sides together and the notches of the waistband facing up,

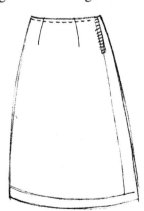

pin the waistband to the skirt. Start by pinning the notches together, then follow with the center back, the center front, and the side seams. Stitch, easing the skirt onto the waistband, starting at one end and finishing at the other. At the ends, fold the waistband in half and sew each end in a ⅝-inch

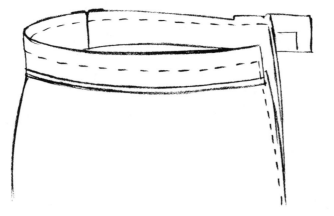

seam. Trim all the seams and turn the ends of the waistband right-side out. This will make the waistband flush with the skirt and zipper on the front of

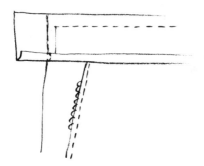

the skirt and form an extension on the back of the waistband. Pin the folded edge of the waistband to the skirt and slip-stitch. Sew hooks and eyes to the waistband.

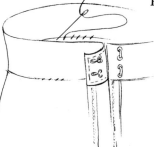

Try the skirt on over your slip and other usual undergarments and this time also wear the shoes you plan to wear with the skirt. Determine the length you want the skirt to be and have someone mark the hem with a yardstick and pins, or chalk it with a skirt marker. Take off the skirt and measure

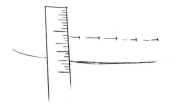

from the marks to the edge of the skirt. If the hem is deeper than three inches, measure the difference from the edge and cut it off. Do the same thing for the lining hem, except that the lining should be ½ inch shorter than the

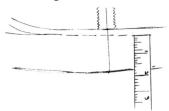

finished skirt. With the right side of the skirt facing up, sew seam binding to the edge of the hem. To finish the lining bottom, turn under ¼ inch and stitch. Pin the skirt and lining hems and sew by hand. With the exception of the use of fusibles (see Chapter 3), hems are always finished by hand.

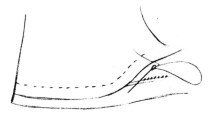

CHAPTER

SEWING CONSTRUCTION

BASIC MACHINE STITCHING

Once your machine is threaded and the tension and pressure are adjusted, you are ready to start sewing, but there are a few rules that you should be aware of before you start. First of all, *never* allow a threaded sewing machine to sew without a piece of fabric under the needle, as the threads will catch on each other and will jam the machine. If this does happen, stop and carefully turn the wheel by hand until the jammed threads become visible. It may be difficult to turn the wheel at first, sometimes it helps to remove the thread plate and pull the threads out of the bobbin case with a pair of tweezers. Once you have loosened the jammed threads, cut them free, and rethread the machine. If you cannot work the jammed threads out, it may be necessary to call the repairman.

If your machine has a foot control, place it on the floor in the position that is most comfortable for you to press it with your right foot. If the machine has a knee control, place your left foot forward and press the control with your right knee. Practice with a scrap of fabric and a threaded machine until you find the speed that is most comfortable for you. Don't try to sew at full speed at first. Start slowly and evenly, and you will build up your speed gradually as you acquire more experience. Use a seam guide (see page 15) and/ or the guide lines on the throat plate to keep the seam straight. Place the largest part of the fabric to the left of the needle. Use your left hand to gently

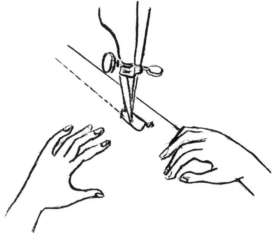

control the bulk of the fabric and keep your right hand a few inches in front of the needle to guide the seam edge. Never let your left arm lean on the fabric. Above all, be sure that you are comfortable. Lean slightly forward from your chair, but do not hunch your shoulders over the work, otherwise you will get muscle cramps in your shoulders and back and will tire easily.

To sew a straight seam, raise the pressure foot and turn the wheel until the needle reaches its highest point. Gently pull the needle and bobbin threads out for a few inches and place them under the pressure foot diagonally to the back of the machine. Place the fabric under the pressure foot and lower the needle into the fabric, holding the threads (but not pulling them) toward the back. Lower the pressure foot. Sew the first few stitches for about half an inch and stop with the needle lowered into the fabric. Put the stitch regulator in reverse and backtrack over the stitches you have made. When you reach the first stitch, set the machine for forward stitching and sew over the previous stitches and sew the rest of the seam. When you get to the end of the seam, backtrack in the same way to finish the stitching. Raise the needle to its highest point and raise the pressure foot. Pull the fabric away from the needle, leaving about three inches of thread, and clip the threads close to the fabric.

If you do not backtrack at the beginning and end of a seam, it will be necessary to leave three or four inches of thread at each end so that you can tie the threads in a double knot. If you sew the seam without finishing the ends with one of these methods, the seam will open as soon as any strain is placed on it. .

Before you start a sewing project, always practice with a scrap of the fabric to determine the tension and pressure needed, and the amount of guidance the fabric will need. Use two layers of the fabric on the lengthwise grain and sew them together in a seam ⅝ inch from the edge of the fabric. Place the seam guide ⅝ inch away from the needle, using the guides on the throat plate, or measure the distance with a ruler and mark it on the throat plate with a small piece of adhesive tape. Set the stitch regulator for 10 or 12 stitches per inch and sew the seam as described. If the thread forms loops on the top or bottom of the fabric, the tension is too loose. If the seam puckers, the tension is too tight. If a ripple forms in the top layer of the fabric, the pressure is too heavy. To make any of these adjustments, see page 21.

Most fabrics need only gentle guidance with the left hand as you sew. If the stitching is not even or straight, place your right hand behind the needle and gently guide the fabric with your right hand from the back, and with your left hand from the front of the needle. (See below.)

To sew curved seams, place the seam guide at an angle so that the one corner is in line with the needle at the proper distance. Use a smaller stitch and sew the seam in the same way as a straight seam, carefully guiding the fabric as you go along.

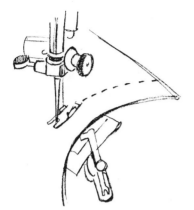

To pivot a stitch to form a point or right angle, sew the seam until you reach the pivot point. Leave the needle in the fabric, but raise it by turning the wheel until the needle just starts to leave the fabric. Raise the pressure foot and turn the fabric the amount needed to form the point or right angle. Continue stitching in the normal manner.

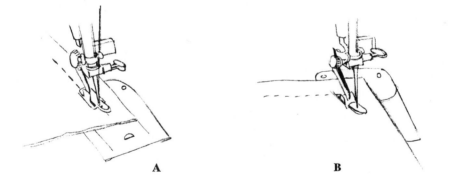

A   B

When pivoting, it is very often advisable to reinforce the stitching at the pivot point. To do this, change the stitch regulator to smaller stitches one inch before the pivot point, turn the fabric, and continue with the smaller stitches for one inch after sewing the pivot point.

For machine basting, set the stitch regulator for the largest stitch possible and loosen the needle tension. Machine basting can be removed easily by clipping the top thread every few stitches and pulling the bobbin thread out. If you have loosened the needle tension while basting, the thread will pull out easily.

You can pin-baste the fabric by placing pins a few inches apart, at right angles to the edge of the seam, and sewing right over them. Never sew with the pins on the underside of the fabric.

Machine gathering is done by making two rows of machine stitching with a long stitch and loosened tension through a single layer of fabric. When you have completed the rows of stitching, remove the fabric from the machine, leaving several inches of thread at each end. Gently pull the bobbin threads from both ends toward the middle, adjusting the gathers as you go. Tie off the ends of the thread when the proper amount of gathering has been obtained.

HAND SEWING

Despite the fact that you will do the major part of your sewing by machine, almost every garment you make will require some hand sewing to finish it. In some cases, such as inserting zippers, you may want to do the job by hand to give the garment the couture touch that you can find only in the most expensive ready-made clothes. Although sewing by hand can be a chore, if you do it carefully the results will be well worth the effort. The most important factor in sewing by hand is to have the correct size needle and the correct thread for the job you are doing.

As a general rule, the kind of thread you should use is determined by the fiber of the fabric you are working on. For cotton, wool, and linen fabrics, use a cotton thread. Silk thread can be used on all fabrics and is especially important for basting on delicate fabrics, as it leaves no marks. Use silk thread when sewing silk fabric. For synthetics or fabrics made of natural and synthetic fibers, use a cotton-covered polyester or a polyester thread.

Choose needles as follows: for light to medium lightweight fabrics, use betweens, sharps, and embroidery size 8 or 7; for medium-weight fabrics, use betweens, sharps, and embroidery size 7 or 6; for heavyweight fabrics, use betweens, sharps, and embroidery size 5 or 4.

When selecting a needle for hand sewing, choose the size that is appropriate to the fabric weight and the length that you find comfortable to work with. Be sure that the eye of the needle is large enough to thread easily. If you find it difficult to thread the needle, you can use a needle threader, which is a little wire loop attached to a metal disc. (Most notions departments sell them.) Pass the loop through the eye of the needle, insert the thread through the loop, and pull the loop with the thread through the eye of the needle.

If you have chosen the proper weight of thread for the job you are doing, you should rarely have to use the thread doubled. Never try to use too long a piece of thread, as it will weaken and tangle and you will only have to cut it off before you come to the end of the thread. For most jobs, the thread should not be longer than twenty inches. Cut the thread at an angle with sharp scissors, never break or tear it, and pass the cut end through the eye of the needle. Leave an end of six or seven inches on one side of the needle and tie a knot in the end of the thread that has passed through the eye of the needle.

To tie the knot, see illustration for right-handed and left-handed sewers.

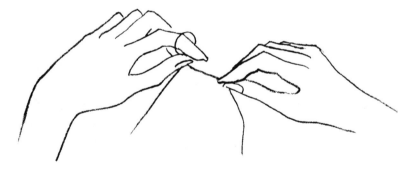

When you have reached within six inches of the end of the thread, you will have to form another knot to fasten the stitching. To do this, make a backstitch, leaving a small loop, then pass the threaded needle through the loop and pull the thread tight. Repeat this process a second time to reinforce the knot.

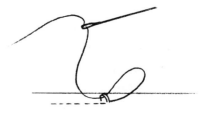

Hand Basting

Basting by hand is used to hold two pieces of fabric together temporarily. It can also be used to mark stitching lines and buttonholes through one layer of fabric. When machine stitching after hand basting, never sew directly over the basting stitches, but to one side of them. Never press over basting stitches, as this will leave permanent marks in the fabric. When working with delicate fabrics that mark easily, use silk thread that will not leave an impression on the fabric.

Even Basting

Even basting is used for seams that require a secure temporary stitch, for example, when seams have to be matched and when one layer of fabric has to be eased to fit on to another. When easing a piece of fabric, that is, when the piece to be eased is slightly larger than the other, place the larger piece on top and ease it gently with your hand as you sew. It will help to pin-baste it first by placing a pin at each end of the seam, then one in the middle of the seam, and then one pin each in middle of the two sections formed. Continue, placing pins in the middle of each section of fabric until the entire seam is pinned. Then baste, using an even basting stitch.

To make an even basting stitch, take a ¼-inch stitch through the fabric and then another and another, spacing them evenly. If the seam is to be subjected to strain while fitting, make the stitches closer together.

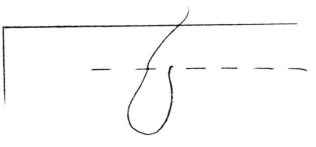

Uneven Basting

Uneven basting is used for seams that are not going to be subjected to strain and for marking the fabric. Take a short stitch through the fabric and a longer one on the top of the fabric and then another short stitch through the fabric, and so forth.

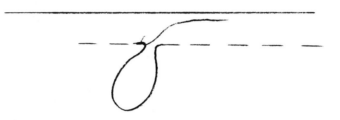

Diagonal Basting

This is used for interfacings, facings, and linings. Take short stitches through the fabric, evenly spaced, at right angles to the edge of the fabric.

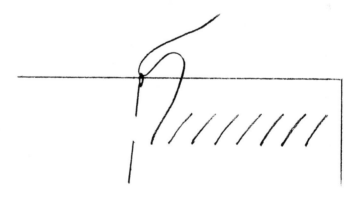

Slip-Basting

Slip-basting is used for matching plaids and prints. See page 309 for instructions on slip-basting.

End all basting stitches by making a few backstitches that can be easily removed.

BASIC HAND STITCHES

Running Stitch

The running stitch is used for seams that are not subject to much strain and for easing and gathering. Make a few even stitches, weaving the needle in and out of the fabric. Make the stitches quite small ($\frac{1}{16}$ inch to $\frac{1}{8}$ inch) for seams and slightly longer for easing or gathering.

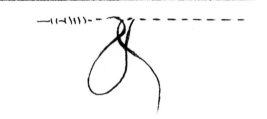

Backstitching

Backstitching is a very strong stitch used for seams. Make a stitch from the underside of the fabric about $\frac{1}{8}$ inch from the edge of the seam. Take a stitch backwards $\frac{1}{8}$ inch and bring the needle up through the fabric $\frac{1}{8}$ inch from the original stitch. Take another stitch backwards through the end of the last stitch and bring it out through the length of the next stitch. This will produce a stitch which overlaps the thread on the back of the fabric.

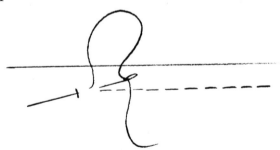

Half Backstitch

Use the same procedure as for the backstitch, carrying the needle only half of the length as the last stitch, but continue to bring the needle out one stitch ahead.

Prick-stitch

The prick-stitch, which is often used to insert zippers, is a version of the backstitch. Carry the needle back only a few threads of the fabric and forward the length of a normal stitch.

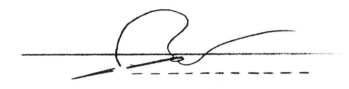

Slip-stitch

The slip-stitch is used very often for attaching trims, pockets, hems, and linings, and wherever an invisible finish is wanted. Slip the needle through the folded edge of the fabric, and at the same time, pick up one or two threads of the underneath layer of fabric. Continue, being sure to keep the stitches evenly spaced.

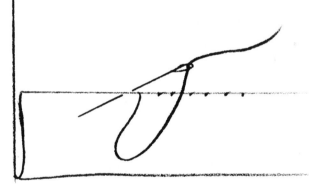

Hemming Stitch

Make a small stitch in the outside of the garment, being sure that the thread does not go all the way through the fabric, and bring the needle up at a diagonal through the edge of the hem. Keep the stitches evenly spaced, constantly checking that the thread does not go all the way through the outside of the garment fabric.

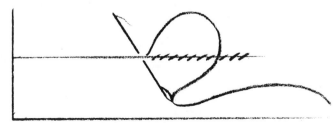

Blind-stitch

The blind-stitch is used whenever you don't want the stitch to show on either side of the fabric. To begin with, sew the edge of the fabric about ¼ inch in with a row of machine stitches. Hold the edge back and take a small stitch through one thread of the fabric on the bottom and then take the same stitch through the underside of the upper layer. Don't pull the thread tight.

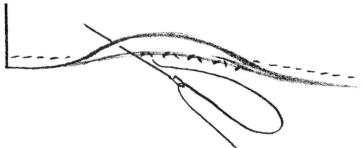

Overcast

The overcast stitch is used to finish the raw edge of a seam. Make diagonal stitches from front to back over the edge, keeping them the same size and evenly spaced.

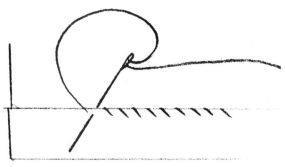

Overhand Stitch

The overhand stitch is used to sew two finished edges together. Working from back to front, use small stitches like the overcast stitch, taking up a few of the fabric threads in each stitch.

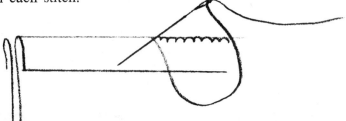

Whip-stitch

The whip-stitch is made in the same way as the overhand stitch with the needle held at a right angle, producing slanted stitches.

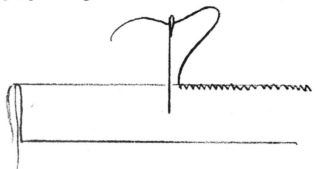

Catch-stitch

The catch-stitch is used most often for holding a piece of interfacing to the outside fabric. Work from left to right, taking a small stitch in the outside fabric. Making sure that the needle catches only one thread of the fabric very close to the edge of the interfacing. Make a stitch in the interfacing, crossing the first stitch. Make the following stitches forming a zigzag pattern. Keep the thread very loose. It is very important to work these stitches from left to right.

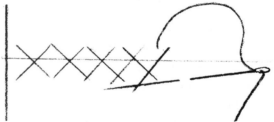

Blanket Stitch

The blanket stitch is used to finish the edges of seams. Work from left to right, take your first stitch at the edge, and take the next stitch ¼ inch from the edge. Bring the needle toward you with the thread under the needle.

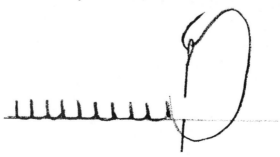

Buttonhole Stitch

The buttonhole stitch is made in exactly the same way as the blanket stitch, but the stitches are placed very close together.

When making all hand sewing stitches, never pull the thread tight, as this will cause the seam to pucker. Other specialized hand stitches are shown in other sections of this book where they apply. For example pad stitching, which is used for tailoring, is discussed on page 322. The chain stitch, which is used to form loops, and bar tacking are found in the section on loops, page 261.

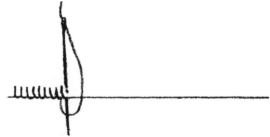

After a little practice, you will find that you will be able to make these stitches quickly and easily, and you will understand their various applications.

PRESSING AS YOU SEW

As mentioned before, pressing as you complete each section of your garment is absolutely essential. Remember that in pressing while you sew, you must lift the iron and gently lower it onto the section to be pressed. Do not slide the iron along the fabric. In order to avoid jumping up to press every seam as you go along, sew a basic unit—for example, all the darts or the side seams—and then press that before you go on to the next unit. All seams that are to be joined to another piece of fabric and any seams that are crossed by another seam must be pressed first. Sometimes the instructions will say that the outer edge of the garment is to be extended beyond the seam by a fraction of an inch. This is done so that the seam will not show from the outside of the garment.

The pattern instructions will tell you when and which direction to press the seam or other detail. Always follow these instructions carefully, using the drawings as a guide.

Always have your ironing board and other pressing equipment set up and ready to use before you start to sew. Test a scrap of the fabric you are using before you press the actual garment, to be sure that you know how the fabric reacts to the heat and steam. If the fabric water-spots or puckers when it comes in contact with the steam, you will have to use a dry iron.

Almost all of your pressing will be done on the wrong side of the garment. If you have to press on the right side of the fabric, use a pressing cloth between the fabric and the iron. Never allow the full weight of the iron to rest on the fabric; the heat and steam will usually be enough to do the job.

Flat Seams

To prevent the seam allowances of a flat seam from making an impression on the fabric, slip two pieces of brown paper between the seam allowances and the garment. If you have a seam roll, use it by placing it under the seam and press with the tip of the iron touching the actual seam.

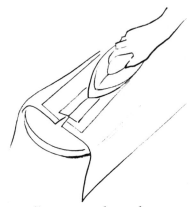

For pressing sleeve seams and other small seams, place them over a sleeve board and press carefully along the seam only, so the sides of the sleeve board don't leave an impression on the fabric.

Curved Seams

Curved, or contour seams must be pressed over a curved surface, such as a tailor's ham or a pressing mitt slipped over the edge of a sleeve board. Open the curved seam over the tailor's ham or pressing mitt and press the seam open, using the tip of the iron.

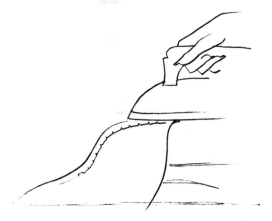

Darts

Hold the dart in the same position as it was sewn, and using the sleeve board, press it flat. Do not press beyond the point of the dart. Then place the dart over a tailor's ham or pressing mitt and press the dart in the direction indicated on the sewing instructions. In general, skirt darts are pressed toward the center front and back, bodice darts are pressed toward the center front and back, bust darts are pressed downward, and sleeve darts are pressed down toward the wrist.

For darts made in very heavy fabric, press them holding the fabric as you did when they were sewn and then slash the dart open to within one inch of the point. Press the dart open over a tailor's ham or pressing mitt, using the point of the iron to open the dart. If the fabric tends to leave an impression as you press, place strips of brown paper between the sides of the dart and the outside of the garment.

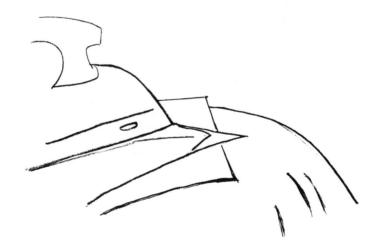

Enclosed Seams

Enclosed seams, like those on a neckline or cuff facing, or in a collar, must be pressed open before the garment is turned right-side out. First press the seam, holding the garment in the same direction as it was when sewn. Then place the garment on the sleeve board and with the point of the iron, press it open. If you have a pointer and creaser, use it instead of the sleeve board for this operation.

For curved seams, press with the point of the iron, completing a small section at a time. Turn the section of the garment right-side out and lay it on the ironing board with the underside facing up. You should now be able to see the line of stitching. Press along the stitching on the under side so the outside edge of the garment extends just above the seam.

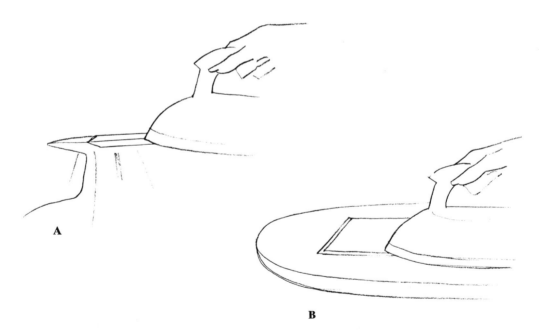

A

B

Sleeves

For set-in sleeves, press the underarm seam open with the sleeve slipped over the sleeve board. Then draw up the ease in the sleeve cap and pin it into the garment armhole to determine the fit. When the sleeve fits into the arm-hold, unpin it and lay it over the pressing mitt or edge of the sleeve board. Using the iron set for steam, gently press the cap between the edge of the sleeve cap and the rows of easing stitches. This will shrink the ease in the sleeve cap so that it will fit into the armhole of the garment smoothly. After you have sewn the sleeve into the garment, place the armhole seam on the narrow end of the sleeve board, and with the point of the iron, press the seam only as far as the stitching. For plain set-in sleeves, turn the sleeve allowance into the sleeve. From the right side of the garment, steam the shoulder lightly.

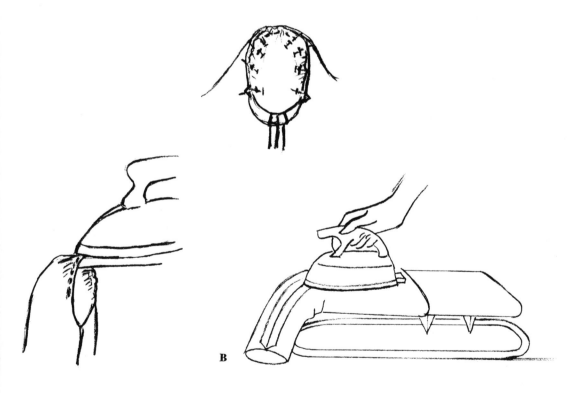

B

Gathers

After the seam is stitched, press on the wrong side of the garment, using the point of the iron to get in between the folds of the gathers. Do not lay the iron on top of the gathers as this would press the soft folds flat.

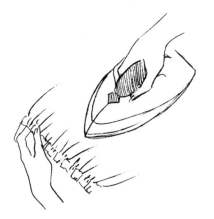

Tucks

When the tucks are made on the wrong side of the fabric, press them in the direction indicated in the pattern instructions with the point of the iron. Be sure not to press beyond the stitching. If the tucks are on the outside of the garment, press them in the same manner, using a pressing cloth.

For pressing other special areas, such as hems and pleats, see the sections on construction of these details.

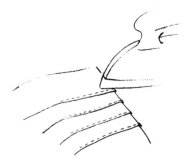

Final Pressing

After the garment is finished, you will have to give it a final touch up. If you have pressed the garment properly during construction, you will not have to do much pressing now. Place the garment on a hanger and stuff the shoulders, sleeves, and collar with tissue paper, or place the garment on a dress dummy if you have one. Steam these areas with a steam iron, but don't allow the iron to touch the garment. The steam alone will do the job. Allow the garment to dry completely before removing it. Something tailored, such as a jacket or coat, you may want to give to a dry-cleaner for a professional pressing job, but remember that there is no substitute for pressing the garment as you make it. You cannot sew the garment without pressing and then expect to press it thoroughly after it has been finished.

SEAMS AND SEAM FINISHES

Seam refers to a row of stitching, used either to hold two pieces of fabric together or for decoration. The basic shape and line of every garment is totally dependent on the construction of the seams. Because of this, seams must be made straight and even, and if you do slip while making a seam, stop and correct the mistake immediately. If you try to ignore the mistake, or think that you can correct it later, you will find that the garment will never have the professional look you are striving for.

The seam allowance is the fabric from the raw edge to the row of stitching. In all but very firmly woven or knitted fabrics, the seam allowance must be finished to prevent the fabric from ravelling. In most cases the seam is made ⅝ inch from the edge of the fabric, thus creating a ⅝ inch seam allowance. See the section called Basic Machine Stitching, page 147, for instructions on using a seam guide to keep the seam straight as you sew.

Plain Seam

A plain seam is made with the right sides of two layers of fabric facing each other and is sewn with the wrong side of the fabric facing up. For instructions on machine sewing a plain seam, see Basic Machine Stitching, page

146. If you have basted a seam, sew the row of permanent stitches to one side of the basting stitches, not on top of them.

There are different ways of finishing the seam allowance in order to keep the fabric from ravelling.

Pink, or Stitch and Pink

For use on firmly woven fabrics that don't ravel badly, pink the edge of the seam allowance with pinking shears, *after* the seam has been stitched and pressed. For a stronger finish, stitch a single row on the seam allowance only, ¼ inch from the edge before pinking.

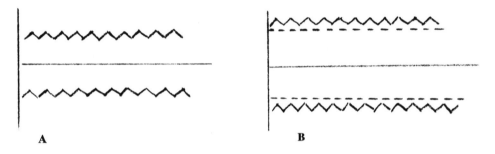

A   B

Stitch

For casual clothes that ravel easily, simply make a row of machine stitching ¼ inch from the edge of the seam allowance.

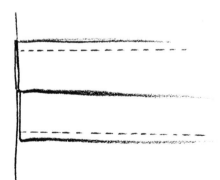

Overcasting

By hand: press the seam open and stitch ¼ inch from the edge of the seam allowance. Trim off ⅛ inch of the fabric and overcast by hand, having the stitches lined up with the row of machine stitching.

By machine: if you have a zigzag machine or a zigzag attachment for your machine, run a row of zigzag stitches just inside the raw edge of the seam allowance.

Turned Edges

This is recommended for use on lightweight fabrics. After the seam is stitched and pressed, press the edge of the seam allowance under ¼ inch and machine stitch as close to the edge as possible.

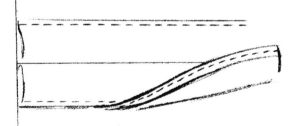

Self-Bound

This is recommended for light-weight fabrics used in children's clothes and sheer curtains. After the seam is stitched, cut off one seam allowance so that ¼ inch remains. Make a small fold on the other seam allowance and fold that seam allowance over so that it encases the trimmed one. Slip-stitch into place.

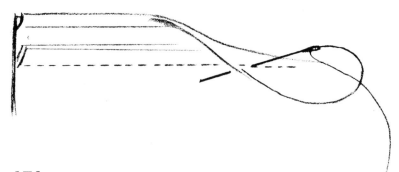

Bound Edges

This is recommended for use on heavy fabrics used in an unlined jacket or coat. Buy double-fold bias tape in a matching color and insert the raw edge of the seam allowance into the tape, with the narrower tape fold on the top. Stitch along the edge.

Some seam allowances require special handling in order to make the seam lie smoothly in the finished garment.

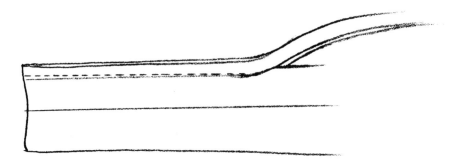

Trimming

Whenever the pattern instructions call for a seam to be trimmed, cut off the seam allowance, following the line of stitching and leaving a ¼ inch seam allowance.

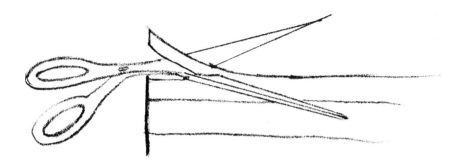

Grading

Grading is used for enclosed seams, such as those found in facings, and whenever there is more than one layer of fabric. Each seam allowance is trimmed to a different width, leaving the seam allowance of the outside garment piece the widest.

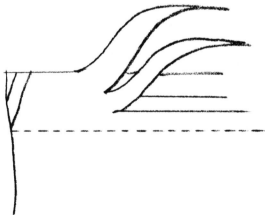

Notching

Seams with an outside curve must be notched to allow the seam to lie flat when turned and pressed. To do this, fold the seam to the position it will be in when finished. Ripples will form in the fabric; cut them away in the form of notches made in the seam allowance at regular intervals. Be careful not to cut the notches too deep.

Clips

Seams with an inward curve must be clipped along the seam allowance. Place the clips close together for deep curves, farther apart for gentler curves. Be sure not to clip into the seam itself.

Understitching

Understitching is used on facings and in other areas when the seam is folded. Grade the seam, and in a curved seam, clip or notch where necessary and press both seam allowances toward the facing. Machine stitch through the facing and both seam allowances ¼ inch from the seam line. Press the facing in and you will find that with the help of the understitching, it will not roll out.

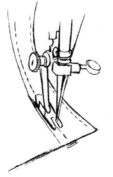

OTHER SEAMS

Intersecting Seams

When two seams intersect, or cross, such as those at the waist of a dress or the underarm of a sleeve, they must be sewn so that the seams match. Press the seams open and lay them on top of one another, right sides of the fabric together. At the seam line (usually ⅝ inch from the edge), place a pin through the top seam and then through the bottom seam, at right angles to the fabric. Place another pin in the fabric on either side of the first pin. Remove the first pin. If the fabric is very slippery, run a few hand basting stitches through the seams, just above the seam line. Stitch along the seam line as you would for a regular seam. Cut the seam allowances at right angles.

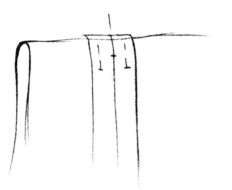

Curved Seams and Princess Seams

Stay-stitch both edges of the fabric ⅜ inch from the edge. Pin the sections together, clipping the inward seam allowance so that the end of the clips reach the stay-stitching. Sew the seam, using the seam guide. After the seam is finished, notch the outward curving seam allowance to the stay-stitching.

Bias Seams

Hand baste the seams of the two pieces of fabric that have been cut on the bias. Hang the garment up and leave it for at least eight hours. Then machine stitch next to the basting in the usual manner, but use a smaller stitch and stretch the fabric as you stitch.

To sew a piece of fabric that has been cut on the bias to one that has not, work with the bias piece on top. Pin and hand baste the seam. Stitch in the usual manner with the bias piece on top.

Corner Seams

Before making the seam, reinforce the inward corner (see the section called Basic Machine Stitching, page 149, for instructions on reinforcing), pivoting at the point. Make a small clip at the point, being careful not to cut the stitching. Pin the sections together wih the reinforced section on top and stitch as shown. Press a corner seam in one of the following ways, according to the pattern instructions.

(a) Press the seam open and cut away the excess fabric on the outward corner and stitch the edges together by hand.

(b) Press the seam toward the outside corner. You will have to trim the extra fabric away from the outside corner and hand stitch the edges together.

(c) Press the seam down, toward the reinforced corner.

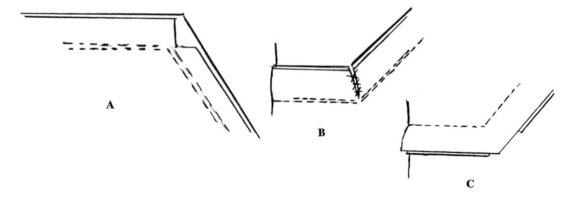

Taped Seams

For curved seams and shoulder seams in knits, and wherever extra strength is wanted, a taped seam is the answer. For straight seams, use seam binding or preshrunk twill tape. For curved seams, use purchased bias seam binding that has been pressed into the shape of the curve. Pin the tape so that ⅛ inch lies over the seam line. Stitch the seam permanently, catching the tape in the seam. When clipping a curved seam that has been sewn with a tape, be sure not to clip the tape.

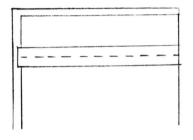

Seam with Ease

Easing is always done when you are sewing two pieces together that are not of equal length. When easing is called for in a seam, there will be markings on the pattern to indicate the area to be eased. Machine stitch through one layer of fabric with a long stitch just inside the seam allowance and leave several inches of thread at each end. Pin the pieces of fabric with the right sides together, with the section to be eased on top. Pull the machine stitches gently from each end and adjust the folds that form evenly. Do this by putting a pin at each end of the area to be eased, then in the middle, and then in the middle of the sections formed. Stitch along the seam line; be sure not to catch the folds of the fabric in the seam.

French Seams

French seams are most often used on sheer fabrics. They make a seam that looks like a regular seam on the outside, but form a tuck on the inside. French seams can only be made on straight seams. Pin the pieces of fabric together with the *wrong* sides facing. Stitch ⅜ inch from the edge. Cut off the seam allowance to within ⅛ to ¼ inch of the stitching. Turn the fabric so that the *right* sides are facing and press along the stitched seam. Stitch along the original seam line, enclosing the previous stitching.

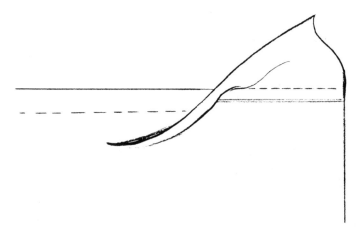

Simulated French Seam

Make a regular plain seam but do not press it open. Fold in ¼ inch on both seam allowances and press. Stitch along the folded edges.

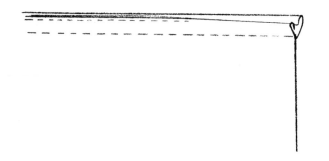

Lapped Seam

Fold in the seam allowance on the side to be lapped and press. With the right sides of both pieces of fabric facing you, pin the folded section to the seam allowance on the other section. Stitch as close to the edge of the fold as possible.

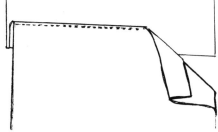

Topstitched Seam

Make a regular seam and press it open. With the right side of the fabric facing you, stitch to one side of the seam, through the seam allowance, the distance indicated on the pattern instructions.

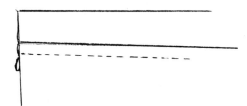

Double Topstitched Seam

Make a regular seam and press it open. Topstitch through the seam allowances on both sides of the seam in the same way as for a topstitched seam.

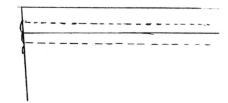

Welt Seam

Make a regular seam and press both seam allowances in the direction indicated on the pattern instructions. Trim the underneath seam allowance to ¼ inch. Stitch through the garment and wider seam allowance, enclosing the trimmed seam allowance.

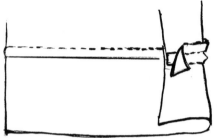

Double Welt Seam

Make a welt seam as instructed. Topstitch on the right side of the fabric as close to the seam as possible.

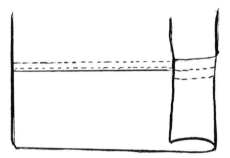

Felled Seam

Sew a regular plain seam with the *wrong* sides of the fabric facing. Press both seam allowances to the side. Trim the underneath seam allowance to ⅛ inch. Fold the edge of the wide seam allowance under ¼ inch along the edge and pin over the trimmed seam allowance. Machine stitch on the folded edge, or for heavy fabrics, slip-stitch.

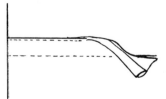

Slot Seam

Make a plain seam, but baste it instead of sewing it permanently. Press the seam open. Cut a strip of matching fabric as long as the seam and wider than the width of both seam allowances. Pin it under the pressed seam. Working with the right side of the fabric facing you, top-stitch an equal distance from both sides of the seam, making sure that the stitching penetrates the garment fabric, the seam allowances, and the strip of fabric. Remove the basting stitches from the seam.

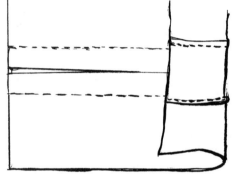

Piped Seam

With the right side of one section of the fabric facing you, baste the piping to the fabric along the seam line. Place the second section of fabric over the first, with the right sides together, with the seam line on the piping. Baste, and then stitch along the seam line, penetrating through all the layers of fabric.

Be sure to review the section called Pressing as You Sew for instructions on pressing straight and curved seams properly. (Page 158.)

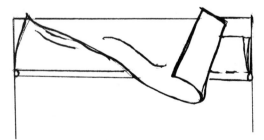

DARTS

Darts are used to make the flat piece of fabric conform to the three-dimensional human body. The length and placement of the darts is essential to the fit of the garment. In Chapter 2, you learned how to shorten or lengthen darts and how to reposition them when necessary. Now you have to learn how to make them properly so that they lie flat against the body and are not noticeable or bumpy.

One of the most important factors in getting an accurate dart is to be sure that you carefully transfer the marking on the pattern to the fabric. Use dressmaker's carbon paper where possible, making sure that you follow the stitching line of the dart. Most darts form a straight line from the top of the dart to the point, but sometimes they are slightly concave or convex. Follow the line given on the pattern. If your fabric will not take carbon paper markings, use tailor's tacks or tailor's chalk to mark the main points given on the pattern.

To make the dart, fold it in half, being sure that the marks on the side of the fabric facing you are directly over the marks on the underside of the fabric. To do this, insert a pin, placed at right angles to the fabric, through the markings on both layers of the fabric. Then place another pin at a right angle to the first pin, with the point of the pin facing the fold of the fabric. Repeat this process for each mark on the dart.

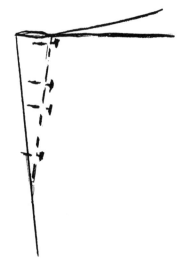

Start stitching the dart at the widest part, at the top of the fabric. Stitch along the stitching line, tapering the stitching to nothing at the point of the dart. Do not backtrack, but gently pull the dart away from the needle, leaving several inches of thread. Knot the ends of the threads.

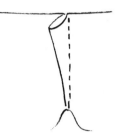

For long, contour darts at the waistline, fold and pin the fabric in the same way as for regular darts. Stitch in the same way, starting the stitching at the middle of the dart, and sew toward the point. Turn the garment over and sew the other half of the dart in the same way. Tie the threads at both ends in a knot. Make a clip in the dart at the waistline to relieve strain placed on the dart in wearing.

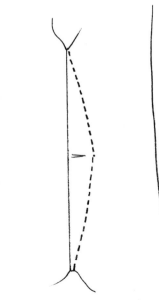

For darts made on the outside of the garment or in sheer fabrics, use a "continuous-thread" dart that is made with only one strand of thread. Fold and pin the dart as described. Remove the thread from the needle and the top thread guides of the machine. Thread the bobbin thread through the needle and the top thread guides in the usual manner and tie the end of the bobbin thread to the top spool of thread. Wind the thread on the spool, pulling it up from the bobbin for about a yard, to give you enough thread to sew the dart without having the knot go through the thread guides. Start stitching the dart at the pointed end and slowly guide the needle into the point of the dart at the very edge of the fold. Turn the spool to take up any slack in the thread, lower the pressure foot, and slowly stitch the dart from the point to the widest part of the dart. Backtrack at the end of the stitching. Cut off the knot and re-thread the machine with bobbin thread for each dart.

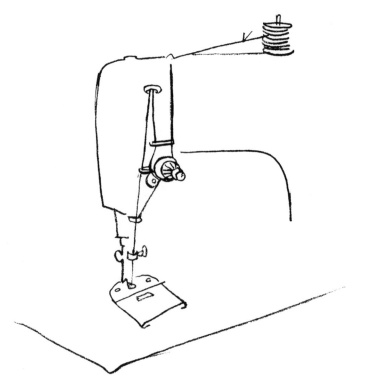

Darts made in heavy fabrics should be slashed open to within one inch of the point of the dart. If the fabric ravels easily, overcast the edges of the dart by hand.

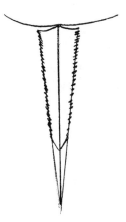

For darts made in sheer fabrics that do not use the continuous-thread method, stitch ⅛ inch away from the original stitching and trim the extra fabric away. Overcast by hand.

Darts must be carefully pressed over a pressing mitt or tailor's ham. See the section called Pressing as You Sew for instructions. (Page 158.)

ZIPPERS

Zippers are the most convenient way to make a closure in a garment. There are several types of zippers available and several methods of inserting them. The type of zipper and the application you use will depend on where the zipper is inserted into the garment.

All zippers are made with either metal teeth or synthetic coils, which are attached to a cloth tape. A zipper made with a synthetic coil is softer and more flexible than the metal one, and it wears more comfortably. The newest zippers are "invisible" or "hidden." They are made with either metal teeth or synthetic coils and do not show in the finished seam.

Neck and skirt zippers open at the top and are used for garments with an opening at the top of the seam, such as the back of a dress or the opening in a skirt or pair of pants.

Dress zippers have a metal stop at the top of the zipper and are used for enclosed seams at the side of a dress under the arm.

Separating zippers are made of metal only and are used for the fronts of coats and jackets, as they have seams that open top and bottom.

Trouser zippers are made of metal only and are used on men's trousers and sportswear (not for women's pants).

Slipcover zippers are also made of metal only and are used for slipcovers.

When selecting a zipper for use with clothes, buy the length and style listed on the pattern envelope under "notions." If the length is indicated, but not the type of zipper, buy a neck or skirt zipper in the length required (skirt zippers are shorter than neck zippers). The length of the zipper given is the measurement from the metal bottom stop to the top of the slider when the zipper is closed, or to the top bar tack on dress zippers. The length measurement does not include the cloth zipper tape. If you can't find the length called for on your pattern, buy a zipper that is longer than you need and shorten it.

To shorten a zipper, measure the length you need and whip-stitch ¼ inch below that with a doubled thread or buttonhole twist. Cut off the bottom of the zipper with scissors or with a single-edged razor blade.

Regular zippers are applied in two ways: with a center or slot seam open-

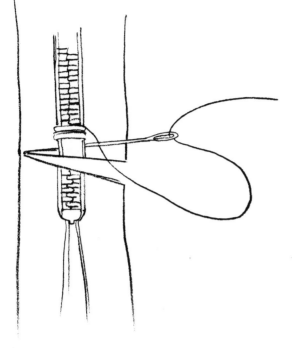

ing which shows one row of stitching on either side of the zipper, or with a lapped seam opening which shows a single row of stitching on one side of the zipper.

Before you can insert the zipper, you must prepare the seam. Your pattern will have a mark above which the zipper is to be inserted, but check to see that the length is correct by holding the zipper to the seam, with the bottom stop of the zipper just above the marking. There must be a seam allowance plus a little more above the top of the zipper with the tab turned up. For a skirt or pants opening, leave the seam allowance (⅝ inch). For the neck opening on a dress or blouse, leave the seam allowance, plus ½ inch for a hook and eye. (The seam allowance is left to allow for the facing, which will be sewn on after the zipper has been inserted.) For a dress side opening, leave just enough opening to allow for the metal bar tack at the top of the zipper.

To prepare the seam, stitch to the bottom opening, backtrack to reinforce the seam, and baste the length of the zipper opening. For a dress side opening, stitch the seam above the basting, backtracking at the start of the seam to reinforce it. Press the seam open.

For a neck opening that is to be interfaced, baste the interfacing to the neckline seam and trim off ⅝ inch of the seam allowance on the inside of the interfacing. If for some reason the seam allowance of the zipper opening is less than ⅝ inch, stitch a piece of seam binding, the length of the zipper opening, to the seam allowance. Stay-stitch the seam allowances of the zipper opening ¼ inch from the raw edge.

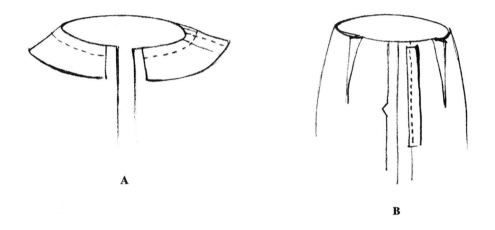

A   B

Your pattern instructions will tell you at what point during the construction of the garment to insert the zipper. It is usually easier to insert the zipper before the main garment seams are finished, as it is easier to work with a flat section.

For applying all but the invisible zippers, you will need an adjustable zipper foot, which will replace the usual pressure foot on your machine. The zipper foot can be moved to either side of the needle and allow you to sew closer to the teeth of the zipper than is possible with the regular pressure foot.

Before you insert the zipper, press the zipper tape to remove any folds. Always press the zipper with it closed and do not place the iron directly on the teeth. This is very important when pressing a zipper with a synthetic coil, as the heat of the iron may cause it to melt. The teeth of a metal zipper may scratch the sole plate of your iron. Press the zipper from the wrong side or use a pressing cloth between the zipper and the iron.

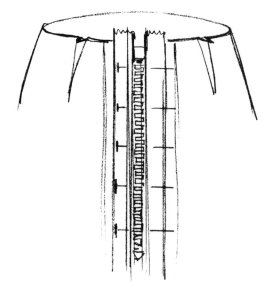

Centered, or Slot-Seam Application

This application is usually used to insert a zipper in the back neckline of a dress or blouse. It can also be used in the back opening of a skirt or pants and at the wrists for a sleeve opening in a tight-fitting sleeve.

With the wrong side of the garment facing you and the basted seam pressed open, mark the bottom end of the basting with a pin sticking up through the seam. With the zipper closed and the pull tab up, pin the zipper to the seam, with the teeth or coil directly over the seam, and the bottom stop of the zipper ⅛ inch from the pin that marks the bottom of the basting. The pull top (not the tab) should be ¼ inch below the seam allowance of the neckline seam. Place the pins at right angles to the zipper teeth, penetrating through all the layers of the garment and going under the teeth. Alternate the directions of the pins as shown.

Replace the pressure foot of your machine with the adjustable zipper foot, with the foot to the left of the needle. Have your machine set to the longest stitch, and working with the wrong side of the garment facing you, follow the guide lines on the zipper tape and baste just to the outside of the guide line. Start the basting down the left side of the zipper, pivot below the bottom stop, pivot again, and baste up the right side of the zipper. Turn the garment to the right side and change the length of the stitch for regular sewing. Following the basting stitching as a guide, stitch right inside the basting, pivoting at the bottom. Count the number of stitches across the bottom of the zipper; be sure to have the same number of stitches on each side of the seam. Stitch up the other side of the zipper. Remove the machine basting stitches from the zipper tape and seam.

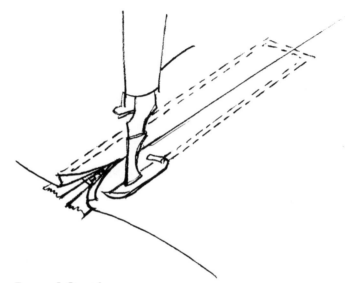

Lapped Opening

This is used for skirts, pants, and neckline openings.

Baste and press the seam open as described. Replace the regular pressure foot with the zipper foot, with the foot adjusted to the right of the needle. With the garment wrong-side out, place it on the machine. Have the top of the garment facing you, with the right-hand seam allowance spread under the needle and the rest of the garment to the left. Open the zipper and place it face down on the seam, with the bottom of the zipper stop just above the basting stitches. The top stop of the zipper should be just below the seam allowance for skirts and pants, or ½ inch below the seam allowance for a neckline opening. The zipper teeth or coil should be on the seam line. Pin at right angles along the right-hand zipper tape, adjust the machine to baste, and stitch along the zipper tape from the bottom to the top, following the guide line on the tape. Remove the pins as you sew.

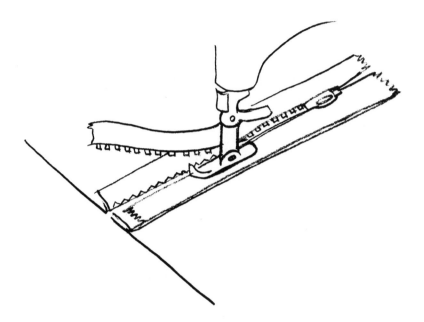

Close the zipper and turn it face up, thus folding the seam allowance where the zipper is basted to it. Adjust the zipper foot to the left of the needle and change the machine to a regular stitch. Smooth the seam allowance to the left of the zipper teeth, and starting at the bottom, stitch through the fold and the zipper tape.

Still with the garment wrong-side up, spread it out with the zipper face down over the unattached seam allowance (left hand). Smooth the zipper so that it is perfectly flat. A small pleat will form at the bottom of the zipper. Pin, again with the pins at right angles to the needle. Starting with the needle at the seam allowance, stitch, pivoting at right angles along the guide line on the zipper tape, and stitch to the top of the skirt. You have sewn through the zipper tape, the seam allowance, and the front of the garment. At the bottom of the zipper, pull the top thread through to the wrong side of the garment and knot the ends of the thread. Remove the basting stitches from the seam.

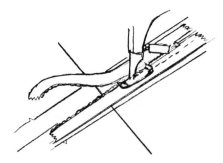

Lapped Opening in a Dress Seam

This application is used to insert the zipper into the left-side seam of a dress under the arm.

Baste and press the seam open. Replace the regular pressure foot with the zipper foot, with the foot adjusted to the right of the needle. With the dress wrong-side out, place it on the machine. Have the top of the dress facing you, with the right-hand seam allowance spread under the needle and the rest of the dress to the left. Open the zipper and place it face down on the seam, with the bottom of the zipper stop just above the basting stitches, and the top bar tack just under the basting stitches. The zipper teeth or coil should be on the seam line. Pin at right angles along the right-hand zipper tape, adjust the machine to baste, and stitch along the zipper tape from the bottom to the top, following the guide line on the zipper. Remove the pins as you sew.

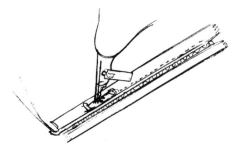

Close the zipper and turn it face up, thus folding the seam allowance where the zipper is basted to it. Adjust the zipper foot to the left of the needle and change the machine to the regular stitch length. Smooth the seam allowance to the left of the zipper teeth, and starting at the bottom, stitch through the fold and the zipper tape.

With the garment wrong-side up, spread it out with the zipper face down over the unattached seam allowance (left hand). Smooth the zipper so that it is perfectly flat. A small pleat will form at the top and bottom of the zipper. Pin, again with the pins at right angles to the needle. Starting with the needle at the seam allowance, stitch, pivoting at right angles along the guide line on the zipper tape, and stitch to the top of the zipper. Pivot again, taking the same number of stitches that you made across the bottom of the zipper. At the top and bottom of the zipper, pull the top thread through to the wrong side of the dress and knot the ends of the thread. Remove the basting stitches from the seam.

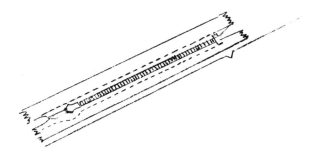

To Insert a Zipper by Hand

Inserting a zipper by hand is a nice way to give a couture touch to any garment you are making. For delicate or stretch fabrics, and for pile fabrics like velvet and corduroy, it is often easier to insert the zipper by hand.

Follow the instructions for the application desired, machine stitching until you get to the final step where the stitching goes through all the layers to the right side of the garment. Machine or hand baste the final step, and then sew the zipper in permanently from the right side of the garment, using a prick-stitch. Use buttonhole twist or regular thread doubled. Take just a few threads in each stitch on the right side of the fabric and take a normal-length stitch on the underside of the work through all the layers of the fabric.

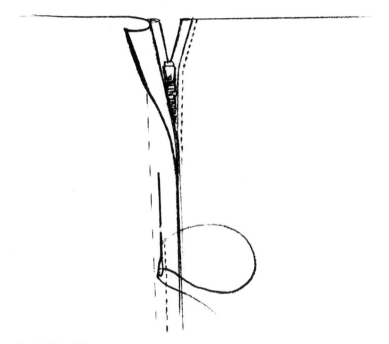

Invisible Zippers

The relatively new invisible zippers are available with metal teeth or a synthetic coil. The synthetic coil is the most practical, being soft and flexible enough for the lightest fabrics, but sturdy enough for heavy fabrics. When properly inserted, the invisible zipper does not show from the right side of the garment because it looks like a seam, with no zipper teeth showing. The invisible zipper is also the easiest and fastest to insert.

If you have to shorten an invisible zipper, open the zipper to the length needed. Whip-stitch an inch below the slider as instructed for shortening regular zippers.

To apply the invisible zipper correctly, you will have to buy a special plastic zipper foot to replace the pressure foot. This special foot is sold with the zipper, in the notions department. Make sure that you buy the same *brand* foot as your zipper, and that the foot is correct for a zipper with metal teeth or a synthetic coil (there is a different foot for each). Check the package carefully when you buy the plastic foot. The package will have instructions on assembling the foot, adapting it to fit your particular machine.

How to Apply an Invisible Zipper

When working with an invisible zipper made with a synthetic coil, press the back sides with the point of the iron to flatten the coils, so that you can see the stitches holding the coils to the tape.

The seam into which the zipper is to be sewn must be completely free; do not sew or baste it together. Slide the zipper foot so that the needle is aligned with the center indicator. Open the zipper and place it on the right side of the fabric as shown, with the coil of the zipper on the seam line and the top of the zipper ¼ inch from the cut edge of the garment. Pin the zipper tape in place, with the pins at right angles to the needle. Line the coil up with the right-hand groove in the zipper foot and lower the foot. Stitch, making sure to get the stitches as close to the coil as possible, and stop sewing when the foot touches the zipper slider. Backstitch to reinforce the seam.

Close the zipper and pin the loose zipper tape to the right side of the other piece of fabric, with the top of the zipper tape ¼ inch from the edge of garment and the coil on the seam line. Line up the coil with the left-hand groove of the foot and lower the foot. Stitch down the zipper tape as before, until the foot touches the zipper slider. Backstitch.

If the plastic zipper foot slides, slide it to the left of the needle so that the needle passes through the notch, or if it doesn't slide (some brands don't), replace it with the adjustable zipper foot adjusted to the left of the needle. Close the zipper and place the right sides of the fabric together, pinning along the seam so that the seam is lined up. Start the stitching ¼ inch above and slightly to the left of the previous stitching. Stitch the length of the seam. When you have finished the seam, there will be one inch of the zipper extending beyond the seam opening. Stitch through the zipper tape and the left seam allowance for one inch. Adjust the zipper foot to the right of the needle and stitch through the zipper tape and right seam allowance for one inch.

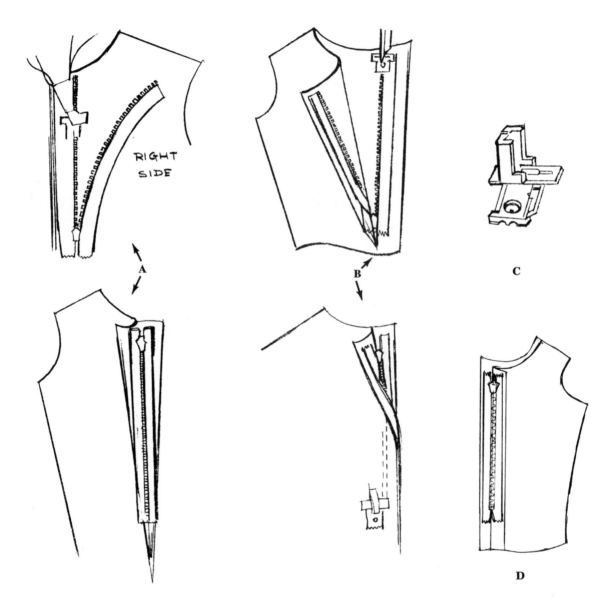

When applying the invisible zipper to a garment with a crosswise seam, or on a fabric with a stripe or plaid to be matched, stitch the first side of the zipper and allow the unstitched side of the zipper to lie facedown on the right side of the fabric. Mark the seam, stripe, or plaid with a pencil mark on the zipper tape. When you pin the second side of the zipper to the right side of the fabric, match the seam, stripe, or plaid to the pencil mark. Stitch as described.

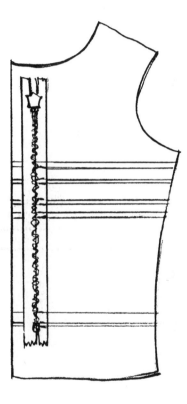

Applying a Shaped Facing

Apply a shaped facing after the zipper has been inserted. Pin the prepared facing to the neckline in the same way as instructed in the section on facings, but fold under the seam allowance on the back of the facing as shown, so that the folded edges of the facing are even with the folded edge of the zipper opening. Stitch, trim, grade, and clip the neckline seam. Turn the facing to the inside of the garment and press. Fold under the raw edges of the

facing to the inside of the garment and press. Fold under the raw edges of the facing and pin them to the zipper tape. Slip-stitch the facing into place and finish the closure with a hook and eye as shown.

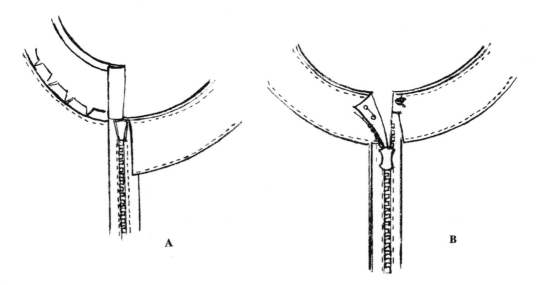

UNDERLINING

The underlining, which can range from very lightweight to quite firm when used as a backing for a tailored jacket or coat, is cut from the same pattern pieces as the outside of the garment. When you cut the outside of a garment piece which is to be underlined, do not transfer the markings to the outside fabric. All markings will be made on the underlining. The underlining is basted to the individual garment pieces and the two layers of fabric are handled as one during the construction of the garment. For simple dresses made of medium- to lightweight fabrics, the facings may be underlined to eliminate the need for interfacing. Part of a garment may be underlined to give strength to areas which will receive strain, for example: underline the body of a dress, but not the sleeves; underline part of the back of a straight skirt when it is not lined, to prevent the skirt from "sitting out" at the back when worn.

To Underline the Body of a Dress

Cut the outside fabric of the dress and remove the pattern pieces without transferring the markings to the fabric. Using the pattern pieces of the dress (front and back of the dress and facings), cut out the underlining and transfer the markings to the fabric. Lay the outside of the front of the dress, wrong-side up, on a flat surface large enough to support the entire piece. Take the matching underlining piece and with the markings facing you, pin it on top of the front of the dress. Pin first at the corners, then at the notches, along the curves and long seams and bottom edges. Without lifting the two layers, hand baste through them, down the center of the dress and through the centers of the darts. Place the piece on the machine and stitch through the two layers ½ inch from the edges. Repeat for the back of the dress. Pin the underlining to the facing pieces, carefully matching the edges, and stitch without hand basting. Make the darts in the usual manner, sewing through both layers as if they were one. Trim the underlining as shown, and slash and press the darts open. Make the dress as instructed by the pattern primer. Mark the hemline and use a long running stitch (by hand) to hold the underlining to the outside fabric. Finish the edge of the hem and turn up the hem. Pin into place and stitch the hem to the underlining fabric only. No stitches should show on the right side of the dress.

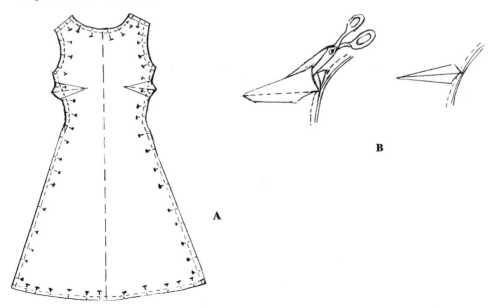

A

B

LINING

The lining for a garment is either cut from special pattern pieces marked for lining or from the same pieces as the outside of the garment, except those for the facings, collar, and trims. Make the lining as if it were a separate garment. After sewing the darts and main seams, press it and insert it into the almost completed garment with the wrong sides of the fabrics facing. After the lining has been basted to the garment, apply the facings, waistband, and so forth. Instructions for making a full-skirt lining are given in Chapter 4.

Linings are hemmed separately from the garment with the exception of jackets and some coat linings, which are slip-stitched to the finished hem of the outside fabric. Jacket and coat linings are finished separately and are inserted into the garment by hand. See Chapter 6, Tailoring, for instructions on coat and jacket linings.

Lining the Body of a Dress

Cut the outside fabric of the dress and transfer the markings to the fabric. Using the pattern pieces for the main sections of the dress (bodice front and back, skirt front and back), cut out the lining and transfer the markings to the lining fabric. Sew and press the main seams and darts of the dress and lining. Insert the zipper into the dress and leave the lining open above the mark for the bottom of the zipper. After pressing the outside of the dress and the lining thoroughly, turn the lining wrong-side out. With the dress right-side out, slip the lining into the dress, with the wrong sides facing, and pin the lining to the dress at the neckline and armholes. Baste the lining to the dress at the neckline and armholes. Fold back the seam allowance on the lining seam over the zipper and slip-stitch the lining to the zipper tape. Make the facings at the neckline and armholes as instructed by the pattern. Finish the hemline edge of the outside of the dress and hem it to itself. Finish the hem edge of the lining and hem it to itself one inch shorter than the dress, with the inside of the hem facing the wrong side of the dress. If the dress has a waistline seam, hand tack the seam allowance of the lining to the seam allowance of the dress at each side.

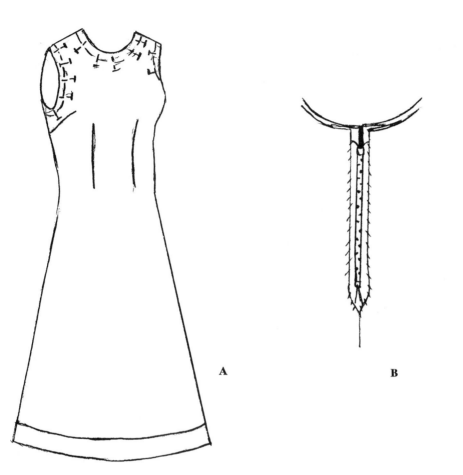

A   B

INTERFACING

Interfacing is used to add body and firmness to small areas of a garment. Interfacings are placed between two layers of the outer fabric, for example, between the upper and under collar and between two sections of a cuff. The weight of the interfacing ranges from a light organza to a heavy hair canvas. See pages 123-125 for a guide to the selection of interfacing fabrics.

Your pattern pieces will specify "to be interfaced," which means that the piece is to be used to cut the interfacing as well as the outside of the garment.

Certain areas, such as collars and most cuffs, should always be interfaced. Any area which will have buttonholes must be interfaced, whether the pattern calls for it or not. Facings are usually interfaced if they are not underlined. Use the facing pieces to cut the interfacing. For interfacing heavyweight woolens in coats and jackets, see Chapter 6, Tailoring, for the techniques to be used on these garments.

For light- to medium-weight fabrics, prepare the interfacing by trimming the corners off on the diagonal and trim away the ⅝ inch seam allowances on the edges that will not be sewn into the seam. Trim off ⅝ inch on neck interfacing, on the edges that will extend into a zipper. If there is a seam in the interfacing, lap one edge over the other and sew along the seam line. Trim the seam allowances to ⅛ inch. Unless otherwise instructed, lay the interfacing over the wrong side of the garment and pin and machine baste ½ inch from the edges.

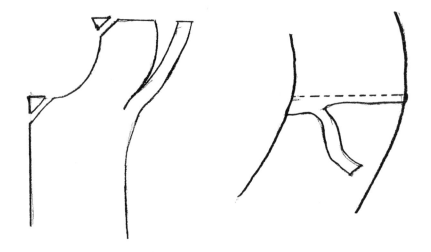

If you are using an iron-on interfacing, test it first by applying it to a swatch of fabric with an iron, following the manufacturer's instructions. Be sure that the combined piece is not too stiff, and that the outline of the interfacing does not show on the right side of the fabric. Prepare the iron-on pieces by trimming them in the same way as described. Carefully place them on the wrong side of the piece to be interfaced, with the treated side of the interfacing facing the fabric, and press them into place with a *dry* iron.

When interfacing an area with a fold line, such as an extended facing or cuff, catch-stitch the interfacing to the fold line from the wrong side, taking up just one thread of the outside fabric as you sew, so that the stitches will not show from the right side.

Once the interfacing is in place, continue with the construction of the garment and remove any basting stitches that show from the right side.

FACINGS

Facings are used to finish the raw edges of a garment, such as those at the neckline, the armholes in sleeveless dresses and blouses, and the openings of jackets. The undersides of collars and cuffs are also called facings. Most facings are cut from the same fabric as the outside of the garment, but for very heavy fabrics or scratchy fabrics, you can cut the facings from a lighter fabric. Facings must be cut, stitched, and pressed accurately to achieve a smooth, clean line on your clothes.

In order to give the body that is necessary for the garment to maintain its line, most facings must be interfaced. The interfacing is usually cut from the same pattern piece as the facing. Sometimes special pattern pieces are included for cutting the interfacing; the pattern instructions will include the information necessary.

Facing Finishes

The raw edges of the facing must be finished to prevent the fabric from ravelling. There are several methods of doing this, depending on the weight and nature of the fabric.

1. For lightweight fabrics—fold under ¼ inch and machine stitch along the edge of the fold.

2. For medium- to heavyweight fabrics—stitch seam binding to the edges of the facing, on the right side of the fabric.

3. For heavyweight fabrics that don't ravel easily—stitch ¼ inch from the edge, and if you wish, pink the edges.

4. For heavy fabrics that ravel easily—overcast the raw edge by hand or by machine, using a zigzag stitch.

5. For knits that don't ravel—machine stitch ¼ inch from the edge.

Shaped Facing

Shaped facings are used for necklines with or without a collar, for sleeveless armholes, and for skirts or pants without a waistband. The instructions given below are for a shaped neckline facing without a collar or zipper. For finishing a neckline facing with a zipper, see page 193.

1. Trim ½ inch from the outer edge of the interfacing and baste the interfacing to the neckline of the garment in a ½-inch seam.

2. Prepare the facing by stitching the seams at the shoulders and press the seams open. Turn under ¼ inch on the outside raw edge and stitch.

3. Pin the facing to the garment, with the right side of the garment facing you and with the wrong sides of the fabric facing each other. Match the seams at the shoulders. Stitch at the neckline on the seam line (⅝ inch from the edge), sewing through the garment, the interfacing, and the facing.

4. Trim the seam allowances, grading the seam by trimming the facing closest to the seam, leaving the interfacing the next widest, and leaving the garment seam allowance wider than the other seam allowances. Clip along the curve at regular intervals, making sure not to clip into the stitching.

5. Press the seam allowances toward the facing and understitch along the facing, having the stitch penetrate through the seam allowances.

6. Turn the facing to the inside of the garment and press. Tack the facing by hand to the inside at the shoulders. Be sure that the facing lies flat and does not pull at the area you have tacked.

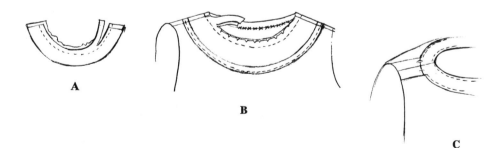

A   B   C

Slashed Facing

The slashed facing is a variation of a shaped facing and used when an opening is wanted in the front or back of the garment. Prepare the interfacing and facing as for a shaped facing. Pin the facing and stitch around the neck and down the mark for the slash, tapering the stitching to a point at the end of the slash, and reinforce the stitching at the point. Trim and grade the seams, cutting the points at the neck edge at right angles to the corner as shown. Slash the opening to the point, being careful not to cut the stitches, and trim the seam allowances as close to the stitching as possible. Clip the seam allowance at the curve of the neckline and understitch as for a shaped facing. Turn the facing right-side out, carefully pushing the points at the corners, from the inside, with a point presser (never use the points of scissors as you may tear through the fabric), or gently pull the points out with the tip of a pin from the right side. Press the facing and tack it at the shoulder seams.

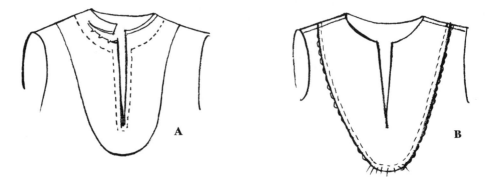

Bias Facing

Bias facings are used on very heavy fabrics or on sheers, where you don't want a full facing that would show through to the right side. Use a purchased single-fold, wide bias tape in a matching color, or cut bias strips from the same fabric as the garment for sheers and cut from the lining or underlining fabric for heavyweight fabrics. For instructions on cutting bias strips, see page 257. Cut the strip four times the width you want the final facing to be, plus ¼ inch. If you are using commercial bias tape, cut it the length of the garment edge plus 2 inches. For a cut bias strip, fold it in half lengthwise and press it, gently stretching it to the shape of the edge to be faced. For commercial tape, open one of the folded edges and press it, stretching it to shape. If you are facing a neckline edge with a zipper, insert the zipper before attaching the facing. Trim the tape of the zipper to just below the seam line. Pin the wrong side of the bias to the right side of the garment, placing the pins ½ inch apart, and shaping the bias to fit. Turn under ½ inch of bias at each edge. Stitch, trim, and clip the seam allowances. Turn the facing to the inside and press, so that the folded edge of the garment extends slightly above the facing seam.

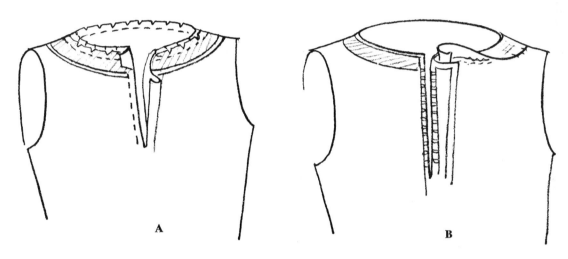

One-Piece Facing for Garments with a Narrow Shoulder Strap

Sew the side seams of the garment and press them open. Sew the side seams of the facing, press them open, and finish the raw edges of the bottom of the facing in the way best suited to the fabric. Baste the interfacing to the wrong side of the garment. Pin the facing to the garment with the right sides facing and sew the neckline and underarm seams. Stitch to the seam line on the shoulders. Understitch the facing as deeply into the shoulder area as possible. Turn the facing to the right side and press. Fold the facing back at the shoulders as shown. Pin the shoulder seams together and sew them, being sure not to catch the facing in the stitching. Backtrack the stitching at each end of the seam so that the ends of the thread are not at the edge. Press the shoulder seams open and fold the facing seam allowances to the inside, and slip-stitch them together.

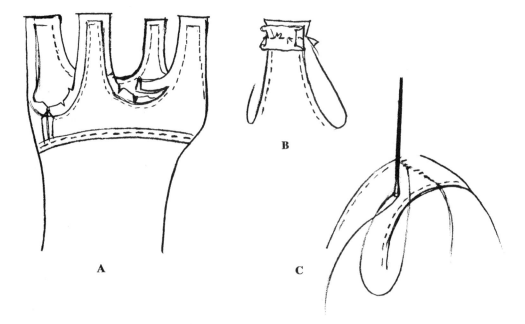

A   B   C

One-Piece Facing for Garments with Wide Shoulders

Sew the shoulder seams of the garment, press them open, and baste the interfacing to the wrong side of the garment. Sew the shoulder seams of the facing and finish the raw edges of the bottom of the facing. Pin the facing to the garment, with the right sides together, at the neckline and armholes. Stitch the neckline and armhole seams. Trim, grade, and clip the seam allowances.

Turn the facing to the right side by sliding your hand from the front under the facing and pulling each back section through the facing to the right side. Understitch the facing through the seam allowances as far as possible into the shoulder sections and around the neckline. Pin the side seams together, matching the underarm seams, and lifting up the facing as shown. Sew the side seams, starting at the edge of the facing. Press the facing at the neckline and armholes with the folded edge of the garment extended slightly above the seam.

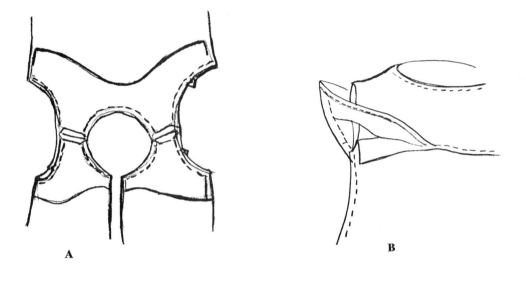

A

B

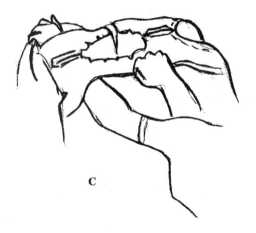

C

Extended Facing

Extended facings are included in the same pattern piece as the area to be faced and are folded to form the facing. They are most often used to face the front of a blouse or jacket and are combined with a shaped facing at the back of the neck.

Baste the interfacing to the wrong side of the garment and stitch the side and shoulder seams. Stitch the back shaped facing to the shoulder seams of the extended facing and press all seams open. Finish the edge of the facing in the way best suited to the fabric. Turn the facing back along the fold line and pin the facing to the garment at the neck, with the right sides of the fabric together, catching the seams at the shoulder. Stitch the neckline seam through all the layers of fabric. Trim and grade the seam, clipping at the curve. Trim the corner at a right angle and turn the facing right-side out. Understitch at the neckline as far into the corner as possible. Tack the facing to the garment at the shoulder seams.

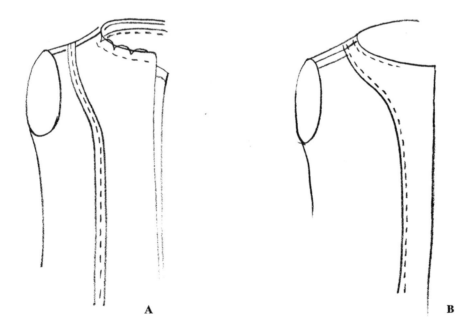

A   B

COLLARS

Listed below are three basic types of collars, versions of which are used on blouses, shirts, dresses, jackets, and coats.

Flat Collars—Flat collars follow the curve of the garment and lie flat along the neckline.

Rolled Collars—Rolled collars, which can be notched or not, stand up from the neckline and fold over at the roll line to form a frame for the face. They can range from very soft to quite stiff, depending on the style of the garment.

Standing Collars—Standing collars are usually firmly backed and stand up from the neckline.

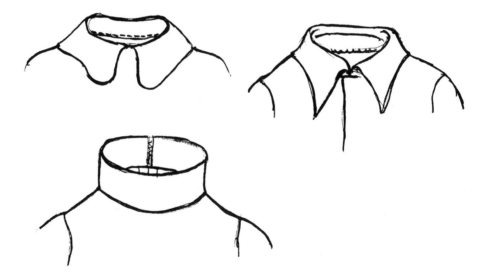

Your pattern may include a separate piece for the under collar, or the upper and under collar may be made from the same piece. When laying out the pattern pieces for a collar, be sure that you follow the instructions for cutting. When cutting the upper and under collar from the same piece, you will have to cut two or four pieces of fabric from the same pattern piece. If there is one, mark the roll line of a rolled collar with basting stitches or tailor's tacks. Collars are nearly always interfaced; there are almost no exceptions. Follow the pattern instructions to use the correct pattern piece for cutting the interfacing.

To be sure that the collar is perfect, you must observe a few rules. Be sure that the seams are perfectly accurate so that both curves or points of the collar are symmetrical. Pressing is very important. Before you turn the sections of the collar right-side out, press both sections of the collar from the wrong side of the fabric. When you press the turned collar, extend the outer edge of the upper collar over the seam so that the seam falls slightly underneath the finished edge from the right side.

Simple Enclosed Collar

The enclosed collar, which may be flat or slightly rolled, is the simplest collar to make and is usually found on dresses and blouses. The collar is made and sewn to the garment along with a shaped facing.

This kind of collar can be made in one or two sections, depending on the pattern. Trim off ½ inch from the edges of the interfacing and baste the interfacing to the upper or under collar according to the pattern instructions. Pin the upper collar to the under collar. Reinforce the stitching at the corners by reducing the number of stitches on the machine one inch before the pivot and one inch after. Trim and grade the seams; clip the curves and trim the points at right angles. Press the seam open and then press it toward the under collar. Turn the collar right-side out and press along the seam line, extending the edge of the upper collar beyond the seam. Shape the collar by pinning it to the garment, overlapping at the edges ⅝ inch to allow for the seam line. Determine the fold of the collar at the roll line and pin along the roll line above the neck seam. Leave the pins in the collar and remove it from the garment. Baste the neckline edges together as they fall with the pins in the roll line. A small ripple may have formed in the upper collar. If the edges of a two-piece collar meet at the center, hand baste them together at the seam line. Pin the collar to the neck edge of the garment and machine baste it to the garment. Prepare the shaped facing and pin it to the neck edge of the garment over the collar. Stitch the neckline seam and trim and grade the seam allowances. Understitch the facing through the seam allowances as you would for a shaped facing. Turn the facing to the wrong side of the garment and tack at the shoulder seams.

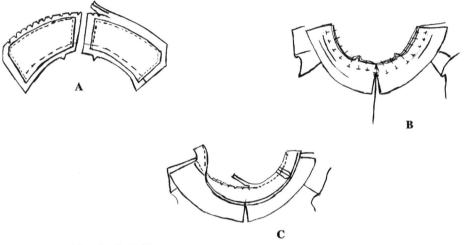

Notched Collar

The notched collar with lapels is most often used for shirts, jackets, and coats. There are two ways to make this collar, depending on the weight of the fabric and the instructions given with your pattern.

For Lightweight Fabrics

Stitch and turn the collar section, following the instructions given for the enclosed collar. Stay-stitch the neckline of the garment ½ inch from the edge. Pin the collar to the right side of the garment, easing or stretching the collar where necessary to follow the markings on the pattern. The facing for this kind of collar may be an extended facing (see page 206), or it may be a separate piece. Both are handled in the same way. Prepare the facing by sewing the back shaped facing at the shoulder seams, pressing the seams open, and finishing the raw edges of the facing. Turn the facing along the fold lines for an extended facing, or pin the separate facing piece to the garment, with the right sides of the fabric facing, over the collar, matching the shoulder seams with the shoulder markings on the collar and at the center back. For an extended facing, stitch at the neckline. For a separate facing, stitch at the neckline and down the front of the garment, pivoting and reinforcing the stitching at the corners. Trim, grade, and clip the seam allowances. Turn the facing to the right side of the garment and press, extending the outer edge of the garment edge on a separate facing.

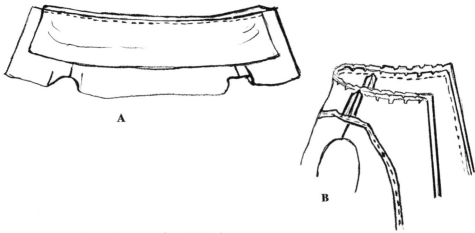

A

B

For Heavyweight Fabrics

Baste the interfacing to the under collar and the garment. Sew the shoulder seams of the garment and press them open. Stitch the under collar to the garment, with the right sides of the fabric together, matching the markings. Trim the seam allowances to ¼ inch and clip where necessary. Press the seam open. Prepare the facing by sewing the shoulder seams, pressing the seams open, and finishing the raw edges. Pin the upper collar to the facing, matching the markings, and stitch. Clip the seam allowance along the curves and press the seam open, but do not trim the seam allowance. Pin the upper collar and facing section to the garment, with the right sides of the fabric together. Stitch the collar from the marking, pivoting at the corners. Stitch along the back of the collar, pivoting at the other corner, and stitch to the mark. Stitch the facing from the mark, having one stitch go right over the stitch made when you sewed the collar. It is very important to get the stitching accurate. Continue stitching down the front of the facing, pivoting at the corner. Repeat for the other side of the garment. Trim, grade, and notch all seams. Press the seams open and then press them in the direction they will be in when they are turned right-side out. Extend the upper collar and lapel edge of the garment when pressing. Turn the collar and facing right-side out and press the entire section. Lift the back facing and pin the back neckline seams together as they fall. Stitch them together with a loose hand stitch. For more detailed instructions on making this style of collar, see Chapter 6, Tailoring.

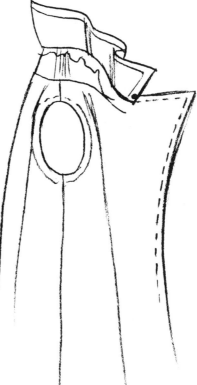

Collar with Band

This collar is used on shirts, blouses, and shirtwaist dresses, and is usually made with a front opening.

Prepare the garment by stitching the shoulder seams, press them open, and finishing the front of the garment. Make the collar section as you would for a simple enclosed collar. Baste the interfacing to the wrong side of the neckband. Pin the neckband with the interfacing to the under collar, with the right sides of the fabric together, matching the notches. Baste the other section of the neckband to the upper collar, with the right sides together. Stitch the neckband to the collar, following the basting, and stitch the edges of the neckband at the front ends. Trim and grade the seam allowances and turn the band right-side out. Press the collar and neckband. Pin the interfaced neckband to the neckline of the garment, with the right sides of the fabric together. Match the notches and markings at the shoulder seams. Stitch the neckband to the neck edge of the garment. Trim the interfacing close to the stitching, trim and grade the seam allowances, and clip along the curve. Press the neckband down toward the garment. Turn under the seam allowance of the neckband and slip-stitch it to the garment at the neck edge. If the pattern calls for it, topstitch the collar and neckband.

A

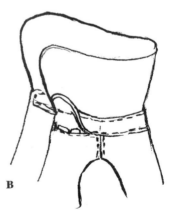

B

Stand-up Collar

Prepare the shaped band as you would for a simple enclosed collar. Press the collar, extending the outer edge over the seam. Pin the collar to the neckline of the garment, matching any marks and notches, and clip where necessary on the collar to ease it. Stitch the collar to the garment. Trim and grade the seam allowance. Press the neckline seam toward the collar, fold under the seam allowance on the raw edge of the under collar, and pin it into place where it falls. Slip-stitch it to the garment.

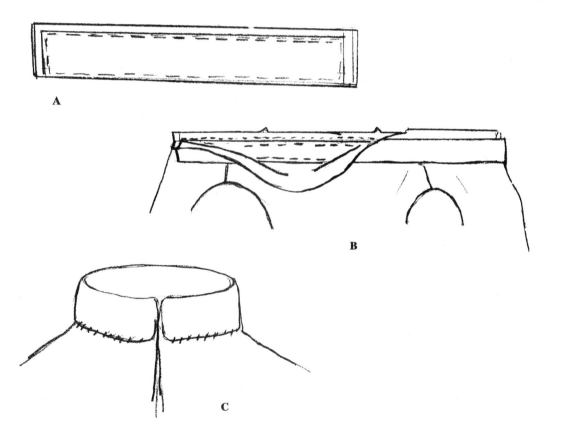

Bias Turn-over Collar

This is a version of the stand-up collar which folds over to form a turtle-neck collar.

The collar and the interfacing are cut on the bias, following the pattern instructions. Baste the interfacing to one-half of the collar on the wrong side of the fabric. Catch-stitch the top of the interfacing to the fold line of the collar. Fold the collar in half lengthwise and sew the side seams. Trim the seam allowances, turn the collar right-side out, and press at the side seams *only*. Pin the collar to the garment and stitch, following the instructions for a stand-up collar. Pin at the fold line, turn under the seam allowance of the raw edge of the collar, and pin into place. Slip-stitch the folded edge to the garment. Finish by sewing hooks and eyes to the back opening of the collar as shown.

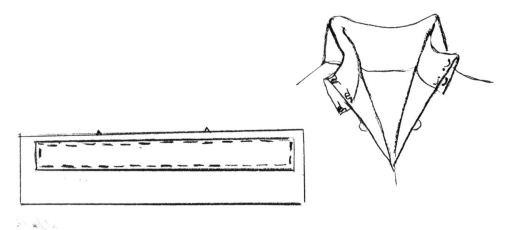

SLEEVES

A well-constructed sleeve is the mark of a professionally made garment. Designers use sleeves in a variety of ways to give different looks to clothes, but all sleeves are versions of one of three basic styles. Once you have mastered these styles, you will be able to make any style sleeve that fashion comes up with.

Set-in Sleeve

The set-in sleeve is cut separately from the garment and is sewn into the armhole (sometimes called "armscye") of the garment. The set-in sleeve may be perfectly smooth at the shoulder, or it may have a dart in the sleeve cap, which is also set into the armhole smoothly. It can also be gathered at the top of the sleeve cap, so that it forms a puffed sleeve when sewn into the armhole.

Raglan Sleeve

The raglan sleeve is also cut separately from the garment, but the top of the sleeve extends up to the neckline. Thus the top of the sleeve also forms the top of the shoulder and part of the neckline of the garment. It is stitched in a continuous seam from the back neckline under the arm and up the front shoulder to the front of the neckline. Raglan sleeves are darted or seamed at the shoulder to form the curve at the shoulder of the finished garment.

Kimono Sleeve

The kimono sleeve is cut in one piece with the front and the back of the garment. If the sleeve is relatively loose-fitting, it is reinforced under the arm. If the sleeve is tight-fitting, the pattern will have a separate piece for a gusset, which is sewn into the underarm to allow the sleeve to fit. Batwing and dolman sleeves are versions of the kimono sleeve.

Sewing Set-in Sleeves

There are a few rules to follow for inserting a set-in sleeve perfectly. The matching points on the sleeve must line up exactly with those on the garment. The notches, underarm seams, and the top of the shoulder must be matched perfectly. This means that when cutting and marking the garment and the sleeves, these markings and notches must follow the pattern accurately.

The ease in the sleeve cap must be distributed evenly. Follow the instructions given below, paying special attention to the pressing instructions.

The row of stitching around the sleeve and the garment must follow the seam line exactly. Use a seam guide and sew the seam very slowly and carefully to be sure that you sew directly on the seam line (⅝ inch from the edge of the fabric).

The top of the sleeve cap of a set-in sleeve is slightly longer than the armhole into which it will be fitted. This is to allow for ease when moving the arm. With the right side of the sleeve facing you and the machine set for a long stitch (8 to 10 stitches to the inch), stitch a single row just outside the seam line along the top of the sleeve cap, between the notches. Make another row of stitches parallel to the first one, ¼ inch away, inside the seam allowance. Pin and sew the underarm seam, and press it open over a sleeve board. Finish the bottom of the sleeve according to the pattern instructions, or see the section called Sleeve Finishes and Cuffs, pages 220-233. Turn the sleeve right-side out.

With the wrong side of the garment facing you, and working with the inside of the sleeve facing you, pin the sleeve to the armhole, with the right sides of the fabric facing. Pin the sleeve at the top of the shoulder seam, at the underarm seams, and at the notches on each side. Place two more pins at the top of the sleeve, ½ inch to each side of the shoulder seam. Gently pull the easing threads at the notch to ease the sleeve between the notches and the pins at the top of the sleeve cap. Don't pull the threads too tight, just until the sleeve loosely fits the armhole. Repeat, pulling the threads on the other side of the sleeve. Wrap the threads around a pin, placed at the notch on each side, to prevent the easing from slipping out. Unpin the sleeve and carefully remove it from the armhole. Place the sleeve cap over the edge of a sleeve board and touching the sleeve with the point of the iron only, steam out the fullness. Do not press folds into the sleeve cap; the steam will shrink out the fullness. Do not ease for ½ inch at either side of the top of the shoulder seam mark.

Pin the sleeve back into the armhole, the same way as before. Pin at the underarm, matching the seams, at the notches, and at the shoulder seam. To place the pins for easing, start by pinning at the notch and at the end of the ease at the top of the shoulder. Then place a pin in the middle of the section between the pins. Then place another pin in the middle of each of the two sections formed. Continue placing the pins in the middle of the section formed by the previous pins until the pins are about ¾ inch apart. Place the pins with the points facing the seam allowance, as shown.

If you are a beginning sewer, machine baste the sleeve to the garment at this point. Once you have sewn set-in sleeves several times, you will be able to stitch the sleeve directly without basting. Place the garment on the machine with the sleeve up, as shown. Baste, or stitch slowly, removing each pin as you come to it.

Check by turning the sleeve right-side out to be sure that you have not formed a pleat in the sleeve or in the garment while stitching. If you have, cut the row of stitching for about an inch and resew along the seam line. Stitch a second row ¼ inch away from the first, inside the seam allowance. Trim off ⅛ inch of the seam allowance and turn the seam allowance into the sleeve without pressing.

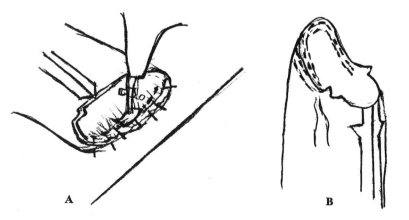

A   B

Sewing Raglan Sleeves

Prepare the sleeve by stitching the underarm seam and top seam or dart. If the sleeve has a top seam, press it open. If it has a dart at the top of the shoulder, slash it to within one inch of the point of the dart and press it open. Complete the hem or cuff of the sleeve. Turn the sleeve right-side out, and holding the wrong side of the garment facing you, pin the sleeve into the armhole. With the right sides of the fabric facing each other, start by pinning the underarm seam first and then pin the sides of the sleeve to the sides of the garment, matching the notches and other marks. Baste, being sure not to stretch the seam. Stitch to one side of the basting, along the seam line. Remove the basting. Make another row of stitches within the seam allowance, between the notches, under the arm. Make a clip in the seam allowances at the notches, being careful not to cut the stitches, and press open the seams above the notches. If the fabric ravels easily, overcast by hand or with a zigzag stitch on the seam allowance under the arm.

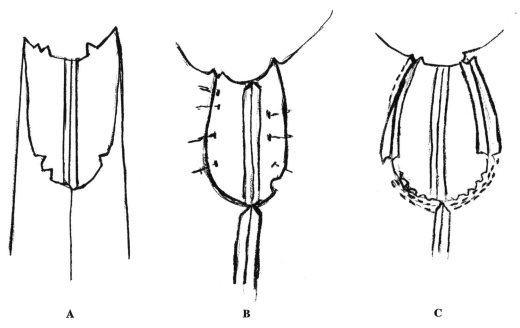

A   B   C

Sewing Kimono Sleeves

Kimono sleeves are made either with or without gussets under the arm. These days, sleeves made with gussets are very rare. If the pattern calls for an underarm gusset, follow the pattern instructions to insert the gusset.

If the pattern does not call for an underarm gusset the seam will have to be reinforced in one of the following ways.

Pin a 4-inch long piece of seam binding to the curve of the underarm on the seam line. Stitch the seam, using a shorter stitch (12 to 15 stitches to the inch) when sewing the curve, sewing the seam binding into the seam. If the seam forms a very sharp curve fold the seam binding in the middle of the curve and stitch it into the seam. Clip the seam allowances at the curve, being careful not to clip the tape. Press the seam open. Sew the top of the sleeve and press the seam open.

Second Method: Stitch the underarm seam, using a smaller stitch when you sew the curve. Clip the seam allowance and press the seam open. Baste a four-inch piece of seam binding over the curve of the seam. From the right side of the garment, stitch the length of the seam binding ⅛ inch to each side of the seam. Stitch the top seam of the sleeve and press it open.

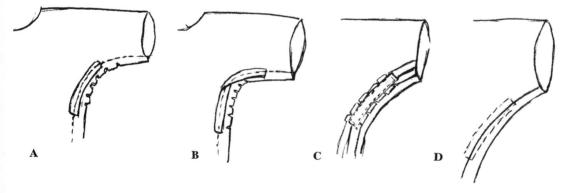

A   B   C   D

SLEEVE FINISHES AND CUFFS

Whether a sleeve is finished with a simple hem or with a cuff, it should be finished before it is inserted into the garment. It is easier to work with each individual sleeve than it is to apply the finish with the entire garment hanging off the sleeve. The length of the sleeve will have been determined by the length of the pattern piece when you cut it out. Therefore any necessary changes have to be made in the pattern before the fabric is cut. (See Chapter 2.)

Plain Hem

Finish the raw edge of the sleeve by sewing seam binding to the right side, or overcast the edge by hand or with a zigzag stitch. Fold the edge of the sleeve to the wrong side of the sleeve along the fold or hemline. Slip the sleeve over the edge of a sleeve board and measure the depth of the hem all around the sleeve. Make sure that it is even. Pin into place and blind-stitch the hem into place. If the sleeve is underlined, stitch it to the underlining only.

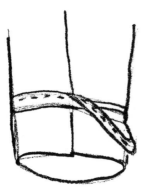

Snapped Wrist Closing

Sew the sleeve seam to the marking. Make a clip in the back seam allowance ½ inch above the marking and press the seam open above the clip. Sew seam binding to the right side of the bottom of the sleeve and fold back along the hemline. Blind-stitch the hem to the sleeve. To the edge of each of the seam allowances, pin a piece of seam binding that is long enough to extend ½ inch beyond each edge of the seam allowance. Stitch the seam binding to the seam allowance, turning under the ends of the seam binding. Press the front seam allowance open along the seam line. Press the back seam allowance to the inside, just along the edge of the seam binding. Lap the back seam allowance over the front to the inside. Slip-stitch the seam binding to the sleeve and slip-stitch the upper edges which are lapped into place. From the right side of the sleeve, sew the snaps into place by hand.

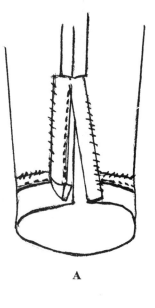

A

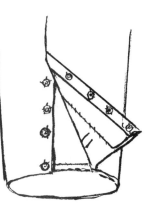

B

Zipper Closing

Stitch the seam to the marking and baste below it. Finish the raw edge of the sleeve with seam binding or by overcasting. Pin the zipper over the seam, face down on the wrong side of the sleeve, and insert it by using the slot seam method. (See the section called Zippers, page 182.) Finish the final step by machine or by hand with a prick-stitch from the right side. Remove the basting from the seam and turn the hem up. With the seam allowances folded in, stitch the ends to the zipper tape and blind-stitch the rest of the hem to the sleeve.

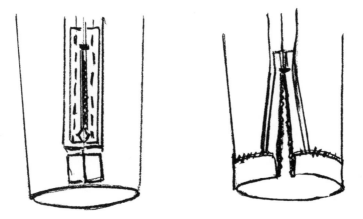

Fabric Loops and Buttons

Sew the seam to the marking. Clip the back seam allowance ½ inch above the mark. Finish the raw edge of the sleeve with seam binding or by overcasting. Turn the hem up and blind-stitch it to the sleeves. Make the fabric loops, following the instructions given in the section called Loops and Other Closures, page 257. Pin and baste the loops into place on the right of the front of the sleeve, being sure to leave enough of the loop free for the button to pass through. Press the seam open above the marking. Cut a piece of seam binding long enough to cover the loops, plus ⅛ inch at each end.

Turn under the ends of the seam binding and pin it over the loops, as shown. Stitch along the edge of the seam binding, stitching through the seam binding, the loops, and the hem at the lower edge. Cut another piece of seam binding the length of the other seam allowance below the marking, plus ⅛ inch at each end. Turn under the edges of the seam binding and stitch it to the back seam allowance. Press the back seam allowance at the edge of the seam binding. Slip-stitch the ends of the seam binding to the sleeve and at the upper ends. Turn the sleeve right-side out and sew the buttons in place.

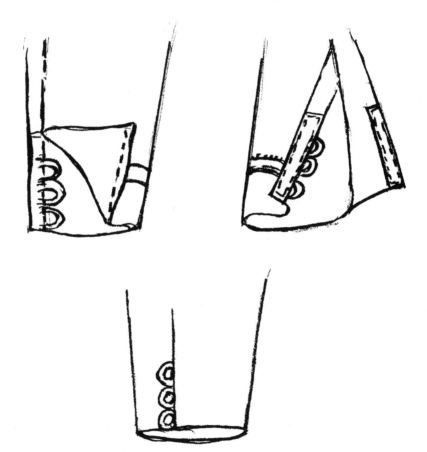

Elastic in a Casing

Press under ¼ inch along the lower edge of the sleeve. Press the edge along the fold line to the inside of the sleeve. Stitch close to the folded edge, leaving a 1-inch opening at the seam. Cut to size a piece of elastic the width called for on the pattern envelope. Attach a small safety pin to one end of the elastic and draw it through the casing until both ends of the elastic show at each end of the casing. Overlap the ends of the elastic and sew them by machine or by hand securely. Allow the elastic to go into the casing; sew the casing closed along the edge of the fold as before.

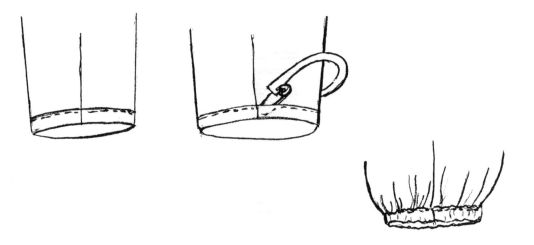

Bias Facing

Sew the sleeve seam and press it open. Cut a strip of bias out of the fabric of the garment if it is lightweight, or out of the lining fabric if the garment fabric is heavy. Cut the strip 1½ inches wide and 2 inches longer than the finished sleeve, following the instructions on page 257 for cutting the bias strip. Pin the bias to the sleeve to determine the length needed. Unpin and sew the bias in a diagonal seam. Press the seam open. Pin the bias to the right side of the sleeve, with the right sides of the fabric facing. Stitch in a ⅝-inch seam. Trim the seam allowances. Turn the bias to the wrong side and press, extending the outer edge of the sleeve below the seam. Turn under the raw edge of the bias and slip-stitch it to the sleeve.

Shaped Facing

Stitch the sleeve seam and press it open. Prepare the facing by sewing the seam and pressing it open. Finish the raw edge by sewing seam binding to the right side, or by overcasting by hand or with a zigzag stitch. Turn the facing wrong-side out, pin, and stitch to the sleeve, with the right sides of the fabric facing. Trim and grade the seam allowance. Turn the facing to the wrong side of the sleeve and press, extending the edge of the sleeve over the seam. Blind-stitch the facing to the sleeve.

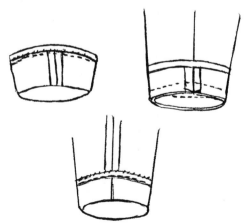

Openings in Sleeves

Sleeves made with a cuff that opens have to be made with an opening in the lower part of the sleeve itself. There are several ways of making this opening and they are given below.

SLASHED OPENING

Unless a separate piece is given for the facing, cut a facing out of the same fabric as the garment, making it 2½ inches wide and 1 inch longer than the slash opening. Finish the raw edges of the facing by turning them under ¼ inch and stitch along the edge, or overcast the edges. Leave the bottom edge raw as shown. Pin the facing over the slash marking on the right side of the sleeve, with the right sides of the fabric facing. Stitch along the stitching line, reinforcing the point by making the stitches smaller (12 to 15 stitches to the inch). Make one stitch across the point and stitch down the other side. Carefully cut through both layers of the fabric to the point of the stitching. Turn the facing to the wrong side and press. Baste together the raw edges at the bottom. The sleeve is now ready to be finished with a cuff or a binding.

CONTINUOUS LAPPED PLACKET

To reinforce the slash, stitch along the stitching line on each side of the slash, using smaller stitches near the point and taking one stitch across the point. Cut the slash to the point. Cut a strip of the same fabric as the garment twice, making it as long as the slash and 1½ inches wide. With the right sides of the fabric facing, open the slash and stitch the sleeve to the strip, using small stitches to one side of the previous stitching. With the right side of the sleeve facing you, press the strip away from the sleeve. Turn under ¼ inch on the long raw edge of the strip and turn the strip to the inside of the sleeve. Slip-stitch the facing to the sleeve.

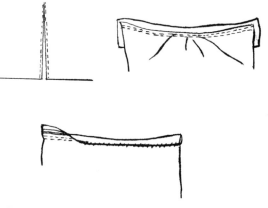

LAPPED CLOSING WITH A ROLLED HEM

Stitch with small stitches between the markings through the bottom of the sleeve. Clip to the markings, being sure not to cut the stitches. Trim the seam allowance to ⅜ inch and turn the seam allowance to the wrong side, rolling it to form a rolled hem. Slip-stitch to the sleeve on the wrong side. The sleeve is now ready to be sewn.

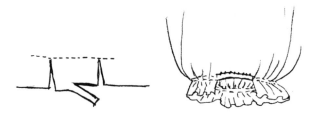

SHIRT SLEEVE PLACKET

Prepare the sleeve by reinforcing the opening with small stitches along the seamlines, pivoting at the corners, as shown. Cut the slash and clip to the corners of the stitching. Stitch the underlap to the back seam allowance, with the right side of the underlap to the wrong side of the sleeve. Press under ¼ inch on the long edge of the underlap and press the underlap toward the seam allowance. Trim the seam allowance. Fold the underlap over the seam allowance and edgestitch through all the layers of fabric.

Stitch the overlap to the other seam allowance. Trim the seam allowance and stitch across the top. Turn in the edges of the overlap and baste. Press the seam allowance toward the inside of the overlap. Press and pin the overlap over the seam allowance. Edgestitch on the overlap through all the layers of the fabric at the point of the overlap. Keeping the overlap free, edgestitch along the long edges of the overlap in the direction indicated by the arrows. Tie all the top threads through to the wrong side.

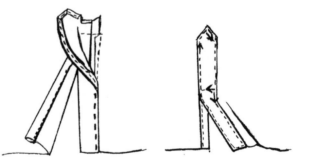

CUFFS

Band Cuff

This cuff is made with no opening in the sleeve. Cut an interfacing one-half the width of the cuff piece. Baste it to the wrong side of the cuff. Sew the cuff seam and press it open. Sew the sleeve seam and press it open. Gather the bottom of the sleeve. With the sleeve right-side out and the cuff wrong-side out, pin the gathered edge to the interfaced edge of the cuff. Adjust the gathers to fit. Stitch the cuff to the sleeve.

Trim the seam allowance and press it toward the cuff. Turn the cuff to the inside along the fold line. Turn under the raw edge of the cuff and slip-stitch it to the sleeve.

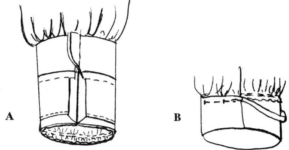

Lapped Cuff with an Opening in the Sleeve

Make the opening in the sleeve called for in your pattern, following the instructions already given.

Prepare the cuff by basting the interfacing to the wrong side of the cuff. If you are making bound buttonholes in the cuff, make them now. Fold the cuff in half lengthwise, with the right sides of the fabric facing, and stitch the side seams, stopping the seam ⅝ inch from the edge. Trim the seam allowance and turn the cuff right-side out and press. Stitch the sleeve seam and press it open. Gather the bottom of the sleeve. With the sleeve right-side out, pin the cuff to the sleeve, with the right sides of the fabric facing. The front of the sleeve opening should be even with the edge of the cuff. Pin the sleeve to the marking on the cuff so that an extension is formed. Adjust the gathers evenly and sew the sleeve to the cuff. Turn the cuff to the inside of the sleeve and turn under the raw edge of the cuff. Slip-stitch the cuff to the sleeve. Finish the cuff by completing the bound buttonholes, or make machine or hand-made buttonholes. Sew the buttons into place.

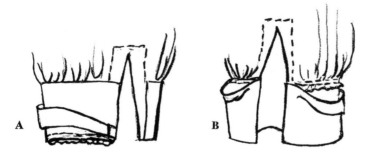

SHIRT SLEEVE CUFF

The shirt sleeve cuff is used with a shirt sleeve placket. Prepare the cuff as you would a buttoned cuff, interfacing half of the cuff. Sew the sleeve seam and press it open. Gather the bottom of the sleeve. With the sleeve *wrong*-side out, pin the cuff to the gathered edge of the sleeve, with the edge of the sleeve opening even with the edges of the cuff. Sew the cuff to the sleeve opening even with the edges of the cuff. Sew the cuff to the sleeve, adjusting the gathers evenly. Trim the seam allowance and press it toward the cuff. Turn under the raw edge of the cuff and pin it to the sleeve. Baste the cuff to the sleeve. Topstitch around the entire edge of the cuff. Make another row of stitches ¼ inch inside the previous stitching. Finish the cuff by making a machine-made buttonhole, and sew the button into place.

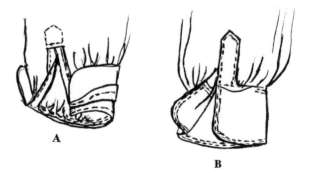

A

B

French Cuff

This cuff is worn folded back on itself and is held together with cuff-links. Cut the interfacing out of the same piece as the cuff and baste it to the wrong side of the cuff. Stitch the two sections of the cuff together, ending the seam ⅝ inch from the long notched edge of the cuff. Trim and grade the seam allowances. Turn the cuff right-side out and press it. Sew the sleeve seam and press it open. Prepare the sleeve opening according to the instructions given and gather the bottom of the sleeve. With the sleeve right-side out, pin the noninterfaced side of the cuff to the sleeve, with the right sides of the fabric facing. Adjust the gathers evenly and stitch the cuff to the sleeve. Press the seam allowance toward the cuff, turn under the raw edge of the cuff, and slip-stitch it to the sleeve. Make the buttonholes on the markings by hand or by machine. Fold the cuff back along the roll line and press it lightly. Fasten with cufflinks.

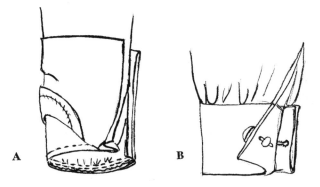

Turned-Back Cuff Cut in One with the Sleeve

If your pattern calls for this kind of cuff, the sleeve pattern piece will be several inches longer than the finished sleeve. The amount of this extra length will depend on the depth of the finished cuff. Finish the edge of the sleeve by stitching seam binding to the right side of the raw edge, or overcast the raw edge by hand or with a zigzag stitch. Turn the cuff along the fold line to the wrong side of the sleeve. On the right side, fold along the second fold line to form the cuff. Blind-stitch the edge of the sleeve to the sleeve. Lightly press the cuff from the right side.

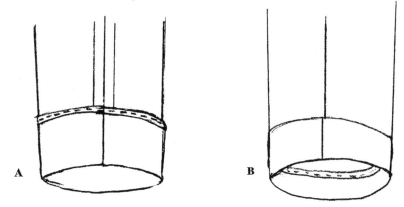

Shaped, Turned-Back Cuff

Sew the sleeve seam and press it open. Prepare the cuff by basting the interfacing to the wrong side of one of the cuff sections. Stitch the second section of the cuff to the interfaced one, trim and grade the seams, and turn the cuff right-side out. Press. With the sleeve right-side out, pin the cuff to it, with the interfaced section facing the sleeve. Baste the cuff to the sleeve. Use a piece of single-fold bias tape that has been cut one inch longer than the lower edge of the sleeve, and with one edge of the tape unfolded, pin it to the cuff along the basting stitches. Lap the edges of the bias tape over each other and stitch through the tape, the cuff, and the sleeve. Trim and grade the seam allowances, but do not cut the tape. Press the bias to the inside, extending the outside of the sleeve over the seam. Slip-stitch the bias to the sleeve.

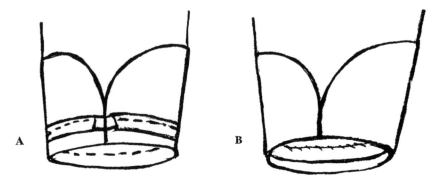

Turned-Back Cuff Cut Separately

Sew the sleeve seam and press it open. Baste the interfacing to the wrong side of the cuff. Stitch the cuff seam and press it open. Finish the raw edge of the cuff by sewing seam binding to the right side along the edge, or overcast by hand or with a zigzag stitch. With the sleeve right-side out, pin the cuff to the sleeve, with the right sides facing. Stitch the cuff to the sleeve. Trim the seam allowance and press the seam open. Turn the cuff inside the sleeve along the fold line. On the outside of the sleeve, fold along the second fold line to form the cuff. Blind-stitch the edge of the cuff to the sleeve on the inside. Lightly press the cuff from the right side.

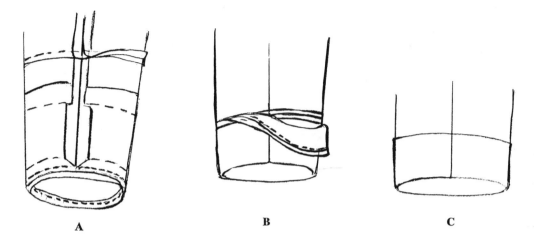

A   B   C

POCKETS

There are two basic kinds of pockets: those that are made of the lining fabric and are hidden inside the finished garment, and those that are made either from the same fabric as the garment or a contrasting fabric and are sewn to the outside of the garment.

Seam Pockets

Seam pockets are made of lining fabric and are hidden in the seam of the garment. Sew the pocket pieces to the pocket extension on the garment, with the right sides of the fabric facing. Press the seam allowances toward the pockets and pin the pockets together, with the right sides facing. Baste the seam along the fold line. Stitch the garment seam and around the pocket. Reinforce the stitching at the pivot at the top and bottom of the pocket. Clip the back seam allowance at the top and bottom pocket extensions, and press the seams open. Press the pocket to the front of the garment and remove the basting.

For dresses made of light- to medium-weight fabrics, the pocket will be cut in one with the garment. Pin the two sections of the dress together, with the right sides of the fabric facing. Stitch the seam and around the pocket, reinforcing the stitching at the pivots. Clip the back seam allowance just above and below the pockets. Press the seam open and press the pocket to the front of the dress.

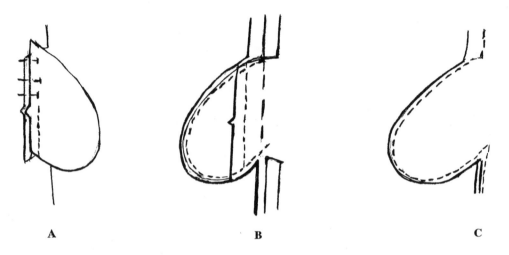

A   B   C

Buttonhole Pockets

Finished buttonhole pockets look like large bound buttonholes from the outside of the garment. Carefully transfer the markings from the pattern to the right side of the garment with basting. Fold the edges of the strip lengthwise so that the edges meet in the center. Press center the strip with the folded edges facing you, over the pocket markings and baste in a line, following the markings. Cut through the center of the strip, being careful not to cut the garment. Take the pocket piece cut from the lining mark and baste it over the strips between the markings. Stitch to one side of the basting lines, counting the stitches, and backtracking at the beginning and end of the stitching. Line the second row directly under the first on the markings and sew the second row of stitches in the same way, making the same number of stitches. With the wrong side of the garment facing you, cut through the garment, starting ½ inch from the edge of the stitches and ending ½ inch in from the other edge. Clip at the corners, being careful not to cut the stitches. Turn the strips and pocket to the wrong side of the garment and press. Fold the right side of the garment back to expose the pocket, and stitching through the triangle, sew around the pocket to the other triangle. Sew the upper edge of the pocket to the garment with stitches that do not show on the right side. Trim and overcast the edge of the pocket.

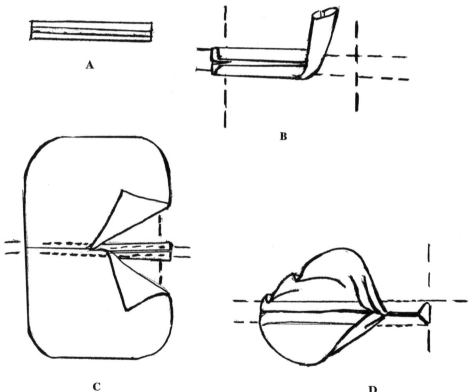

A

B

C

D

Welt Pocket

Welt pockets are made of lining fabric and turned to the inside of the garment with a welt made of the garment fabric that shows on the outside of the garment.

Cut the welt out of the garment fabric using the pattern piece given, cut the interfacing out of half of the pattern piece folded lengthwise. Baste the interfacing to one half of the wrong side of the welt and catchstitch to the fold line. Fold the piece in half lengthwise and stitch to within ⅝ inch of the edge. Trim the seam allowance and turn to the right side. Press, extending the outer edge slightly. Baste along the seam line of the unfinished edge.

Baste mark the pattern markings for the pocket placement on the right side of the garment, being sure to keep the markings accurate. Place the welt on the markings with the basted seamline even with the lower stitching line and the finished edge of the welt down. Have the outside of the welt facing the right side of the garment.

Take the pocket piece cut from the lining fabric and pin it over the pocket markings. With small stitches, backtracking at the beginning and end of the row, stitch along the upper stitching line, counting the stitches. Line the second row directly under the first on the markings, and make the second row of stitching in the same way, making the same number of stitches. With the right side of the garment facing you, cut through the garment, being careful not to cut the welt, starting ½ inch from the edge of the stitches and ending ½ inch in from the other edge. Clip at the corners, being careful not to cut the stitches. Turn the pocket to the wrong side and turn the welt up.

Press the edges of the pocket as close together as possible (they may not match exactly). From the right side of the garment expose the edge of the pocket and stitching through the triangle, sew around the pocket to the other triangle. Sew the upper edge of the pocket to the garment with stitches that do not show on the right side. Trim and overcast the edge of the pocket.

Place a piece of brown paper under the welt and press it up. Slip stitch the edges of the welt to the garment.

Flap Pocket

The flap pocket is made in the same way as the welt pocket with a few changes. Prepare the flap and interfacing as for the welt. Baste mark the pocket placement lines on the right side of the garment as for the welt pocket. Place the flap on the marking with the basted seam line even with the upper stitching line and the finished edge of the flap facing up. Make the pocket as for the welt pocket. When you turn the pocket to the wrong side turn the flap down. Sew around the edges of the pocket to the wrong side and turn the flap down. Sew around the edges of the pocket as for the welt pocket. Place a piece of brown paper under the flap and press it down. Tack the edges of the flap at the top edge on both sides.

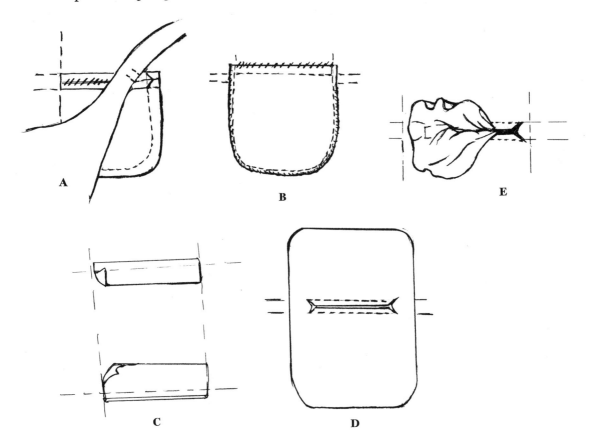

Patch Pockets

Patch pockets which are cut either from the same fabric as the garment, or from a contrasting fabric, are sewn to the outside of the garment.

UNLINED PATCH POCKET

Turn under ¼ inch on the top of the pocket and stitch. Turn the top hem allowance to the outside (right sides of the fabric facing) and stitch along the seam lines. Trim the seam allowances and turn the top right-side out and press.

The bottom of the pocket can be either rounded or straight. For a rounded edge, stitch with long stitches (8 to 10 to the inch) on the edge of the pocket. Press along the seam line and pull the thread to ease the corner. Notch where necessary. For sharp corners, press along the seam allowance and miter by sewing at an angle along the seam allowance at the corner. Trim the seam allowance and press the seam open. Turn the corner to the wrong side and press the corner, side, and bottom seam allowance to the wrong side.

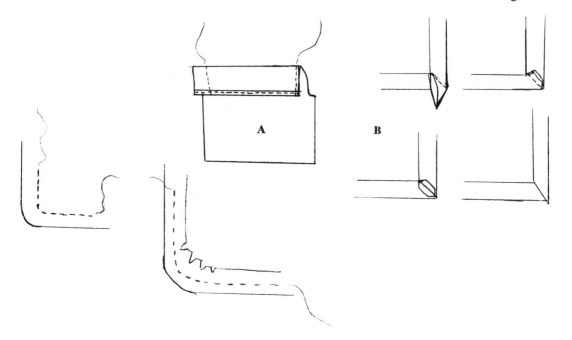

LINED PATCH POCKET

Use the pattern piece for the pocket and cut the lining from the fold line to the bottom of the pocket. Place the lining on the top of the pocket piece with the right sides of the fabric facing. Stitch along the top seam line, leaving a 1 inch opening in the middle of the row of stitching. Fold the pocket along the fold line, bringing the lining down so that it is even with the bottom of the pocket. Stitch around the pocket and trim the seam allowance. Turn the pocket right side out through the opening left in the first row of stitching. Press the pocket, extending the outer edge of the pocket beyond the lining. Slip stitch the opening in the lining to the pocket.

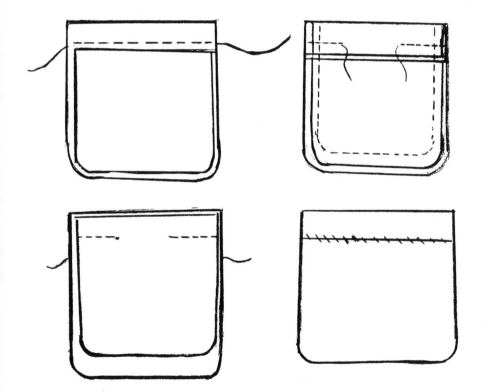

Attaching the Patch Pocket

Mark the pocket placement on the right side of the garment with tailor's tacks or basting. Pin the pocket to the markings, placing the pins parallel to the pocket edges and ¼ inch from the edges. Turn the pocket back to the pins and slip-stitch the pocket to the garment. For a decorative effect, top-stitch on top of the pocket by machine.

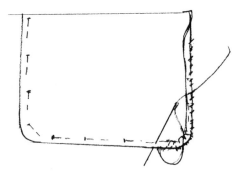

BELTS

Belts made of the same fabric as the garment they are to be worn with give a finished look to your clothes. There are several kinds of fabric belts, those that tie, those that are fastened with snaps or hooks and eyes, and those that are finished with a buckle.

Sashes or Tie Belts

The self-tying or sash belt can be as narrow (½-inch wide) or as wide (10 inches) as you want. They can also be just long enough to tie at the ends, or they can have ends that are long enough to reach the hem or extend it. The width and length are determined by the style of the garment and the weight and nature of the fabric used. Follow the pattern as a guide, or use your own judgment.

The fabric for a tie belt can be cut on the bias or on the straight grain of the fabric. A bias-cut belt will be softer than a straight cut belt. To make the belt, cut a piece of fabric twice as wide as the finished belt, plus ⅝ inch on each side for the seam allowances, and as long as needed to go around your waist and tie with the ends as long as you want, plus ⅝ inch at each end for the seam allowances. If it is necessary to get a piece long enough, piece the fabric by sewing a seam on a section of the belt that will not be too noticeable (see the section called Loops and Other Closures, page 257, for piecing bias) and press the seam open. Fold the belt in half lengthwise and start the stitching at one edge of the belt. Continue stitching, pivoting at the corner, along the long edge of the belt. Two-thirds of the way along the edge, stop the stitching and backtrack over the stitching for one-half inch. Leave a two-inch opening and start stitching again along the edge, backtracking over the beginning of the stitching. Pivot at the other corner and stitch up the side of the belt. Trim and grade the seam allowances, and cut off the seam allowances at the corners in right angles, as shown. Use the opening in the long edge to turn the belt right-side out. Press, extending the outside of the belt over the seam, and slip-stitch the opening closed.

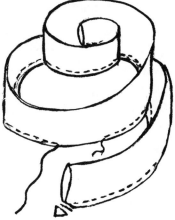

Corded Belt

Use soft fabrics, such as silk, soft satin, or crepe cut on the bias, to cover cords of any size you want, following the instructions for tubular cording in the section called Loops and Other Closures, page 259. For a single-cord belt, make the cording long enough to go around your waist, and tie with the ends extending out. Finish the ends by tying the cord in a knot. Tack the knot with hand sewing to keep it from opening. You can make an interesting belt by making three cords, using either different colors of the same fabric or the same color, and braiding the cords. Leave the three cords unbraided at each end and tie a knot as you would for a single-cord belt.

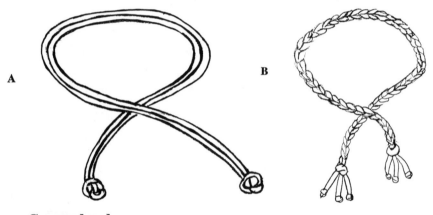

Cummerbund

You will need four pieces of featherboning to make the cummerbund. Cut a piece of bias fabric 9 inches wide and long enough to go around your lower ribcage, plus ½ inch. Overcast the long edges of the fabric by hand or with a zigzag stitch. Turn the edges to the inside of the fabric and press. Make two rows of machine gathering stitches ¼ inch in from each end and do the same on the band, where it will be at the sides when you hold it up to you. Pull the gathering threads until the band is the width you want it to be. Remove the casing from the feather-boning and cut it into four pieces, ½ inch shorter than the depth of the band at the gathering. Cover two pieces of the boning with seam binding and stitch the seam binding. Place the bones over the gathering at the sides and sew into place by hand. Sew two pieces of ½ inch wide grosgrain ribbon to the right sides of the ends of the band. Place the two remaining pieces of boning over the gathering, next to the ribbon, and sew them into place. Turn in the ends of the ribbon, fold it over the boning, and sew into place securely. With the ends of the band meeting, sew hooks and eyes at the ends to close it.

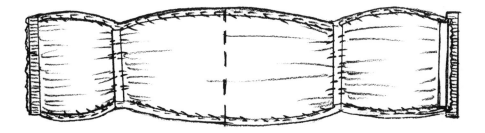

Straight Belts

Cut all straight belts as long as your waist measurement plus seven inches.

Straight Belt Made with Interfacing

Cutting on the straight grain of the fabric, cut two pieces the width and length of the belt, plus ⅝ inch all the way around for the seam allowances. Cut one end of the belt shaped as wanted, pointed or rounded. Cut two pieces of nonwoven interfacing the same length and shape as the outside piece, but do not add the seam allowances. Stitch the two pieces of interfacing together with long rows of machine stitching ½ inch apart. Place the interfacing on the wrong side of the belt fabric and pin into place. Turn down the seam allowance of the belt over the interfacing and press. Using running stitches, hand sew the seam allowances to the interfacing. Stay-stitch the underside of the belt ½ inch from the edges and turn the edges under ¾ inch and press. Pin the underside to the interfaced belt and slip-stitch to the belt. Finish with a buckle.

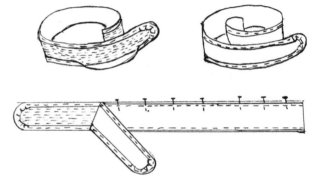

Straight Belt Made with Purchased Belting

Along the selvage of the fabric, cut the belt twice as wide as the belting, plus ⅝ inch for the seam allowances, and as long as needed. Cut the belting as long as needed and shape one end into a point. Fold the belt fabric in half lengthwise, with the right sides of the fabric facing. Stitch the end, trim and press the seam open, and turn the seam to the inside, forming the point. Insert

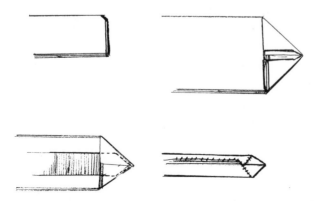

the pointed end of the belting into the point of the fabric and fold the raw edge of the belt over the belting. Press. Fold the selvage edge over the belting and press. Slip-stitch the folded and selvage edges. Finish with a buckle.

Straight Belt Made with Purchased Belting and Made by Machine

Cut a strip of the fabric along the straight grain of the fabric as long as needed and finish one end in a point or round it off. With the right sides of the fabric together, fold the fabric lengthwise over the belting and pin at right angles to the long edge. Replace the pressure foot on the machine with an adjustable zipper foot. Stitch as close to the belting as possible, but be sure not to stitch through the belting. Trim the seam and move it to the center of the belting and press it open. Stitch the end of the fabric that is in a point or rounded off, being careful not to stitch through the belting. Pull the belting out and turn the belt right-side out. With the shaped end of the belting first, insert it into the belt. Finish with a buckle.

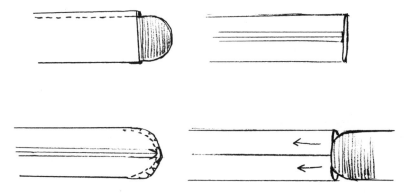

Contour Belt

Cut out the fabric for the belt, using the pattern piece given. Cut out two layers of nonwoven interfacing from the same pattern piece and trim off the seam allowances. Make the belt, using the instructions for a straight belt made with interfacing, and finish with a buckle.

Buckles

Buckles come in a variety of materials, from metal to wood. They come in three basic styles: full buckles with a prong, half buckles with a prong, and clasp buckles. Kits for covering full- and half-prong buckles with your fabric can be purchased in the notions department. To make the buckle, follow the instructions that come with the kit.

To attach a full-prong buckle, make an eyelet (see page 253) at the center marking of the belt. Pierce the eyelet open through all the layers of the belt. Slip the belt through the buckle and insert the prong into the eyelet. Turn under the edge of the belt and slip-stitch it to the belt.

To attach a half-prong buckle, make an eyelet as for a full-prong buckle and make a fabric loop large enough for both layers of the belt to go through. Slip the prong of the buckle through the eyelet and sew the loop to the belt just below the buckle. [Sew the end of the belt over the loop.]

Finish the other end of the belt with hand-worked eyelets, or buy a kit for attaching metal eyelets in the notions department. If you are using a metal buckle, be sure that the eyelets have the same finish as the buckle (gold or silver).

Clasp Buckles

If you are using a clasp buckle, make the straight belt with unfinished edges at both ends. Slip the unfinished edges of the belt through the ends of the buckle and turn under the edges. Hand stitch the ends to the belt.

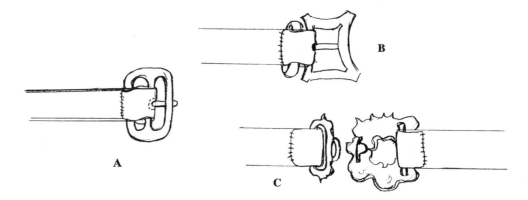

Carriers

Belt carriers are used to hold the belt in place. For inconspicuous carriers, use buttonhole twist in a color that matches the belt. Sew it at the sides of the dress at the waistline, using a blanket or chain stitch as instructed in the section called Loops and Other Closures, page 260.

Fabric carriers are usually part of the design of the garment, as they show very noticeably. Cut the fabric loops long enough for the belt to go through, plus ¼ inch. Cut the fabric along the selvage; it should be three times the width of the finished loop. Fold the loop lengthwise twice, with the selvage edge on top. Slip-stitch the selvage edge to the loop. Topstitch along the edges of the loop, by machine if desired. Sew the ends of the loop together by hand and place the loop on the garment, on the marks for the loops. Slip-stitch to the garment.

BUTTONS

The selection of buttons available is vast. Unless the buttons are to be used for decoration only, the size needed will be given on the pattern envelope. Buttons are measured in "lines." Forty lines is equal to one inch. They may also be measured in fractions of inches, equal to the diameter of the button.

Sizes of Buttons in Lines and Equivalent Inches

Line	Inches
18	⅜
20	½
30	⅝
36	⅞
40	1
45	1⅛
55	1⅜
60	1½
70	1¾
80	2

The size of the button is also determined by the thickness of the button. A line 20 full ball button will require a longer buttonhole than a flat line 20 button. For this reason, it is important to buy the buttons before you start to make the buttonholes. The designer of the pattern has determined the size of button that is most suitable for the garment you are making. Don't try to use a larger or smaller button than the one called for until you are experienced and can cope with the change of buttonhole sizes and general proportions involved.

When you go to buy the buttons, take a large swatch of your fabric with you. That way you will be able to try different styles and colors of buttons to get an idea of how they will look on the finished garment. As a general rule, dressy or tailored buttons go with dressy or tailored fabrics, and sporty buttons —horn or wooden ones—go with sporty, tweedy fabrics. But, like most rules in fashion, this one can be broken if you find a button that you feel works with your fabric and the style of the garment—buy it regardless of any rules. You can also make, or have made, buttons covered with the same fabric as the garment, so that the buttons will not be too prominent. If you wish, you can buy a kit in the notions department and make your own covered buttons. Follow the instructions that come with the kit. If you want to cover a button with a sheer fabric, use a piece of lining under the fabric so that the button form doesn't show through the fabric. For garments that call for loop closures, use ball, half-ball or dome-shaped buttons.

There are two basic kinds of buttons, regardless of their shape: sew-through buttons, which have holes in them through which they are sewn on, and shank buttons, which have a metal or cloth shank at the back, or as part of the structure of the button, and it shows only on the back. The kind of button will determine the method to be used in sewing the button on.

Before you sew the buttons on, you will have to determine where they will be placed. Do not attempt to sew the buttons on until the construction of the garment is finished. The exception to this is buttons on a sleeve cuff, which should be sewn on before the sleeve is inserted into the garment.

If the button is for decoration only, simply sew it on, following the mark on the pattern for the placement.

For "working" buttons (those that will actually button and unbutton), use the following method. Pin the overlap of the garment so that looks as if it were buttoned. Place a pin straight down through the outer edge of a horizontal buttonhole, or in the center of a vertical buttonhole. Place another pin through the fabric at the point of the first pin. This determines where the button will be sewn. Carefully unpin the overlap of the garment; make sure that you don't disturb the pins.

For medium- to heavyweight fabrics, use buttonhole twist or heavy-duty thread to sew on the buttons. For lightweight, delicate fabrics, use silk thread. For all other fabrics, use regular-weight thread. Pass it through beeswax to strengthen it.

Sew-through buttons will have to be sewn on, forming a thread shank to allow the garment to button without pulling. The length of the shank is determined by the thickness of the fabric. Place the button on the right side of the fabric where it is to be sewn on and place a heavy pin or a toothpick over the button, between the holes. Sew two-hole buttons with the threads parallel to the buttonhole; sew four-hole buttons with the threads parallel to each other or crossing over each other to form an X. Starting from the underside of the fabric, sew the button on, passing the thread through the holes and over the pin or toothpick. Once you have made enough stitches to hold the button on, remove the pin or toothpick and pull the button straight up until it reaches the end of the threads. Pass the thread through the hole to the underside of the button and wind it around the threads several times to form the thread shank. Bring the thread through to the wrong side of the fabric and backstitch a few times to secure the thread.

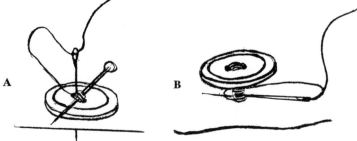

For coats and jackets, place a small button on the underside of the fabric directly under the top button, for reinforcement. Sew the button as directed, passing the thread through the small button as well as the top button.

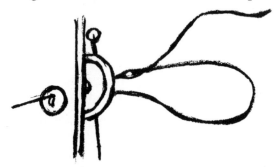

For buttons sewn on very delicate fabrics, use a small square of seam binding in place of the small button.

Shank buttons with a metal shank will not need a thread shank; simply sew them on with the shank aligned to the buttonhole and the thread parallel to the buttonhole. Shank buttons with a cloth shank will need a thread shank when sewn onto heavy fabrics. Use the method described above, inserting the toothpick between the shank and the fabric.

BUTTONHOLES

There are two kinds of buttonholes: thread-worked, which are made by machine or by hand, and fabric-bound, which are made with the use of the machine. Machine-made, thread-worked buttonholes are most often used on dresses, blouses, children's clothes, and casual, tailored clothes. Hand-made, thread-worked buttonholes are used on dresses and blouses made of delicate fabrics and wherever a fine finish is wanted. Bound buttonholes are usually found on tailored jackets and coats, and in some cases, tailored dresses and blouses.

Buttonholes are usually horizontal to the garment. They are sometimes vertical, and occasionally, on the diagonal. They are all made in the same way, regardless of their direction.

The size of the buttonhole is determined by the diameter and thickness of the button; therefore you must purchase the buttons before you make the buttonholes. Always make a test buttonhole on a scrap of your fabric to be sure that the button fits.

If you have altered the length of the pattern, you will have to respace the buttonholes. Leave the top and bottom buttonholes where they are on the pattern and redraw the others at equal distances from each other, being sure to keep the front ends lined up with the original buttonholes. In order to have the buttonholes placed properly, you will have to add to the markings on the pattern. The new markings must be transferred to the right side of the garment piece by basting through the markings added to the pattern.

For horizontal buttonholes, extend the horizontal line of the buttonhole to the edge of the garment in front, and for 2 or 3 inches in the back. Make two vertical basting lines at each end of the buttonhole, starting three inches above the top buttonhole and ending three inches below the last buttonhole.

For vertical buttonholes, make horizontal basting lines at each of the buttonholes, extending 3 inches beyond the buttonhole markings. Be sure that all markings fall precisely on the grain of the garment fabric.

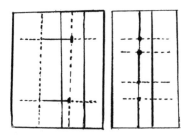

All areas with buttonholes must be interfaced. Thread-worked button-holes are made on the finished garment. Bound buttonholes are made after the interfacing has been attached, but before the rest of the garment is finished.

Machine-Made, Thread-Worked Buttonholes

Buttonholes made with a sewing machine are made with a buttonhole attachment, which replaces the pressure foot and has templates for making different-size buttonholes. For zigzag machines, buttonholes are made without the use of a different attachment. Follow the instructions given in the manual for your machine and be sure to make a test buttonhole before you make one on the actual garment.

Hand-Made, Thread-Worked Buttonholes

Make a row of small machine stitches ⅛ inch from the buttonhole marking, and at each end. Slash the buttonhole open between the stitches. Use a single strand of thread. Start sewing at the upper left-hand corner of the buttonhole, bringing the needle under the slash and up through the fabric just above the row of machine stitches, as shown. Pull the thread toward you, as shown in the second illustration, pulling it slightly to form the purl on the slashed edge. Repeat this stitch, keeping the stitches close together and evenly spaced. Fan the stitches out at the edge nearest the garment edge and continue for the underside of the buttonhole. Make a bar tack, like a blanket-stitched thread loop at the end of the buttonhole. See page 260 for instructions for making the bar tack.

Keyhole buttonholes, which are used on man-tailored garments, are made in the same way, but pierce the edge of the buttonhole near the garment edge with a knitting needle and fan the stitches out around it.

For vertical buttonholes, make the buttonhole in the same way, but make a bar tack at each end of the buttonhole.

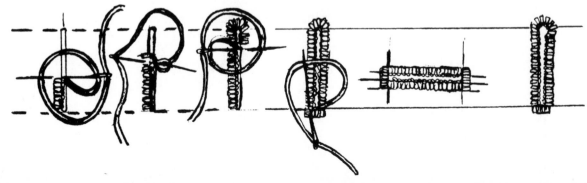

Eyelets

Make a hole of the necessary size in the fabric with a knitting needle or a small pair of scissors. Machine stitch a row of small stitches around the hole. Finish the eyelet with hand-worked buttonhole stitches in the same manner as for buttonholes.

Bound Buttonholes

There are several ways of making bound buttonholes, two of which are given here. Also, there are several gadgets for making bound buttonholes on sale in notions departments. Follow the instructions given with them. Experiment with these gadgets and with the methods given here until you find the way that is easiest for you. The finished buttonhole will look the same no matter which method you use.

PATCH METHOD

Cut a patch of fabric 2 inches wide and the length of the buttonhole, plus 1 inch. You will need one patch for each buttonhole. Follow these instructions step by step for your test buttonhole, but when you make the buttonholes themselves, complete all steps for each buttonhole before you go on to the next.

With the right sides of the fabric facing, center the patch over the place for the buttonhole and baste along the vertical lines marked on the garment. Baste through the horizontal buttonhole marking. Baste or draw with tailor's chalk two lines parallel to the horizontal line, ⅛ inch above and below the line. Set the machine for 20 stitches to the inch and sew around the rectangle formed by the chalk or basted markings. Sew very slowly and count the stitches on the horizontal lines, pivot at the corner, and count the stitches made at the ends of the rectangle. Continue sewing the bottom and other end of the rectangle, making the same number of stitches. Backtrack over the beginning stitches.

With small, very sharp scissors, clip through all the thicknesses of fabric through the center of the rectangle, starting ¼ inch from one edge to ¼ inch from the other edge. Clip diagonally to the corners, being careful not to cut the stitches. Carefully pull the patch through to the wrong side of the garment. Flatten the patch and press lightly. You should have a perfectly rectangular hole. From the right side of the garment, bring up on fold of the patch to the center of the rectangle, so that it forms a ⅛-inch lip. [Stitch it from the right side by hand with prick stitches to hold the lip in place.] Repeat this step to form the top lip. Optional: For a stronger, corded buttonhole, draw two lengths of narrow cording through the lips, using a tapestry needle (a heavy needle with a blunt point), and cut the ends of the cord even with the patch ends.

With hand stitches, overcast the ends of the fold on the wrong side of the patch. Also by hand, baste the lips together temporarily. With the right side of the garment facing you, turn back the edge of the garment to expose the ends of the patch and the triangle of the fabric. With small stitches, machine stitch through the triangle and the end of the patch (and cording, if used). Turn the garment over and repeat for the other end of the buttonhole. See facing page.

Remove all the basting marks, but leave the lips of the buttonhole basted together. They will be removed when the garment is finished. Press over the buttonhole lightly.

ORGANZA PATCH METHOD

This is an alternative method best used for heavy or loosely woven fabrics.

Cut a patch of organza 1 inch longer and wider than the buttonhole. Center it over the buttonhole and stitch a rectangle, following the method described above. Clip the rectangle as described, and turn the patch to the wrong side and press. Make two bias-cut patches 1½ inches wider and

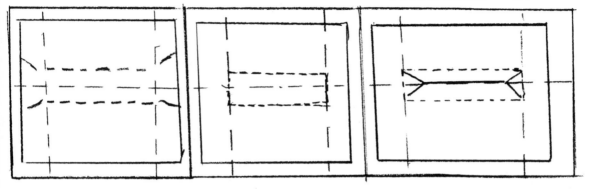

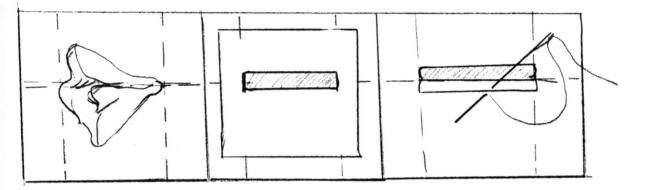

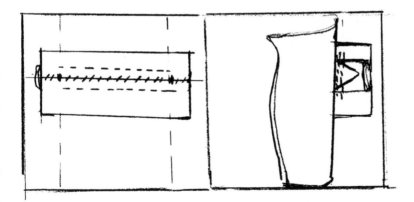

longer than the buttonhole. With the right sides of the patches facing each other, machine baste through the lengthwise center. Press the basted seam open as shown. Pin the patch over the rectangle, lining the basted seam up with the basted position line. Working from the wrong side of the garment, pin the garment to the patch as shown. Stitch with small stitches below the previous stitching, starting ½ inch away and ending ½ inch away from the previous stitching. Repeat for the other side of the buttonhole.

With the right side of the garment facing you, turn back the edge of the garment to expose the ends of the patches and the triangle of the fabric. With small machine stitches, sew through the triangle and the patches. Turn the garment over and repeat for the other end of the buttonhole. Remove the basting markings, but leave the two patches basted together until the garment is finished. Press the buttonhole lightly.

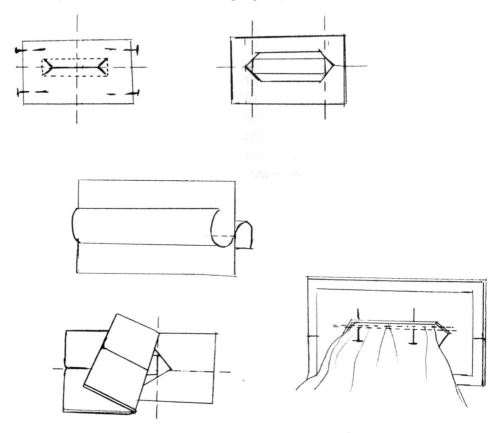

Finishing the Underside of a Bound Buttonhole

Once the garment has been finished and the facing is sewn in place, re-move the basting holding the lips of the buttonhole. From the right side, place two pins at each end of the buttonhole, penetrating through the facing. Cut through the facing from pin to pin and at the corners, as you did when clipping through the buttonhole. Fold the raw edges of the facing to the inside and slip-stitch to the edges of the buttonhole.

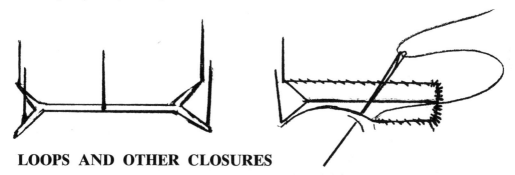

LOOPS AND OTHER CLOSURES

Loops are used in place of buttonholes as part of the design of various garments. These loops are made of bias tubing, which is often used as a trim as well. To make bias tubing, you have to first cut the fabric on the true bias and form the strips of the bias.

To Make Bias Strips

Take a piece of woven fabric that has been made grain-perfect, and make the ends true by pulling out a thread along the crosswise grain and cutting along the pulled thread. Find the true bias by folding the fabric at right angles, as shown. Press lightly along the fold to mark the bias. With a ruler and tailor's chalk, mark the strips to either side of the fold, making the strips as wide as required. With sharp scissors, cut along the markings, keeping the edges straight. In most cases, the strips will be too short to form the length of tubing needed; therefore the strips will have to be pieced. To join the strips, trim the edges of the strips along the grain lines, so that the ends are parallel. Place the strips together, as shown, with the right sides of the fabric facing. The points of the strip will extend past the width of the strip. Machine stitch along the straight grain of the fabric in a ¼-inch seam. Press the seam open and trim off the corners.

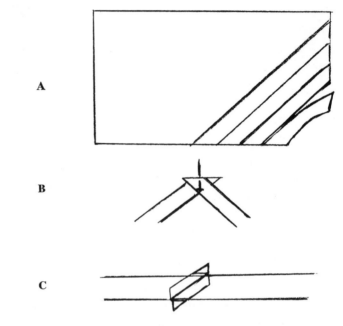

A

B

C

Bias Tubing

To make bias tubing, cut and piece (if necessary) bias strips to the length needed and four times the width of the finished tubing. Fold the stripping in half lengthwise and stitch with a narrow seam allowance. For lightweight fabrics, make a deeper seam allowance than for heavy fabrics; the average seam allowance should be ¼ inch. With small stitches, stretching the fabric as you sew, stitch to within ½ inch of the end of the tubing, and for the last ½ inch, stitch very close to the raw edge, forming a funnel.

The easiest way to turn the tubing to the right side is with a loop turner, which can be purchased in the notions department. Instructions for using the loop turner come with it, and it can be used to easily turn any weight of bias tubing. If you can't find a loop turner, use a heavy needle and heavyweight thread attached to the opening edge of the loop. Work the needle through the tube, with the eye of the needle first, and carefully turn the tubing right-side out. Cut the thread off once the tube has been turned right-side out.

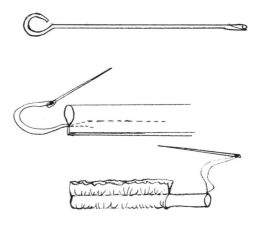

Bias Tubing with Cording

For a firmer tubing, use soft cording as a filler. Cut the cord twice as long as you want the finished tubing to be. Cut the bias strips wide enough to go around the cord and add 1 inch to that width, and cut it as long as needed for the finished tubing. With the right sides of the fabric facing, pin the bias around the cord, with the edges of the bias even, ½ inch beyond the center of the cord. Replace the pressure foot on the machine with an adjustable zipper foot and stitch through the bias and the cord at the end, and then as close to the cord as possible, without catching the cord in the stitching. Stretch the bias as you sew. Trim the seam allowance close to the stitching and turn the tubing right-side out by gently pulling the enclosed cord out. Cut off the excess cord.

Placing the Loops

Pin the loop to the edge of the facing (or a scrap of fabric) to determine how much extension will be required for the button to pass through. Loops are usually used with full ball, half ball, or domed buttons. Once you have determined the extension, pin the tubing to the pattern markings, with the loops facing the inside of the garment. Use the tubing in one long piece, or cut it into individual loops if instructed by the pattern. Baste the loops into place just inside the seam line. The facing will then be stitched over the basted loops, catching them in the seam line, and the loops will be formed when the facing is turned to the right side.

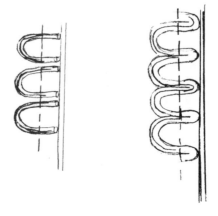

Thread Loops

Thread loops perform many jobs, depending on the placement and length of the loop. There are two ways to make the thread loop, both of them are done by hand.

Blanket Stitch

To make any thread loop, use a single thread of heavy-duty thread or silk buttonhole twist. Thread the needle and knot one end. From the underside of the garment, bring the thread to the right side and make several long stitches. The length of these stitches will determine the length of the final loop. So if the loop is being used to hold a belt or button, be sure that the stitches are long enough for the belt or button to pass through. Start at the top of the long stitches and make blanket stitches as shown. Do not pull the stitches too close together, or the loop will twist. When the blanket stitches cover the long stitches, carry the thread to the back of the garment and tie the thread off in a knot.

CHAIN STITCH

With heavy thread or buttonhole twist, bring the thread from the inside of the garment to the right side of the fabric. Make a small stitch and pull it out to form a loop. Hold the loop in your left hand and the needle in your right hand. Pass the needle thread through the loop and form another loop, taking it in your left hand. Pull the loop tight, and repeat until the chain is as long as desired. Pull the last loop tight to form a knot, and pull the needle through to the wrong side of the garment and tie off the thread.

Hooks and Eyes

Hooks and eyes come in a variety of sizes, from very small, for sheer fabrics, to quite large and heavy, for use on skirt waistbands. They are also made in a very large size for use with furs and fake furs. They are made of metal and come silver colored and with a black enamel finish. Use the silver ones on medium- to light-colored fabrics and the black ones on black and dark-colored fabrics. They come packaged with two shapes of eyelets: straight and rounded. Which you will use will depend on its placement on the garment.

For edges of fabric that overlap, place the hook slightly to the inside of the overlapping edge. Sew the hook on by using overhand stitches over the circular ends and then under the hook. Be sure that the thread penetrates only the layer of fabric facing you, so that the stitches do not show on the right side of the garment.

For overlapping edges, use a straight eyelet. Once the hook has been sewn on, overlap the edges, and determine the placement for the eye by placing a pin under the hook. This will usually be ½ inch in from the edge of the fabric. Sew the eye on with overhand stitches in the same way you did for the circular ends of the hook.

For a delicate finish, the metal eye can be replaced with a thread eye. Follow the instructions given for a blanket-stitch loop.

For edges of a garment that just meet, use the rounded eyelet. Sew the hook on in the same way as for an overlapping edge. Place the rounded eyelet directly opposite the hook, with the curve of the eyelet extending beyond the fabric. Sew with overhand stitches through the circular ends of the eyelet and on the curved edge just inside the edge of the fabric. Be sure that the thread does not penetrate through the right side of the garment.

For the edges that meet, a thread loop may be substituted for the metal eyelet. Make a thread loop, following the instructions for a blanket-stitch loop, and make it long enough to extend past the edge of the fabric.

Very heavy solid hooks and eyes are made for use on the waistbands of skirts and pants. Place them in the same way as for an overlapping edge and sew them on with overhand stitches through the hook and the eye.

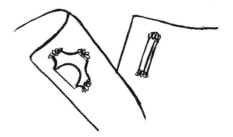

Snaps

Snaps are used to fasten areas of the garment that are not subjected to much stress, for example, in combination with a buttoned front. They should not be used to close waistbands or necklines, as they will open too easily when the garment is worn. Snaps are also made of metal and come in silver and black. They come in sizes from very small to large. Silk-covered ones are available for use on the fronts of jackets and coats where they will show when the garment is open.

The snap consists of two parts, one with a ball and the other with a socket into which the ball fits. Sew the ball part on first, placing it on the overlapping edge slightly inside the edge of the fabric. With overhand stitches, sew through one of the holes, and then pass the thread between the two layers of fabric and bring the needle up through the next hole. Continue sewing through each hole with overhand stitches. End the stitching by sewing a small knot next to the last series of stitches. Rub some tailor's chalk on the ball of the snap, and overlap the fabric and press with your fingers. The chalk will leave a mark on the underlapping fabric. Center the socket of the other part of the snap directly over the chalk mark. Sew it on, using the same method as for the first.

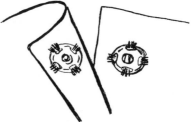

Covered snaps are sewn on in the same way. If you cannot find covered snaps in the same color as your garment, cover regular snaps with a small piece of china silk or other lightweight lining fabric. Cut the fabric into two circles twice as wide as the snap. Make a row of running stitches around the edge of each circle, leaving long ends of the thread loose. Place each part of the snap facedown in the center of a circle of fabric. Pull the threads tight to form the cover. Knot the ends of the threads. Open and close the snaps several times to allow the ball of the snap to work its way through the fabric.

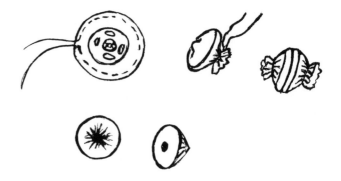

Snap Fasteners

Snap fasteners work in the same way as snaps, but they are much stronger and are not sewn on. (The ball section of the snap shows on the right side of the fabric.) They are generally used on sportswear and children's clothes in place of buttons. When you buy snap fasteners, they often come with a little tool, which is used with a hammer to apply them. You can also buy a separate tool, which looks something like a pair of pliers. To apply, follow the instructions that come with the fasteners.

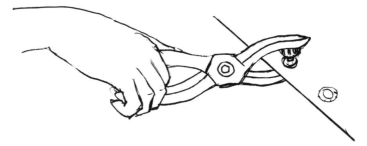

Nylon Tape Fasteners

Nylon tape fasteners consist of two strips of fabric, one with little hooks and one with loops, which stick together and can be pulled apart and stuck together again. They can be used in little pieces or in longer strips to close loose-fitting dresses and children's clothes. They cannot be used in place of zippers or most buttons, as they cannot take much strain. Buy the tape fastener in the color closet to the color of your garment, and cut the strip to the length needed. Hand sew the hook side of the tape to the underside of the overlapping fabric, sewing around the edges of the tape with small overhand stitches. Make sure that the stitches do not show on the right side of the fabric. Place the loop section on the underlap of the fabric, pin it in place, and sew around the edges by machine.

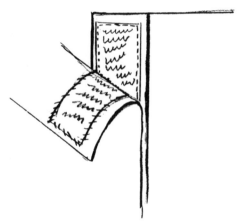

GATHERING AND SHIRRING

Gathering

Gathering is one of the most often used ways of attaching a large piece of fabric to a smaller one. It is always part of the design feature of the garment.

Fabrics are almost always gathered along the crosswise grain. Mark the gathering line carefully and be sure to keep the line on the crosswise grain, or your gathers will be uneven when finished. On all but the heaviest fabrics, the gathering stitches will be made by machine. There are two ways of doing this.

1. Set the machine for a long stitch (8 to 10 stitches to the inch), loosen the needle tension, and use silk or polyester thread in the bobbin. Make two or more (depending on what the pattern calls for) rows of stitches along the gathering lines and leave several inches of thread at the beginning and end of the row. Gently pull the bobbin thread from each end to form the gathers.

2. Replace the pressure foot of your machine with the gathering foot. Set the machine for a long stitch and tighten the needle tension slightly. Stitch along the gathering line, guiding the fabric under the needle carefully. Leave several inches of thread at the beginning and end of the row. Gathers will form as you stitch, but they may not be deep enough. By gently pulling the bobbin thread after you have finished the row of stitching, you can make the gathers as deep as you need.

For very heavy fabrics, make the gathering row of stitches by hand, using silk thread, and make a row of long, running stitches. Do not secure the end of the stitching, but pull along the thread carefully to form the gathers.

Joining a Gathered Section to a Flat Section

Work with the gathered section facing you. Make the rows of gathering stitches and pull along both ends of the fabric to form the gathers. With the right sides of the fabric facing, pin the gathered section to the flat one at the ends of the seam, at matching seams, and at notches. Place the pins at right angles to the fabric, with the points of the pins facing the raw edge of the fabric. Then find the halfway point of the gathered section between the pins, and pin. Then find the halfway point of the remaining sections, and pin them. Continue in this manner, adjusting the gathers by sliding them along the thread until the entire section is pinned, with the pins about ½-inch apart. With the regular pressure foot on the machine and a regular length stitch (10 to 12 to the inch), sew along the seam line over the gathers. Press the seam in the direction indicated by the pattern instructions.

Joining Two Gathered Sections

Cut a piece of seam binding or twill tape the length indicated in the pattern instructions. Mark the seams, centers, and notches on the tape. Make the rows of gathering stitches in both sections of the garment, and gather. Pin the seam binding or tape over the gatherings at the seams, centers, and notches. Adjust the gathers in the same way as instructed for joining a gathered to a flat section. Place the pins under the seam binding or tape, through the two layers of fabric. Once the whole piece has been pinned with the pins about ½ inch apart, remove the seam binding or tape. Stitch through the two gathered sections on the seam line and press the seam as instructed by the pattern guide.

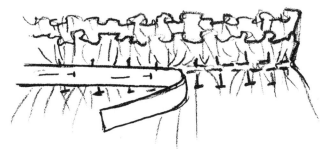

For general instructions on pressing gathers, see the section called Pressing as You Sew, page 158.

Shirring

Shirring is formed by making several rows of parallel gathering stitches to control the fullness of the garment.

For soft, stretchable shirring that will give with the movement of the body, thread the bobbin with elastic thread. To do this, wind the bobbin by hand, being careful not to stretch the elastic as you wind. Use the same thread for the needle that you are using to make the rest of the garment. For effect, especially in children's clothes, shirring stitches can be made with thread in contrasting color. Set the machine for 7 stitches to the inch. After the first row of gathering stitches has been made, the fabric will be puckered. Stretch this puckering out as you feed the fabric under the needle for subsequent rows of stitches. The loose ends of the gathering stitches will be caught in the finished seam of the garment.

To make a shirred section that will not have give, make several rows of gathering stitches, using a row of long machine stitches, and form the gathers by pulling the bobbin threads.

You can also make these rows of gathering stitches by using the gathering foot of your machine. To see the amount of gathering made by the gathering foot, test first on a scrap of fabric, adjusting the stitch length (making the stitches longer) and tightening the tension. The gathers can be made deeper by gently pulling the bobbin threads after the rows of stitching have been made.

Once the necessary number of gathering rows has been made, secure the edges of the stitching by making a row of machine stitches at right angles to the gathering stitches, within the side seam allowance. Make a stay for the shirred section by cutting a piece of the garment fabric or a lightweight fabric the length and width of the shirred area, plus ⅝ inch around the edges. Turn the ⅝ inch to the inside of the stay, and press. Pin the stay to the shirred area, with the wrong sides facing, and slip-stitch into place.

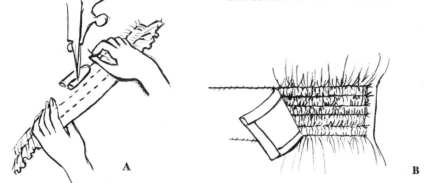

A   B

PLEATS

Pleats, which are usually found in the skirt of a garment, are made by folding the fabric over itself or with an insert piece set into the skirt behind the pleats.

Folded pleats can take several different forms to create many different looks, for example:

Knife or Straight Pleats—which are formed by having all the folds in the pleat face the same direction.

Box Pleats—which are formed with two folds of the pleat facing the same direction.

Inverted Pleats—which are formed with two folds of the pleats facing each other, sometimes with a separate insert set behind the pleats.

Sunburst or Accordion Pleats—which are made by forming folds that do not overlap along the length of the fabric. These pleats must be made commercially, as they require special equipment.

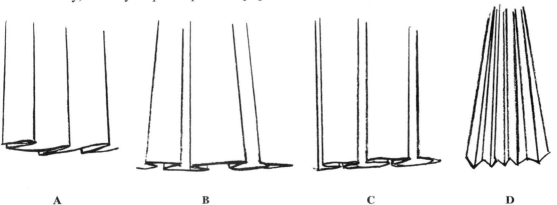

A   B   C   D

Pleats can be pressed and/or stitched along the edges to make them razor-sharp, or they can be soft, unpressed pleats, which are folded and lightly steamed so that they form soft folds along the length of the garment.

When choosing a pattern with a pleated skirt, be sure that you use the correct size for your hip measurement. Choose one of the fabrics called for on the pattern envelope, as these are the fabrics that will hold the pleats best.

A pattern for pleats will have two rows of markings that must be transferred to the fabric accurately. One of these markings is the roll line for unpressed pleats, or the fold line for pressed pleats. This is the line along which the fabric will be folded. The second line is the placement line, along which the folded pleat will be placed. Transfer these markings to the wrong side of the fabric with dressmaker's carbon paper. If the fabric won't take carbon paper marks easily, or if the pleats are to be formed on the right side of the garment, make the marks with thread basting or tailor's tacks. Use two colors of thread, one for the fold line and one for the placement line, to make it easy to determine which is which when the pattern is removed from the fabric. The pleats will be formed from the wrong side or the right side of the garment, depending on the pattern instructions.

Forming the Pleats

For skirts that are pleated all the way around on the straight grain of the fabric, determine the hem depth after you have made the markings for the pleats. Measure the length of a garment—that is, the length you want—and mark the hem at that length, being sure to leave a seam allowance (⅝ inch) at the top of the skirt. Sew all the seams of the skirt except for the one into which the zipper will be inserted. Finish the bottom of the hem in the way best suited to the fabric, and press and sew the hem. After the skirt has been pleated, sew the final seam from the bottom up to the opening for the zipper. Do not press the seam open. Hand whip-stitch the seam allowances together over the hem.

To form the pleats, place the skirt over an ironing board, wrong- or right-side up, according to the pattern instructions. Fold along the roll or fold line, and bring it to meet the placement line. Pin the folded edge to the placement line. Make all the pleats in this manner, pinning as you go. When all the pleats have been formed, hand baste from the bottom up through all the layers of fabric along the edge of the fold. Remove all the pins.

Sew the final seam as described and machine baste over the pleats at the top of the skirt just inside the seam line. Try the skirt on and pin the opening for the zipper shut. If the waistline is too loose or too tight, make an adjustment by shifting the top of the fold just inside or outside of the placement line for each pleat. Remove the machine basting. Be sure to leave at least ½ inch ease all around the skirt.

For pressed pleats, remove the basting except at the top of the skirt. Place strips of brown paper under the folds of the pleats and press from the wrong side, using a pressing cloth under the iron. Press again from the wrong side. Machine baste around the top of the skirt again and try it on. If the pleats open instead of falling straight, raise the skirt until they fall straight, and mark the amount taken up. Sew the skirt to the waistband or bodice, taking a deeper seam allowance along the marking. If the pleats overlap instead of falling straight, lower the skirt until they fall straight. Mark the amount lowered and sew the skirt, taking a smaller seam allowance as marked.

For unpressed pleats, leave the hand basting in until the garment is finished. Lightly steam the pleats without allowing the iron to rest on the fabric. Remove the basting.

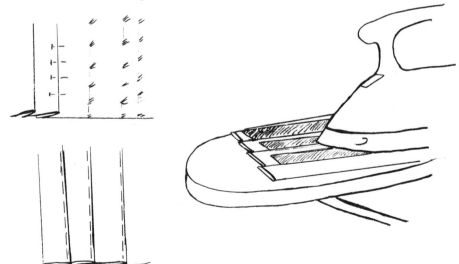

Shaped and stitched pleats are made with the upper section of the pleat trimmed off. Stitch to the markings and form the pleats below the stitching as you would for straight pleats, but sew the hem in place after the pleats have been made. Try the skirt on and make any adjustments as you would for a straight-pleated skirt.

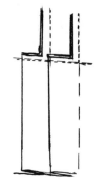

Hemming a Pleated Skirt

Mark the hemline and clip one seam allowance just above the marking. Press the seam open within the hem allowance. Finish the raw edge of the hem in the way best suited to the fabric. Hand sew the garment.

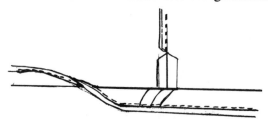

For very sharp pleats, after the garment has been hemmed, stitch along the edge through the fold of the hem, as shown.

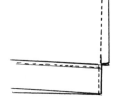

Edgestitching

If the pattern calls for edgestitching, use one of the following methods, whichever is called for in the pattern instructions, after the skirt has been hemmed and before it is attached to the waistband or bodice.

Stitch along the edges of the outside of the folds. For very sharp pleats, stitch along the edges of the inside folds from the wrong side of the skirt.

For pleats stitched down to the hip, edgestitch along the fold from the outside of the garment to the marking, through all the layers of fabric. Stop the stitching at the marking and stitch along the fold of the pleats from the previous stitching.

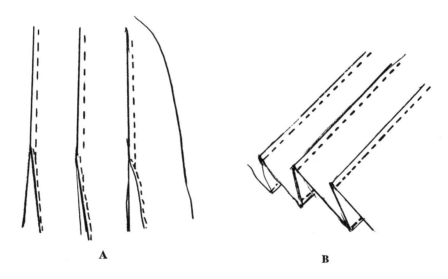

A   B

Inserting a Zipper in a Knife-Pleated Skirt

For a knife-pleated skirt, use a regular skirt zipper, either with a synthetic coil or with metal teeth. The seam into which the zipper will be sewn should be left open. On the underlapping seam, mark a seam allowance $7/8$ inch deep and the length of the zipper. Reinforce-stitch with small stitches at the bottom of the zipper opening, forming a right angle. Clip to the pivot of the reinforcing. Fold the $7/8$-inch seam allowance to the inside and baste it in place. With the right side of the skirt and the zipper facing you, pin the basted seam allowance over the zipper, with the bottom stop of the zipper at the reinforced corner. With the zipper foot adjusted to the right side of the needle, stitch across the bottom of the zipper, pivot, and stitch along the edge of the zipper. Pin the overlapping pleat over the zipper. With the wrong side of the skirt facing you, pin the free zipper tape to the seam allowance. Open the zipper. Pin the seam together, right sides of the fabric facing, and sew the seam from the bottom up, sewing through the zipper tape close to the teeth of the zipper.

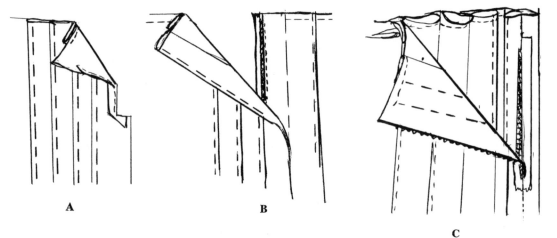

A   B

C

Making a Pleat with an Underlay

Pin the seam together and baste along the fold or roll line. Press the seam open. If the pleat is to be unpressed, use steam only. With the right side of the fabric of the insert facing the wrong side of the skirt, pin the insert to the seam allowances and stitch. Do not press the seams open. Remove the basting.

Accordion or Sunburst Pleats

These pleats must be made commercially. Check the Yellow Pages of the telephone book, or ask at the fabric or notions department for the name of a commercial pleater. Ask him how to prepare the fabric. After the pleating has been completed, stitch the skirt to the waistband or bodice of the garment. Finish the hem with a rolled hem.

GODETS

Godets are pieces of fabric inserted into a seam or cutout, usually in a skirt, to add an extra flare to the garment.

To Sew a Godet into a Seam

Stitch the seam to the marking for the godet and backtrack at the marking. Press the seam open. Pin the godet section into the seam, with the right sides of the fabric facing, matching any marks or notches. It may be necessary to stretch the godet slightly in order to make it fit. Stitch from the mark with the wrong side of the godet facing you, starting the stitching precisely where the seam stitching stopped. Pin and stitch the other side of the godet in the same way, starting at the mark. Do not press the godet seams open, but press the seam from the right side of the garment.

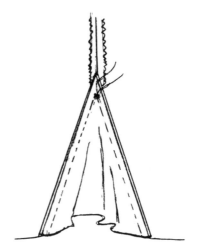

To Sew a Godet into a Cutout

Prepare the cutout by stay-stitching just inside the seam line. With the wrong side of the garment facing you, pin the godet to the cutout, with the right sides of the fabric facing. Start by pinning at the center of the godet to the bottom of the seam. Repeat the pinning, from the center out, for the other side of the godet. Ease where necessary. Using a small running stitch, hand baste from the center down one side of the godet and repeat for the other side, from the center down. Look at the godet from the right side to make sure that the curve is even on both sides. Sew by machine, starting the stitching from the center of the godet down to the bottom. Stitch the other side in the same way, starting from the center and sewing down the side. Clip the garment seam allowance where necessary. Press the seam up, toward the garment.

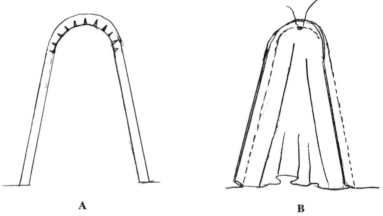

A   B

TUCKS

Tucks are stitched folds of fabric, usually made along the lengthwise grain of the fabric, and used as a decorative feature of the garment. They can be made with the folds showing on the outside of the garment or with the folds on the inside. Sometimes only part of the fabric is stitched, so that the fullness beneath the tuck is incorporated in the design of the garment. Tucks vary in width from narrow pin tucks, which are almost the width of a pin, to those which are almost an inch wide.

Tucks that are placed so that the stitches show from the right side of the fabric are called "spaced tucks," and those that are placed so that the fold of one tuck covers the stitching of the next are called "blind tucks."

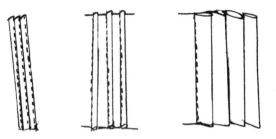

The most important part of making perfect tucks is to transfer the markings from the pattern exactly on the grain line of the fabric and at the proper width from each other. If the tucks are to be made on the right side of the fabric, make the marks with basting or tailor's tacks. If you want to add tucks to a garment and the pattern doesn't call for them, make the tucks in the fabric before you cut the pattern piece out. Make a gauge out of cardboard, cutting a notch in the cardboard the width of the tuck desired. Use the gauge as shown, to keep the width and distance of the tucks equal. After the fabric has been tucked, place the pattern piece over the tucks, being sure to keep the tucks in the same place on both sides of the garment. Then follow the pattern instructions for making the garment.

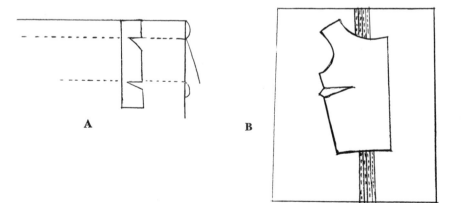

A   B

For patterns that do call for tucks, follow the pattern markings exactly. As soon as you have made a row of tucks, press them in the direction indicated on the pattern instruction. When pressing released tucks (those that are not stitched for the length of the garment piece), press only to the end of the stitching line and do not press the unstitched fold of the fabric. Dart tucks are made to take the place of darts; press them in same way as released tucks.

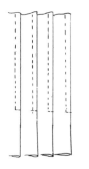

Corded Tucks

Mark the fabric carefully, determining the width of the tuck by pinning the fabric over the cord. Replace the pressure foot with a zipper foot and stitch as close to the cord as possible.

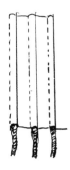

Hand Tucks

For sheer or delicate fabrics, or for dainty baby clothes, sew the tucks by hand, using a small running stitch and silk thread.

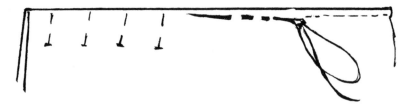

HEMS

The term *hem* is most often used to mean the edge of a skirt which is turned up and sewn on the inside, but it also applies to any edge of a garment which is finished in the same way. Except for some children's clothes and casual sportswear, hems should be sewn in place by hand.

The depth the hem should be depends on two things: the weight of the fabric and the style of the garment. Blouses and very full skirts should have a hem depth of ½ inch. Short sleeves and circular skirts, 1 inch. Pants, the bottom of jackets, and long sleeves, 1½ inches. Most dresses and coats should have a hem depth of 3 inches. Lightweight fabrics can have slightly deeper hems; heavy fabrics should have narrower hems. With very few exceptions, the hem is made after the garment has been completed.

To make a simple hem, press all the seams open, and then determine the hemline by trying on the garment. For skirts, mark the hem with a hem marker or with a yardstick and pins. See Chapter 4, page 145, for instructions on marking a skirt hem. For coats, try the coat on, with the buttons buttoned, and the shoes you plan to wear with the coat. Mark the hem in the same way as for skirts. For sleeves, blouses, pants, and the hems of jackets, try the garment on and turn the hem under so that the proportions of the overall garment are correct. The patterns for these gaments will have a hemline marking printed on them, use this as a guide. But if you feel that the garment looks better with a deeper or narrower hem, follow your own judgment.

Knits and bias-cut and circular skirts should be allowed to hang for twenty-four hours before marking the hem, to let the fabric settle. Once the hemline has been determined, turn the garment wrong-side out and fold along the hemline. Measure the depth of the hem from the fold to the raw edge. If the hem depth is not even, or if it is too wide, trim off the raw edge. Pin the hem in place and press lightly, removing the pins as you go, so that you do not press over them.

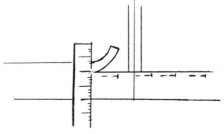

Eased Hem

The hem of a slightly flared skirt will have to be eased at the edge in order to make it fit. Once you have measured and trimmed the hem (if necessary), sew a row of large machine stitches (10 to 12 to the inch) ¼ inch from the raw edge. Place the skirt wrong-side up over the edge of an ironing board, and with a pin, gently pull the bobbin thread every few inches until the hem fits. Place a piece of brown paper between the hem and the garment and steam along the eased edge.

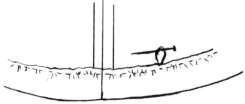

The raw edge of the hem will have to be finished to prevent the fabric from ravelling. The finish you use will depend on the structure of the fabric.

Hem Finishes

Most fabrics can be finished by sewing seam binding to the raw edge. If the garment is washable, preshrink the seam binding before you use it. Lap the seam binding ¼ inch over the right side of the fabric and stitch close to the edge of the seam binding. Turn in the end of the seam binding. Slip-stitch or hem the other edge of the seam binding to the garment or underlining.

For hems that have been eased, use *bias* seam binding to finish the raw edge. Open one of the folded edges of the seam binding and sew it to the right side of the raw edge, lapping it ¼ inch. Stretch the seam binding as you sew. Press the binding up, and slip-stitch or hem the other folded edge to the garment or underlining.

For fabrics that don't ravel easily, make a row of machine stitches ¼ inch from the raw edge. Trim above the stitching with pinking shears. Turn the pinked edge back ¼ inch and blind-stitch the hem to the garment or underlining.

For medium- and heavyweight fabrics, make a row of machine stitches ¼ inch from the edge, and overcast by hand or with a zigzag stitch. Turn the overcast edge back ¼ inch and blind-stitch the hem to the garment or underlining.

For medium- and lightweight fabrics, turn under ¼ inch and machine stitch close to the edge. Slip-stitch or hem the folded edge to the garment or underlining.

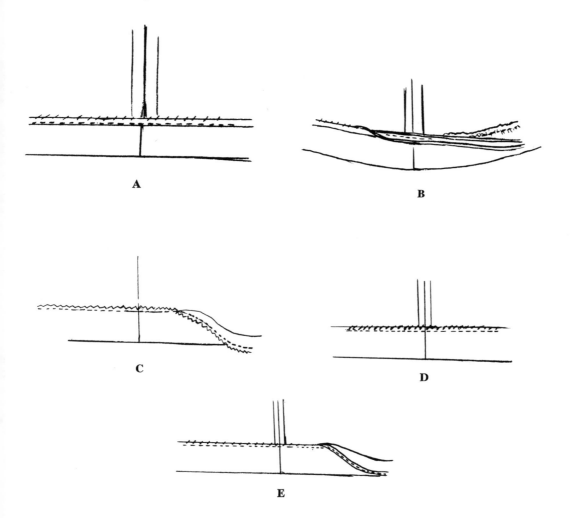

A

B

C

D

E

Circular Skirts

After letting the garment hang for twenty-four hours, mark the hem and trim the depth to 1 inch. Ease, and finish with bias seam binding as you would for an eased hem. Another method used for hemming a circular skirt is the faced hem.

Faced Hem

Faced hems are used for circular skirts, as mentioned, and they are also used for adding length to a skirt and for very heavy fabric. You can buy ready-made hem facing of taffeta or cotton, which comes 2 inches wide and with the edges turned under ¼ inch, or you make a strip of bias facing 2 inches wide out of a fabric lighter than the garment to be hemmed. See the section called Loops and Closures, page 257, for instructions on cutting the bias strips. Make the strip longer than the length of the hem. Turn it under ¼ inch along one side of the length, and stitch. With the right sides together, pin the bias strip to the skirt, opening out the ¼ inch fold if you are using ready-made facing, forming a fold at the beginning of the stitching, as shown. Press the facing down and turn the skirt up along the hemline. Slip-stitch the opening in the facing and slip-stitch or hemstitch the facing to the garment.

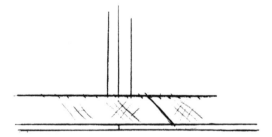

Horsehair Braid

A hem made with a horsehair braid provides extra shaping for long skirts, such as those in evening dresses and wedding dresses. Use purchased braid 1 inch wide and press the folds out of it. Cut the braid the length of the bottom of the hem, plus ¾ inch. Overlap the edges of the braid ¾ inch and enclose them in a piece of fabric. Trim the depth of the hem to ½ inch. Pin the braid to the right side of the fabric ¼ inch from the raw edge and sew ¼ inch from the edge of the braid. Turn the skirt to the wrong side, folding on the hemline, and pin into place. From the right side, stitch through the garment and the braid with a small backstitch. On the inside, tack the braid to the skirt at the seams.

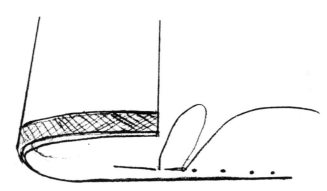

Double-Stitched Hem

Double-stitched hems are used for garments with very wide hems, for knits, and for very heavy fabrics.

Finish the raw edge of the hem in the way best suited to the fabric. For knits, make a row of machine stitches ¼ inch from the raw edge. Mark the hemline, turn up the hem along the hemline, and press. Place a row of pins parallel to the hemline half way up the hem. Turn back the edge of the hem to the row of pins and catch-stitch the hem to the garment. Blind-stitch the finished edge of the hem to the garment.

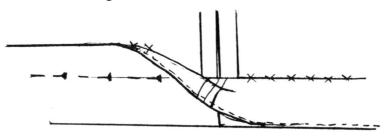

Narrow Hems

Narrow hems are used to finish the edges of sportswear and children's clothes. Turn the raw edge under ¼ inch and press, turn under another ¼ inch and press again. Machine stitch along the edge of the fold (the stitching will show on the right side of the garment).

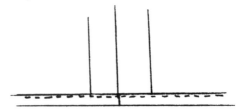

Rolled Hems

Rolled hems are used to finish the raw edges of sheers, some bias-cut fabrics, and scarves. Mark the hemline and make a row of machine stitches ¼ inch between the hemline and the raw edge. Trim the hem allowance close to the stitching. Fold the hem over in a ⅛ inch fold. Start sewing by taking a small stitch in the garment. Take another small stitch in the fold of the hem. Repeat these two stitches for an inch and pull the thread tight. When you pull the thread, the hem will roll over automatically. Repeat the sewing for the length of the hem, pulling the thread every inch.

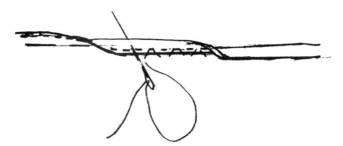

BINDING

Binding made of bias strips of fabric is often used to finish the raw edges of jackets, collars, and sleeves as part of the design of the garment. Self-fabric, or contrasting fabric, or commercial binding can be used for these purposes.

To make bias strips for binding, follow the instructions for cutting bias strips given in the section called Loops and Closures, page 257. Be sure that you cut the strips carefully, with even edges. Purchased binding comes in different widths. For a finished binding ¼ inch wide, buy ½ inch wide bias tape; for a finished binding ½ inch wide, buy 1 inch wide bias tape. When cutting bias strips, decide how wide you want the finished binding to be and then cut them three times as wide, plus ¼ inch. With the right sides of the fabric facing, pin the bias to the raw edge of the garment. Sew in a seam the width of the finished binding. Press the binding up and turn under the raw edge of the binding so that when the binding is folded over, the seam allowances of the fold will fall on the seam line. Fold the binding over the seam allowance and slip-stitch to the seam line so that the stitches do not show on the right side of the fabric.

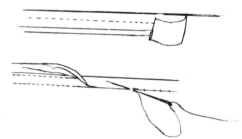

French or Double Binding

This finish can only be used with lightweight fabrics. Make the bias strip six times the width of the finished binding. Fold the strip in half lengthwise, with the wrong sides of the fabric facing, and press. Pin the folded binding to the right side of the fabric and sew in a seam the width of the finished binding. Fold the bias over the seam allowance and slip-stitch to the seam line so that no stitches show on the right side of the fabric.

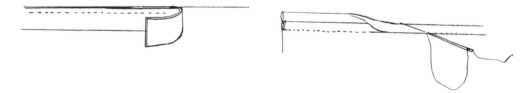

Joining the Edges of Bias Strips

Overlap by folding the end of the strip back ½ inch at the beginning of the stitching, catching the fold in the stitching. When you get to the end of the strip, overlap it over the fold and stitch over the previous stitching for ½ inch.

To join the strip in a seam as you sew the binding to the garment, stop the stitching 2 inches away from either side of the join. Leave 2 inches of the bias strip extending beyond the place where the join is to be. Fold the garment away from the joining at right angles, as shown. Sew the bias strip along the straight grain of the fabric. Trim the seam allowance and the corners of the bias, and press the seam open. Continue stitching the bias to the garment, sewing over the join.

Corners

To sew an inside corner: stitch to the point of the corner and lower the needle at the point for the pivot. Leave the needle in the fabric, turn the garment at a right angle, and pull the bias around the needle. Continue the stitching, forming the corner. Fold the bias to the wrong side, folding in a miter, as shown.

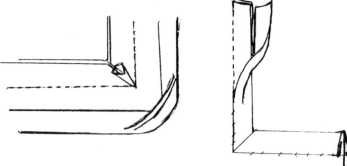

To sew an outside corner: stitch until you are the width of the seam allowance away from the corner, then stop. Backtrack over the stitching to secure it. Fold the bias toward the corner, as shown. Start stitching at the edge of the binding and garment edge. Fold the bias to wrong side, folding in a miter, as shown.

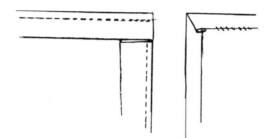

Opening in the Garment

When applying the binding to an open edge of a garment, such as a neckline opening, fold the bias under ½ inch before you start sewing and catch the fold in the stitching. Turn the folded end in when you slip-stitch the binding to the garment.

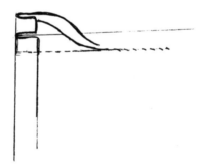

COUTURE TOUCHES

Lingerie Strap Guards

Lingerie strap guards are sewn to the inside shoulder seam of dresses and blouses to prevent bra and slip straps from sliding over the shoulder. Use the smallest snap you can find. Sew the socket section of the snap to the shoulder seam or facing near the neckline and sew the ball section of the snap to a 1½ inch piece of seam binding. Sew the other end of the seam binding to the shoulder seam. When you put the dress on, slip the straps under the seam binding and snap.

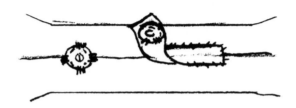

Covered Hooks and Eyes

Covered hooks and eyes add a nice touch to an important garment. Use silk thread or buttonhole twist for larger hooks and eyes. Working from right to left, make a blanket stitch until the hook or eye is completely covered with thread. Match the color of the thread to the garment fabric.

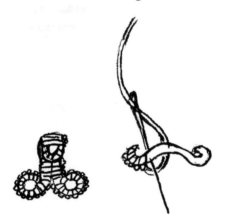

Hong Kong Finish

This finish is used on unlined garments to cover the raw edges of the seam allowances. Cut bias strips of china silk or another lightweight fabric in a color that matches the garment. Sew the strip to the edge of the seam allowance, using a ¼ inch seam. Turn the strip to the back of the seam allowance, and sew through the seam allowance and the strip under the seam allowance.

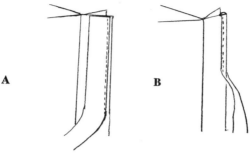

Lace and Other Trimmings Used Instead of Seam Binding

For very special dresses, buy a very narrow lace (¾ inch) and use it instead of seam binding. On a jacket that has been lined, sew a narrow piece of lace or a narrow, embroidered braid over the lining and the facing of the jacket. Pin it in place and slip-stitch both edges of the lace or braid to the lining and the facing. Turn under the edge of the lace or braid at the back neckline of the jacket.

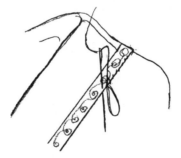

RUFFLES

Ruffles are used to add a soft, feminine touch to many different kinds of garments. They are also used on children's clothes and for curtains and bedspreads. A ruffle is frequently used as part of the design of a garment, and in this case, there will be a special pattern piece for cutting the ruffle. Ruffles can be made from the same fabric as the garment, or from a contrasting fabric or lace. Even if the pattern doesn't call for it, a ruffle can be added as a finishing touch to the collar, neckline, or cuff of a dress or blouse. Cut the ruffle out of a strip of fabric that has been cut on the crosswise grain or true bias of the fabric. You can also purchase ready-made ruffles, usually made of lace or embroidered eyelet cotton, which are handled in the same way as those you make yourself.

The nature of the finished ruffle will depend on the nature of the fabric from which it is made. Soft, light fabrics and medium-weight fabrics lend themselves well to making ruffles, but stiffer sheers, such as organdy, also make good ruffles of a different sort.

Ruffles can be faced, in which case they will not have to be hemmed. When the design of a pattern calls for a ruffle, it will usually be faced. Unfaced ruffles must be finished with a hem. This can be done by making a narrow hem along the edge of the fabric before it is gathered into a ruffle. For sheer and very delicate fabrics, make a hand-rolled hem. For other fabrics, make a narrow hem, as described in the section called Hems, page 284. If your sewing machine has a hemmer attachment, make the hem according to the instructions given in the sewing machine manual.

Making a Straight Ruffle

Cut strips of the fabric to be ruffled on either the crosswise grain of the fabric or on the bias. To obtain the length needed, make seams in the strips where necessary. For instructions on cutting and seaming bias strips, see page 257. The length of the strip needed will depend on the fullness of the ruffle desired. For a very full ruffle, cut the strip three times as long as the piece to which it will be attached. For a ruffle not quite as full as that, cut the strip twice as long. For a moderately full ruffle, cut the strip one and a half times as long. Wide ruffles should be made fuller than narrow ones. If you are not sure how long or how full you want the finished ruffle to be, cut the strip longer than you think necessary. You can always cut off the extra length. Cut the strip as wide as the desired width of the finished ruffle, plus an allowance (⅜ inch) for the hem and ⅝ inch for the seam allowance.

For a faced ruffle, cut the strip twice that of the finished width and add 1¼ inches for the seam allowance. To make the faced ruffle, fold the strip in half lengthwise, with the wrong sides of the fabric facing, and press along the fold.

Gathering the Ruffle

If your sewing machine has a ruffler attachment, follow the instructions given in the sewing machine manual to gather or pleat the strip to form the ruffle.

If you don't use the ruffler, the alternative is to use silk or polyester thread in the bobbin, loosen the thread tension, and using a long stitch (8 to 10 stitches to the inch), make a straight line of stitches on the seam line of the raw edge of a hemmed ruffle, or through the two layers of a folded strip for a faced ruffle. Make another row of stitches ¼ inch inside the first one. Gently pull the bobbin threads, as for gathering, to form the ruffle.

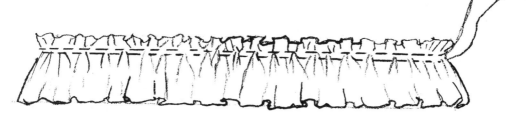

Double Straight Ruffles

Double ruffles have two finished edges. For a double ruffle that will be hemmed, cut the strip as wide as needed, plus ¾ inch for two narrow hem allowances. Make a narrow hem along both of the long edges, using one of the methods described. Make the rows of gathering stitches ¼ inch on either side of the center of the strip.

For a faced, double ruffle, cut the strip twice as wide as needed. Fold the fabric twice, with the wrong sides of the fabric facing, with the raw edges meeting in the center. Make the rows of gathering stitches ⅛ inch inside the raw edges.

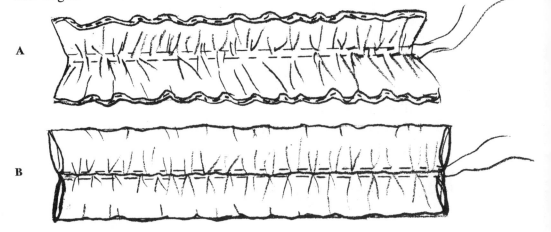

Headed Straight Ruffles

A headed ruffle looks like a double ruffle, but one side of the ruffling is wider than the other. Cut the strips to the same width as required for a double ruffle.

For a hemmed headed ruffle, finish the hems of the long edges of the strips as you would for a double ruffle. Determine the line for the heading and make the gathering stitches ⅛ inch on either side of that line.

For a faced, headed ruffle, determine the line for the heading and fold the edges of the strip to meet that line. Make the gathering stitches ⅛ inch inside the raw edges.

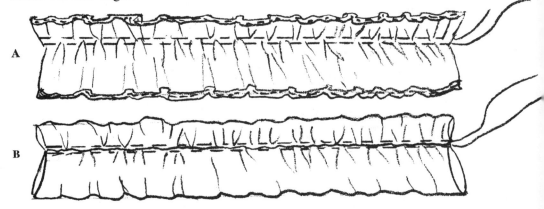

To Attach a Straight Ruffle to a Straight Edge

Pin and sew the ruffle to the seam line and trim the ruffle seam allowance to ⅛ inch. Fold the edge of the garment seam allowance under ⅛ inch and pin the folded edge over the stitching on the ruffle. Stitch close to the edge of the fold, sewing through all the layers of fabric. Steam the ruffle away from the garment without allowing the iron to rest on the ruffle.

An alternative way of applying a straight ruffle to a straight edge is to stitch the ruffle to the garment along the seam line and trim the seam allowance to ¼ inch. Enclose the raw edges with a strip of self-bias, with the edges folded to the inside, or use commercial, double-fold bias tape.

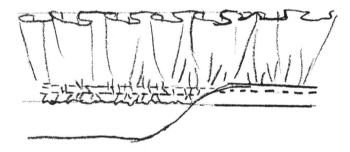

To Attach a Double Ruffle to a Straight Edge

Finish the raw edges of the ruffle by turning the ¼-inch fold under and edgestitching. Pin the ruffle to the garment and stitch on either side of the gathering stitches. Remove the gathering stitches.

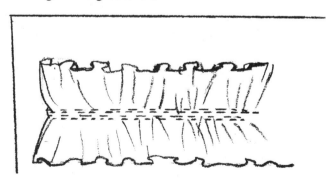

To Attach a Headed Ruffle to a Straight Edge

Fold the edge of the garment under ⅛ inch, fold again in another ⅛ inch fold, and press the fold. Pin the ruffle to the folded edge, with the wrong side of the ruffle facing the right side of the garment fabric, along the line that determines the heading. Stitch between the gathering stitches, sewing through the ruffle and the folded edge of the garment.

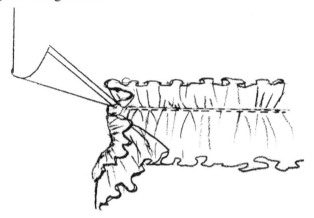

To Attach a Straight Ruffle in a Seam

Pin the ruffle to the seam line of one side of the garment piece and baste it to the garment fabric just inside the seam line. Pin the sections of the garment together, with the right sides of the fabric facing. Sew along the seam line, sewing through the two layers of fabric and the ruffle. Remove any gathering stitches or basting that show from the right side and press the seam open from the wrong side.

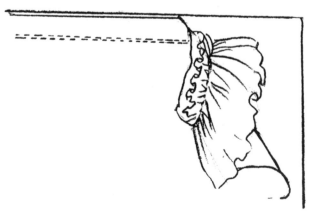

To Attach a Ruffle to a Faced Collar or Cuff

Pin the ruffle to the collar or cuff, with the right sides of the fabric facing, easing the ruffle where necessary. Allow extra fullness in the ruffle at the corner and place the pins ½ inch apart. Machine baste just inside the seam allowance. Pin the facing of the collar or cuff, with the right sides of the fabric facing, matching any marks or notches. Stitch along the seam line, sewing through the two layers of fabric and the ruffle. Trim and grade the seam allowances and turn the collar or cuff right-side out. Press, but do not allow the iron to rest on the ruffle.

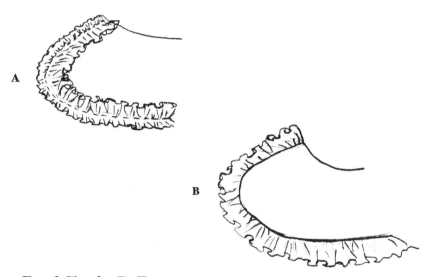

Faced Circular Ruffles

Cut the circular ruffle using the pattern piece given, being very sure to follow the grain line on the pattern piece. Sew any seams in the ruffle and facing sections, and trim the seam allowances and press them open. Pin the ruffle to the facing, with the right sides of the fabric facing, and sew along the seam line. Trim the seam allowance to ¼ inch and turn the ruffle right-side out and press, extending the right side of the ruffle over the seam slightly. Baste the raw edges of the inside of the ruffle together.

Just inside the seam line, stay-stitch the curved edge to which the ruffle will be attached. Stay-stitch the inside of the ruffle just inside the seam allowance. Pin the ruffle to the garment, with the right side of the ruffle up. The seam allowances of the ruffle and the garment should be clipped to the stay-stitching to make the ruffle lay flat. Baste the ruffle to the garment.

Prepare the shaped facing. Pin the facing over the ruffle, with the wrong side of the facing up. Stitch along the seam line, sewing through the facing, the ruffle, and the garment. Trim and grade the seam allowances. Press the facing away from the ruffle, being careful not to let the iron rest on the ruffle. Understitch through the facing, the ruffle, and the garment seam allowances by hand, using a small running stitch. Turn the facing to the inside of the garment and finish as you would for a shaped facing.

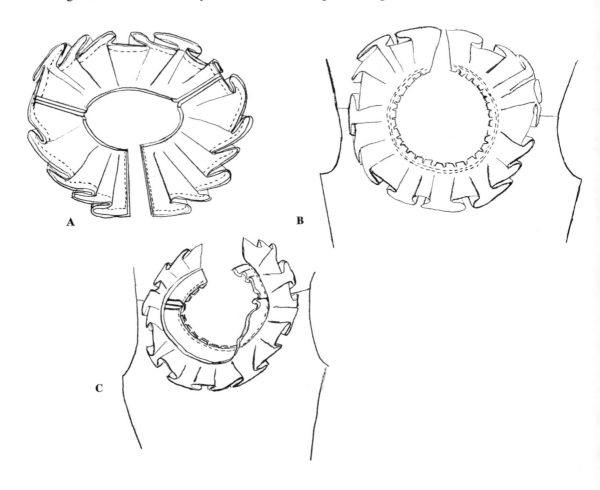

HAND SMOCKING

Hand smocking (which is done on the right side of the fabric) creates a lovely effect when it is used on children's dresses and occasionally on adult dresses. When you buy a pattern that calls for smocking, it will come with an iron-on and transfer sheet. On this sheet there are dots arranged in pattern, which is followed to create the smocking. The smocking is usually done on the fabric before the pattern piece is cut out.

Cut the piece of fabric as instructed in the pattern primer. Transfer the dot pattern by placing the transfer sheet face down over the fabric and pressing with a hot iron. Be sure to place the iron straight down on the transfer sheet. If you slide the iron along the sheet, the dots will not be in the right place.

Use six-strand embroidery thread in one or more contrasting colors to make the smocking. Smocking comes in a variety of patterns—the one shown here is honeycomb smocking, which is the simplest—but the method used here will apply to all smocking.

Bring the needle up from the wrong side of the fabric at the first dot. Make a stitch through the second dot, and another back through the first dot. Pull the thread taut and bring the thread up at the third dot. Repeat as for the first set of dots, pulling the thread taut at each set of dots.

The transfer sheet given with the pattern will include a test section so that you can practice making the smocking before you make it on the dress section. Once the smocking has been completed, follow the pattern instructions for making the dress.

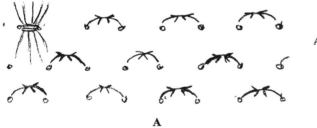

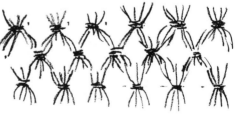

A   B

APPLIQUES

Appliqués are used for all kinds of clothing, usually for children's or teen-agers' sportswear. They can also be quite dressy when made of satin or other elegant fabrics.

There is a vast selection of ready-made appliqués, either embroidered or printed, available. Pin them to the right side of the finished garment and slip-stitch them in place.

You can make your own appliqués out of different fabrics, using shapes of your own design, or cut shapes out of children's coloring books. If you have a printed fabric with large definite motifs, cut the appliqué following the print. For fabrics that ravel, cut the appliqué with a ¼-inch seam allowance and apply in one of the following ways.

1. For soft or lightweight fabrics, cut an underlining of stiff lightweight fabric, such as organdy, and baste it to the edges of the wrong side of the appliqué. Machine stitch the appliqué to the garment along a ¼-inch seam line. Cut the edge of the appliqué close to the row of stitching and sew around the edges with a narrow of zigzag stitch.

2. Back the appliqué with organdy and sew a row of machine stitches around the edge. Fold under the seam allowance of the appliqué and slip-stitch it to the garment.

Felt makes very good appliqués and does not have to be cut with a seam allowance. Pin the appliqué to the garment and sew in place with a blanket stitch, using embroidery thread or very lightweight yarn. Simple appliqués for children's clothes can be cut from iron-on mending fabric and ironed into place without any sewing.

SPECIAL FABRICS

Knits

Knit fabrics are available in many different weights and textures, and because of their knitted construction, they require slightly different handling from woven fabrics.

When choosing knits, take into consideration the same factors you would in choosing a woven fabric—the fiber content, the weight and drapability of the fabric, and the amount of softness or crispness the fabric possesses. You must also consider the amount of give the fabric has, which is not present in woven fabrics. Some knits such as "sweater knits," which are made to resemble hand-knitted fabrics, will have more give than other, more firmly knitted fabrics. You can tell the amount of give by pulling the fabric crosswise and lengthwise and determining how far the fabric stretches before it returns to its original shape.

The sweater knits, which have considerable give in both the crosswise and lengthwise directions, are most suitable for use with patterns designated "for knits only." Soft knits such as jersey and the tricot knits such as ciré are suitable for soft blouses and dresses. The heavier double knits are best used with patterns marked "suitable for knits," or where knits are included in the recommended list of fabrics on the back of the pattern envelope. Avoid patterns with obvious gathers or pieces cut on the bias or that have circular skirts. The bias of a knit fabric is not the most stretchable part of the fabric, unlike a woven fabric.

Knits must be prepared for cutting in much the same way as woven fabrics. You cannot pull a thread to make the ends of the fabric thread-perfect, as you can with a woven fabric, but you can cut along a crosswise row of knitting to achieve the same effect. The lengthwise rib of the knit serves the same purpose as the lengthwise grain of a woven fabric. Be sure when buying knits that the lengthwise ribs have not been twisted or pulled out of shape. Do not follow the fold the manufacturer has made in the fabric, as it may not be exactly on the lengthwise rib. Be sure that the fold will press out; if it does not, you will have to lay out the pattern avoiding the fold. If it does not come out with steam pressing before you cut it, it never will.

Be sure that the fabric has been preshrunk before you start to work with it. You can preshrink washable knits using the same method used for woven fabrics. Give woolen knits to a dry-cleaner to be preshrunk. Wash 100 percent polyester knits before cutting in order to remove the finishing in the fabric, which may stick to the needle when sewing. Always dry knits flat to prevent stretching.

Cut the fabric out on a smooth, flat surface. Don't let it hang over the edge of the table, or it will stretch out of shape. Use a "with nap" layout (all the pattern pieces facing in one direction), as there are differences in the texture of the two directions of the fabric which will show in the finished garment. Use the lengthwise rib of the knit as a guide for straightening the "grain" and for laying out the pattern pieces.

Ball-point sewing machine needles and pins are available and are the best to use with knits because they work by separating the threads rather than by cutting into them. Use all polyester or cotton-covered polyester thread with all knits. Be sure that your scissors are sharp, or you will snag the fabric when cutting. Use tailor's tacks or chalk for marking.

Set the sewing machine for light pressure and loosen needle tension. Use a small stitch (between 10 to 12 stitches per inch) when sewing with a straight stitch. On long seams which will receive strain—such as the sides of dresses, skirts, and pants—you can use a plain straight stitch if you stretch the fabric slightly as it feeds under the needle. Do not stretch the fabric when sewing necklines, facings, armholes, and other small areas of the garment. If you have a zigzag machine, you can use a small zigzag stitch, which will stretch slightly. Some of the new sewing machines have a special "stretch" stitch for use with knits. Always test the stitch you are using on a scrap of the fabric before you begin to sew the garment.

Sew a piece of preshrunk seam binding into the shoulder seams to prevent them from stretching. Use a stretch-lace seam binding to finish the hem, or simply stay-stitch ¼ inch from the raw edge.

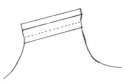

Use an interfacing of suitable weight for facings, under buttonholes, and anywhere else interfacing is called for. You might want to use a lightweight lining for jerseys and other lightweight knits, but most double knits and other medium to heavy knits don't need a lining, except for jackets and coats where it is used for a finished appearance.

Allow the garment to hang for a day or so before hemming to let the shape of the fabric "settle."

Prints

Most printed fabrics can be handled as you would solid colors, but study the print first before you buy it or cut it. When buying a printed fabric, be sure that it is not printed off-grain. If it is, there is no way that you can cut the fabric to make the print look as if it were hanging straight. If the design of the print runs in both directions, it can be cut and sewn as if it were a solid color. For small prints that run in one direction, use a "with nap" cutting layout and buy extra fabric, if no "with nap" layout is given. For larger and/or symmetrical prints, you will have to use a "with nap" layout and match the print as well.

To match a symmetrical print, the first thing to do when laying out a pattern is to press out the fold of the fabric and study the print to determine the length of the "repeat." One "repeat" contains the entire design, which is then repeated throughout the length of the fabric. The length of the repeat will determine how much extra fabric you will need.

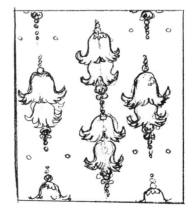

Make the crosswise edges of the fabric thread-perfect and refold the fabric. Be sure that the fold runs through the center of the design, even if this means that you have to fold the fabric without the selvages touching. As long as you keep the crosswise edges even and the distance of one selvage from the other even, you will not make the fabric off-grain. Use a simple pattern, without a center seam if possible. Lay out the center front piece on the fold, placing the design of the print in a pleasing proportion to the overall garment. Do not allow large flowers or other large designs to fall directly on the bust or the buttocks. Lay out the back of the dress in the same place on the repeat, using the notches to match the print. (See illustration.) Lay out the sleeves so that the single notch on the front of the armhole matches the print in the same place as the single notch of the armhole on the front bodice.

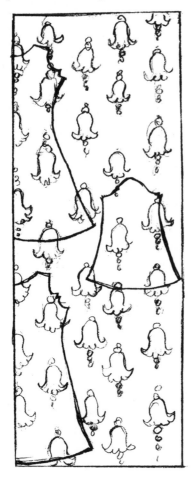

Geometric prints should be laid out in the same manner as striped fabrics, using a row of the geometric design as if it were a stripe. See page 311 for instructions on how to lay out striped fabric.

Border prints are best used with patterns specifically designed to be used with them. Such patterns include a layout for these prints. If your pattern has not been designed for use with border prints, you will have to make your own layout. Avoid styles with flared or A-line skirts. Most fabrics with border prints have the print running on the lengthwise edge of the fabric; therefore, to have the border come out on the hem of the garment, you will have to lay out the pattern on the crosswise length of the fabric. This means that the garment can be no longer than the width of the fabric except when seamed at the waist or bodice. If the border print is also a symmetrical one, follow the instructions given for laying out symmetrical prints. The center of the print must be at the center of the garment.

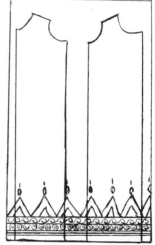

For large prints that are not obviously symmetrical, use your own judgment about matching. If the print runs in both directions, it will not be necessary to follow a "with nap" layout, just be sure to place large designs so that they do not fall directly over the bust or buttocks. If the print has a definite one-way direction, follow a "with nap" layout and use the same rules for laying out the design.

Fake Furs

Fake furs come in a large variety of weights and lengths of surface fur. They are either woven or knitted, but they are handled in the same way. The thin, napped ones can be treated like other pile fabrics, such as corduroy. The longer haired ones require special handling.

The most important factor to take into consideration is the choice of the pattern. More and more patterns are being made to be used with fake furs. These are most suitable because they take into account the fur of the garment, allowing for the thickness of the pile, and give "with nap" layouts, which must be used. If you want to use a pattern that is not specifically designed for fake furs, choose a simple style and avoid complicated seaming and details. Loop closings, frog closings, and large hooks and eyes that are meant to be used with furs are most suitable for fake furs. It is best, however, when using a fake fur for the first time to find a pattern specifically designed for it.

Use polyester or cotton-covered polyester thread. Lay out the pattern using a "with nap" layout on a single thickness of the fabric, pinning the pieces to the wrong side of the fabric. Pin the pattern pieces to be cut on the fold on the fold line and trace around them with chalk or a ball-point pen; reverse the pattern piece for the remaining half. For other pieces, such as sleeves and the front of the garment, be sure to reverse the pattern piece when cutting the piece for the second time so that you get a left and right front and a left and right sleeve, and so forth.

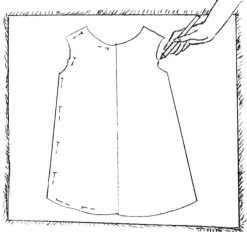

Cut the fabric with dressmaker's shears if the pile is not too long, or use a straight-edged razor blade, working from the wrong side of the fabric. Use a straight stitch or small zigzag stitch and test the stitch on a scrap of the fabric first.

Do not press the fake fur with an iron, but press the seams apart with your fingers and catch-stitch the seams open by hand if they do not stay open by themselves.

At the shoulders and neckline, stitch a ¼-inch preshrunk twill tape into the seam. After sewing the seams, trim the pile off the inside of the seam allowance to reduce the bulk of the seams. For darts, stitch as marked and trim the allowance to ⅜ inch. Catch-stitch the darts open if necessary.

If you must make a buttonhole, use two strips of preshrunk ⅝-inch grosgrain ribbon or leather and stitch parallel to the edges of the buttonhole. Turn to the inside and sew by hand, reinforcing the end of each buttonhole. Sew the ribbon or leather to the back of the fabric. Sew buttons on with long thread shanks.

When the seams are finished, use a darning needle to pull out the fibers of the pile that may have gotten caught in the stitching.

Pile Fabrics

The first thing to do when working with pile fabrics—such as corduroy, velvet, and velveteen—is to determine the direction of the nap. Do this by rubbing your hand along the lengthwise grain of the fabric. If it feels smooth, you are rubbing with the pile; if it feels rough, you are rubbing against the pile. You must use a "with nap" layout to cut out the pattern so that the pile runs in the same direction on all the pieces of the garment. Decide whether you want the pile to run up or down. Hold the fabric up in front of you and decide which effect you prefer (the color will appear slightly different depending on which way the nap runs). You may have to change the pressure on your machine when sewing a pile fabric. Test it first by sewing two scraps of fabric of equal strength together, with the right sides of the fabric facing each other. If the edges of the seam come out even, the pressure is all right. If the top piece forms a bubble at the end of the seam, the pressure needs adjusting. Lighten the pressure on your machine until the seam comes out even.

To press pile fabrics, place a scrap of the fabric right-side up on the ironing board. Place the garment over the scrap, wrong-side down, and press with a steam iron.

Leather

Leather is easy to sew with, but it requires special handling. It is sold by the skin and is measured in square feet rather than in yards.

Choose a pattern specifically designed for use with leather or one with simple seams and small pattern pieces. If the pattern does not have small pieces, you may have to piece the pattern in order to get it to fit on the leather skins. If you cut a pattern piece apart to piece it, be sure to add a seam allowance (⅝ inch) to each of the cut edges. The amount of leather you will need will depend on the size of the skins and your pattern. Measure the pattern pieces, and remember that you have to cut two of everything (two sleeves, both sides of the bodice, and so forth), reversing the pattern pieces to do so. Because changes cannot be made in leather after it has been sewn (the holes made by the needle will show), it is advisable to make the pattern out of another fabric first and make any adjustments necessary before you cut the pattern out of the leather.

Leather does not have a grain, but suede should be cut using a "with nap" layout, with the tops of the pattern pieces facing the "head" of the skin.

Use transparent tape to tape the pattern pieces to a single layer of the wrong side of the leather, avoid making any obvious marks or holes in the leather. For a pattern piece that would normally be placed on the fold of the fabric, tape it to the leather, draw around the piece with a ball-point pen, tape it along the edge that is to be placed on the fold, and reverse the pattern piece. Trace around the other pattern pieces and reverse them to get a right and a left sleeve, a bodice front, and so forth. Make all the markings on the wrong side of the leather with a ball-point pen.

Use a special leather sewing machine needle and silk or mercerized cotton thread. Do not pin the seams, but tape them at the edges with transparent tape to hold them as you sew. Leather garments should be lined with a firm fabric such as taffeta. Leather can be stretched, but it will not return to its original shape; so be careful not to stretch it unless necessary.

Hems and seams can be held in place with rubber cement. Spread a thin layer on both sides of the area to be glued, wait until the glue is slightly tacky, and tap lightly with a wooden mallet. You can also use topstitching to hold seams and hems in place.

If pressing is necessary, use a warm dry iron on the right side, with a piece of brown paper between the iron and the leather. To clean, give leather garments to a dry-cleaner who specializes in cleaning leather.

Lace

Lace can be very expensive or not, depending on the fiber used to make it. Making a dress or blouse of lace requires some special preparation before you cut. Choose patterns that are simple, without too many seams or fussy details. Lace does not usually have a grain, as the back of the fabric is made of net and is not woven.

Lay out the pattern using a "with nap" layout and treat the motif of the lace as if it were a large print, taking into consideration the placement of the main motif. Lace made with one scalloped edge can be used with the finished scallop as a hem. Treat it like a border print. Underline a lace garment with a sheer or semi-sheer fabric such as china silk.

If the underlining is not sheer, use shaped facings cut from the lace; they won't show from the right side of the garment. If the underlining is sheer, cut the facings from the underlining fabric.

Use French seams to sew the main seams of the garment. See page 174 for instructions on how to make French seams.

Vinyl

Vinyl fabrics are handled in much the same manner as leather, because once pin and needle holes are made in the fabric, they cannot be removed. It is therefore advisable to make the garment in a different fabric first so that any adjustments can be made before you cut the vinyl. Choose a pattern designed for use with vinyl fabrics, or one with a minimum of seams and darts. Cut as you would for any other fabric, but tape rather than pin the seams as you sew. You can pin the pattern to the vinyl, but be sure that the pins are placed between the cutting line and the seam line. If your pattern calls for set-in sleeves, remove some of the ease in the pattern before cutting (see the section called Sleeve Pattern Adjustments in Chapter 3). Vinyl must be sponged clean with soapy water, so be sure that any lining you use does not water-spot.

Mark vinyl on the back with tailor's chalk and on the front with a grease pencil that will rub off. Use a long stitch setting (8 to 10 stitches per inch) and mercerized cotton thread. Place tissue paper over the seam as you sew if you find it difficult to feed the fabric into the machine.

Do not use an iron to press vinyl. Press the seams open with your fingers, or tap them lightly with a hammer. Topstitching may be used to hold the seams and hems in place. If your pattern calls for buttonholes, make bound buttonholes and stitch around them from the right side to make them lay flat.

Plaids

Fabrics with plaids, stripes, and certain prints require matching at the seams when the pattern is laid out, and are not recommended for the beginning sewer. Do not attempt to use these fabrics until you have made several simpler garments first—you should be familiar with different construction techniques and used to laying out patterns.

Plaids that are symmetrical in design are called even plaids. Asymmetrical plaids are called uneven plaids, and must be placed so that the design balances in the finished garment. Be sure that you do not use a pattern labeled "unsuitable for plaids," because such a pattern cannot be cut with the plaid design balanced. Choose patterns that have been designed for use with plaids, and that have as few seams as possible. In order to match any plaid, you will need to buy more yardage than is called for on the pattern envelope. Usually, an extra ½ to ⅔ of a yard will do.

Slip basting is done by hand and can be used to match seams when sewing if the garment has been cut out so that the design of the fabric matches. To slip baste, turn under the seam allowance and work from the right side of the fabric. Pin the folded edge on the corresponding piece, with the design matching, and put the needle through the fold and then through the lower layer in a long stitch. Sew the entire seam in this manner; then sew the seam by machine from the wrong side in the usual way. If you cut the pieces of the pattern so that they match, slip basting is rarely necessary.

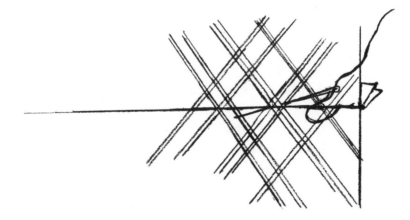

Even Plaids

Make sure that the fold of the fabric runs through the center of the plaid or the dominant line. Match the design by placing the pattern with the seam lines at the same place on the repeat of the plaid design at corresponding notches on the pattern so that they will match when the seam is sewn. The plaid will not match at the underside of the sleeve cap or above the bust darts, but it should match at all other seam points.

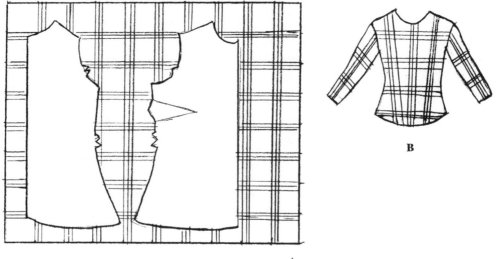

B

Uneven Plaids

A

For cutting uneven plaids, always use a "with nap" layout. Choose the dominant stripe that you want to fall at the center front, and fold the fabric through that stripe. Pin the fabric along the lengthwise edge and be sure that the matching stripes fall directly on top of one another. Pin the front pieces first, then the back and sleeves, making sure that the same stripe is kept in the center and the seams match at corresponding notches. Whenever you pin pattern pieces that are to match, double check the match before you cut the fabric.

Checks

Fabrics with a checked design are matched in the same way as even plaids.

Stripes

Striped fabrics are either even or uneven and must be handled in the same way as plaids. Be sure to place corresponding notches on the same stripe.

Chiffon

Chiffon is a very soft, sheer fabric, made of silk or synthetics, and owing to its slippery quality, it requires special handling. Because chiffon is somewhat difficult to handle, you should not attempt to make a garment out of it until you have had experience cutting and sewing other fabrics.

Choose a simple pattern that does not have too many seams. The bodice of a chiffon dress may be cut double, and then stitched together before the darts and other details are sewn, in the same way as you would handle an underlining. A full skirt may be cut double or triple, with each layer hemmed separately, but attached to the bodice in one piece.

Before you start to cut or sew chiffon, be sure that your scissors, pins, and needles are as sharp as possible. Lay the chiffon out with a sheet underneath it to keep it from slipping. To be sure that it does not slip off-grain while you are cutting, cut the various pieces in sections. That is, cut the bodice sections first, cutting the chiffon along a crosswise thread, and repin the fabric before you cut the skirt or sleeve sections. Use a lot of pins to hold the selvages together and to pin the pattern so that nothing slips.

Eliminate the facings on a chiffon garment. Overcast the edges with a zigzag stitch, turn in the edges ⅝ inch at the neck and other faced edges, and slip-stitch in place. Do not use interfacing on chiffon.

For all straight seams, use a flat felled seam. Do not make a French seam because this will cause the chiffon to pucker. Sew the sleeves into the armhole in an ordinary seam, trim the seam to ¼ inch, and overcast the edges by hand. Cut off the regular hem allowance and finish with a hand-rolled hem.

CHAPTER

6

TAILORING

Making a tailored suit or coat is not as difficult as it may appear, but it must be approached with the proper preparation and patience. Do not attempt to make a tailored jacket or coat as your second sewing project. Once you have had experience making simple skirts, dresses, and sportswear, you will have enough knowledge of fabrics and sewing techniques to make your first tailored garment. This chapter includes instructions for making a tailored suit, but the techniques used for the jacket will apply to making a tailored coat.

Tailoring requires more hand sewing and more involved pressing than you have been doing, and therefore you must be ready to take the time and make the effort required for a really professional job.

The first thing you will need is a pattern that will lend itself to tailoring. A pattern that can be tailored will call for interfacing, lining, and perhaps, underlining. It should include separate pattern pieces for the interfacing. The fabrics called for on the pattern envelope should include medium- to heavyweight woolens. Generally, Vogue patterns are best suited for tailoring.

For your first tailoring project, choose a basic design identical to or similar to the one illustrated here, according to your taste. Leave complicated couture features alone until you have finished this first project. The skirt in this chapter uses a 1-inch grosgrain ribbon in place of a waistband. If you prefer to make a skirt that has a waistband, buy a pattern that has one and follow the pattern instructions and the instructions given in Chapter 4 for applying the waistband. If you want to make the skirt as shown here and cannot find a pattern for a skirt without a waistband, buy one that has one and leave it off, substituting the grosgrain ribbon as instructed here.

Many different fabrics can be tailored, but for the first project a medium-weight, crisp wool in a solid color or tweed will be the easiest to handle. Avoid shiny-surfaced fabrics, or any twill or other wool that has a distinct diagonal weave. Do not waste your time and effort on a cheap fabric. Buy the best you can afford and you will find the results well worth the expense and work involved. When you are finished, you will have a garment that is not only fashion-right, but one that will last through several seasons of intensive wear.

Several pieces of equipment, some of which you probably own by now, are essential to doing a perfect tailoring job. Most of them are used for pressing and they can be used to facilitate your other sewing as well. These items are essential:

A Tailor's Ham—It is used to press curved seams and to shape the collar.

A Seam Roll—It is used to press seams perfectly flat and even.

A Pointer and Creaser or a Tailor's Board—These are made of wood and have points that will enable you to press and shape small, tight areas, such as the points of a collar.

A Sleeve Board and Pressing Cloths—You should already have them because they are essential for a proper pressing job.

Silk Thread—It will be used for all the basting and hand sewing that is used to shape the jacket. Silk is preferable to any other kind of thread, as it is less likely to leave marks on the fabric. Pick a color that matches your fabric.

A Shaped, Man's Suit Hanger or a Dress Dummy—A dress dummy in your size is ideal, but the hanger will serve to help shape and fit the jacket as you construct it.

Once you have chosen your pattern and fabric, you will need the following "underneath" fabrics and notions.

Underlining or Backing—An underlining, or *backing* as it is called when used in tailoring, is not absolutely essential, but it will add body and strength to the garment. It will also make the construction of the jacket easier, as the interfacing can be sewn and shaped to the backing instead of being sewn directly to the garment fabric.

Always choose a backing that is lighter than the suit fabric so that it will add body to the garment without distorting the feel and drape of the fabric. Use the list given on page 118 as a guide to choosing the backing fabric. [Follow the measurements given on the pattern envelope for the outer fabric, checking the width of the backing fabric, as the backing will be cut from the same pattern pieces as the suit.]

Preshrink the backing fabric and be sure that it is grain-perfect before you cut.

Interfacing—Always use hair canvas for interfacing any tailored garment made of wool. The hair canvas should be lighter in weight than the jacket fabric, but heavier than the backing fabric. Buy ½ yard more than is called for on the pattern envelope for use when hemming the jacket.

Preshrink the hair canvas by pressing it thoroughly with a steam iron before you cut it.

Lining—You will need two kinds of lining fabric. For the jacket, you need an opaque, slightly slippery fabric so that the finished jacket will easily slip over any blouse or sweater that you will wear under it. A lightweight, satin-backed crepe, used with the satin-side out, is ideal. Match the color of the jacket as closely as possible, or choose a color that contrasts well with the jacket, because the lining will show when the jacket is worn open.

The skirt lining should be slightly lighter weight than the jacket lining and definitely not slippery. Use the list given on page 116 as a guide to choosing the lining fabric.

Buttons—Buy the size specified by the pattern. Choose a style and a color that complements both the kind of fabric you are using and the style of the jacket. See the section called Buttons, page 247 for a guide to selecting appropriate buttons. Buy one more button than is called for by the pattern, in case you lose one and need a replacement.

1/4-inch Wide Twill Tape—This is used to stabilize the seams in the front of the jacket. Preshrink the tape by soaking it in very hot water for a few minutes.

1/4 Yard of Lamb's Wool or Heavy Cotton Flannel—This will be used to add padding to the jacket at the shoulders. Preshrink it. You may want to use purchased shoulder pads instead.

General Notions—Buy hand sewing needles that are the most comfortable length for you to use. You may find that a short needle is easier to control. You will also need the following items: a skirt zipper, regular or invisible; silk or cotton-covered polyester thread for sewing the suit; silk buttonhole twist to sew on the buttons; hooks and eyes for the skirt; seam binding, and, if necessary, one or two silk-covered snaps.

If you have to make major alterations in the pattern, make a muslin shell for the jacket, using the front, back, and sleeve sections of the pattern, but not the collar and the facings. Make the changes in the muslin, remembering that more ease has been allowed in a jacket or coat pattern than in other patterns because jackets and coats are worn over other clothes. For this reason, buy the pattern in your usual size; do not buy a size larger. When altering the jacket pattern, do not fit this ease out of the pattern, or it will be too tight. Any changes made in the jacket body must be made in the lining pattern. If necessary, make any adjustments in the skirt pattern.

Cutting the Suit

Use the layouts given in the pattern instructions to cut out the jacket and skirt from the outside fabric. Transfer all markings from the jacket pattern to the fabric with tailor's tacks. The markings for the jacket and skirt will be made on the backing as well, but for the front of the jacket, it is important that they be made on the right side of the fabric, precisely marked directly from the pattern. Use the same pattern pieces to cut out the backing fabric. Transfer all the markings from the pattern to the backing fabric with dressmaker's carbon paper and a tracing wheel.

Use the jacket lining pieces, and unless there is a separate piece for the sleeve lining, use the pattern pieces for the sleeve to cut out the sleeve lining. To cut out the skirt lining, use the same pieces used to cut out the skirt. Transfer all markings on the pattern to the wrong side of the lining with dressmaker's carbon paper.

Starting the Suit

The next step is to baste the backing to the outer fabric for all the pieces of the suit. Follow the instructions given for basting an underlining to a garment on page 159 for all the pieces. When you baste the backing to the sections of the jacket, the markings on the backing must fall directly under the markings made on the outer fabric with tailor's tacks. To be sure that they do so, place a pin through a tailor's tack on the jacket at right angles to the fabric, and be sure that the point of the pin goes directly through the marking on the backing.

Now carefully take all the pieces for the jacket and put them in one place, out of the way, as you are going to make the skirt first.

Making the Skirt

Sew the darts, handling the outer fabric and backing as one, and sew the seams as instructed in the pattern instructions. Press the seams open over the seam roll from the wrong side, using the steam to do most of the pressing. Do not rest the iron on the fabric heavily. Insert the zipper in the back seam, using the centered, or slot-seam method given on page 185 for a regular zipper, or follow the instructions for an invisible zipper given on page 190.

Sew the darts and baste the seams in the lining in the same way as for the skirt, leaving the opening for the zipper above the mark on the back seam. With the skirt wrong-side out and the lining right-side out, slip the lining over the skirt and pin at the matching seams at the top of the skirt. Turn under the seam allowance over the zipper. Machine baste the lining to the skirt just inside the seam allowance. Try the skirt on to be sure that the lining fits inside the skirt comfortably. If it bunches slightly, the lining is a little too large. Mark the amount to be taken in at each seam, and baste. Do not take in too much, or the lining will be too tight and the skirt will never be comfortable. Once you are satisfied that the lining fits the inside of the skirt, remove the basting stitches at the waistline, take the lining out of the skirt, and sew the seams permanently. Press the lining seams open. Press the skirt and the lining thoroughly. Put the lining back into the skirt and baste again at the waist. Slip-stitch the lining to the zipper tape.

Finish the bottom of the skirt with seam binding. Finish the bottom of the lining by making a ⅛-inch fold to the inside of the lining. Make another ⅛-inch fold over the first and sew through both folds.

Cut the grosgrain ribbon as long as the waist of the skirt, plus 2 inches. Trim the seam allowance of the skirt at the waist to ¼-inch. Pin the ribbon to the right side of the skirt at the waist, with one edge just over the seam line and 1 inch extending at each end. Turn under the ends of the ribbon over the zipper. Stitch the ribbon to the skirt, sewing just inside of the edge of the ribbon, easing the skirt where necessary. Make another row of stitching ⅛-inch above the first, sewing through the ribbon and seam allowance. Press the ribbon to the inside of the skirt. Slip-stitch the ends of the ribbon to the zipper tape and sew a hook and eye just above the zipper opening. Hand tack the outer edge of the ribbon to the other seams, sewing through the lining and the seam allowance.

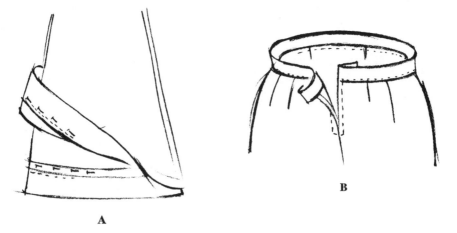

A

B

Pin up the hems of the skirt and the lining, making the lining ½-inch shorter than the skirt. Do not sew the hems in place until you have finished the jacket; you want to be sure that the finished skirt length is in proportion with the finished jacket.

Making the Jacket

Baste the main seams of the body of the jacket and the darts, and try the jacket on over the skirt and a blouse or lightweight sweater. Pin the jacket closed, lapping the front over the buttonhole markings. The jacket should fit comfortably over the blouse or sweater and should be loose enough to allow for movement, but not so loose that it bags. If the seams have to be taken in or let out, mark the changes and rebaste the seams. Make sure that the darts fall in the right place. Once you are sure that the shell of the jacket fits, sew the front side seams and the darts permanently. Do not sew the side or shoulder seams permanently yet. Press the front side seams open, and press the darts as indicated on the pattern instructions.

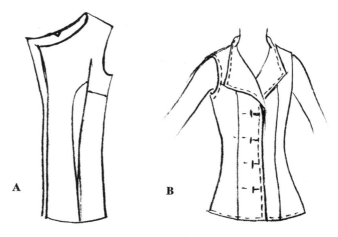

Prepare the Interfacing

If there are darts in the interfacing, sew them in one of the following ways:

(a) Cut out the dart, bring the edges together, and sew a piece of seam binding over the edges.

(b) Cut the dart away, bring the edges together, and sew with a zigzag stitch.

(c) Cut through the center of the dart, lap the edges over each other, and sew through the seam line. Reinforce the stitching at the point of the dart.

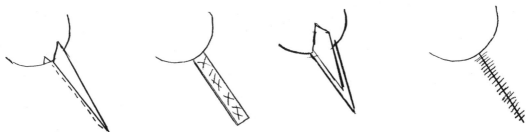

Trim away the edges of the interfacing ⅛ inch *inside* the seam allowances (trim off ¾ inch), except at the armhole edges.

Pin the interfacing to the inside of the jacket shell. Working from the outside of the front of the jacket, fold the lapels back along the roll line and pin the interfacing to the points of the jacket as it falls. If there is no roll line

printed on the pattern, read ahead to the next step before you pin the interfacing to the points of the lapel.

Check that the interfacing and the jacket look like one piece of fabric, that is, that there are no bubbles between the outer fabric and the interfacing. If bubbles do form, repin the interfacing until they are gone. Mark any changes that must be made on the interfacing.

Remove the basting stitches holding the side and shoulder seams of the jacket. Baste the interfacing to the jacket along the edges, using long running stitches (sewn by hand). Attach the interfacing to the backing by using tailor basting. To make the tailor basting, make a small horizontal stitch through the interfacing to the backing, taking up a few threads of each fabric in the stitch. Make another horizontal stitch 1 inch below the first one in the same manner. Repeat these stitches over the entire interfacing, except for the area on the lapel beyond the roll line. Keep the thread loose, and be sure you do not sew through the outside fabric. If your jacket is not backed, eliminate

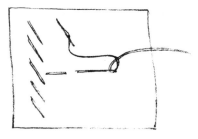

this step, and catch-stitch the edges of the interfacing to the jacket, using a very loose catch-stitch.

Sew the side and shoulder seams permanently and press them open over the seam roll. If the roll line is not printed on the pattern, you will have to determine its exact placement. Do not omit this step even if the roll line has been marked, as the fit of the jacket and the weight of the fabric may make a slight change necessary.

Sew the back seam of the under collar and press it open. Overlap the seam on the back collar interfacing and stitch. Trim the seam allowance from the interfacing (if you have not already done so) and catch-stitch the interfacing to the under collar very loosely. Pin the under collar to the jacket, overlapping the seam allowances. Baste the under collar to the neckline, matching the markings at the front, shoulders, and center back. Try the jacket on and have somebody help you, or if you are working alone, place the jacket on a dress dummy or a shaped, man's suit hanger. Pin the right front over the left, matching the markings for the buttonholes with those for the buttons. Pin the jacket closed at the buttonhole markings.

The collar and lapel will roll back from the top buttonhole and form the shape of the finished jacket, as shown on the pattern envelope. Place pins along the roll line on the lapels and collar, and make sure that the back of the collar (without the seam allowance at the edge, fold it under temporarily) covers the seam line where the collar will be attached to the jacket.

With a row of basting thread, mark the roll line on the lapels and the under collar. Carefully remove the under collar from the jacket, holding it so that it is still folded back from the roll line. Pin the bottom of the under collar to a tailor's ham, maintaining the roll. With a steam iron, steam around the fold of the roll, but be careful not to allow the iron to touch the under collar. Shape the collar with your fingers while it is still wet, making both sides symmetrical. Steam the folded lapel and shape it in the same way. After you have shaped the under collar and the lapels, let them dry completely before you handle them again.

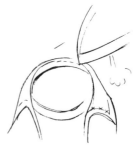

Make bound buttonholes on the right front, following the instructions for one of the methods given on pages 253-257.

For the interfacing in front of the roll line on the lapel, use padding stitches. These are made in the same way as tailor basting, but the stitches are made ¼ inch apart and should catch the outer fabric in the stitch as well as the backing and interfacing. Hold and shape the lapel with your left hand, folding it along the roll line, and sew the padding stitches with your right hand.

A

B

To stabilize the under collar permanently, it will also have to be pad-stitched. Work with the wrong side of the under collar facing you, and hold it with the left hand to maintain the fold away from the roll line. Work from the basted roll line toward the inside of the under collar, making three or four rows of stitches ¼ inch apart, stopping the stitching inside the seam line. Then work from the outside edges of the under collar, making the rows of stitches parallel to the outside edges of the under collar. Be sure to maintain the roll as you stitch.

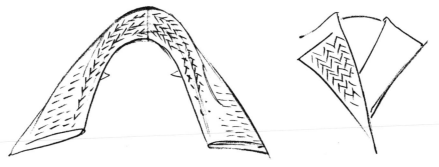

The ¼ inch twill tape is now added to the front edges of the interfacing to stabilize and reinforce the seams. Place one edge of the tape so that it is just over the seam line (which is ⅝ inch from the edge of the jacket). Baste the twill tape to the backing and sew the other edge of the tape to the inter-facing with tailor basting. The edge of the tape will be caught in the front seam when the facing is applied. Place and sew the tape down the front sections of the jacket, as shown. Place another piece of tape along the roll and use tailor basting to hold it in place.

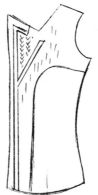

Press the pad-stitched under collar and lapels from the outer fabric side, being careful not to disturb the roll line.

Stay-stitch the neckline of the jacket between the markings, sewing ½ inch from the raw edge. Reinforce the stitching at the pivot points and clip. Pin the under collar to the neckline seam, with the right sides of the fabric facing, and matching at the center back, shoulder marks, any other marks, and at the large marks at each side of the collar. Be absolutely sure that the marks on the jacket and the under collar match exactly. Clip the neckline edge of the jacket where necessary. Begin sewing the under collar to the jacket, starting the stitching precisely through the large marking on the collar. Backstitch over the first few stitches to reinforce the stitching. Stitch along the seam line, pivoting where indicated, stopping the stitching at the large mark on the other sde of the under collar. Backstitch to reinforce the stitching. Press the seam open.

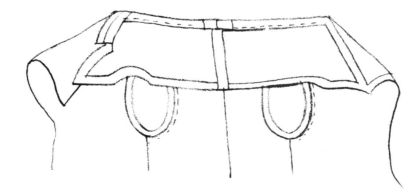

Reinforce the pivot points of the facing along the seam line, as you did for the jacket, and clip to the pivot marking. Sew the back facing to the front facing and press the seams open. Stay-stitch the inside of the back facing. Pin the upper collar to the front facing, matching all the same marks, as you did for the under collar. Clip the facing seam allowance where necessary. Sew the collar to the facing, starting the stitching through the large mark and backtracking to reinforce the stitching. Sew the seam, pivoting at the pivot marks, and stop the sewing at the other large mark, backtracking to reinforce. Press the seam open.

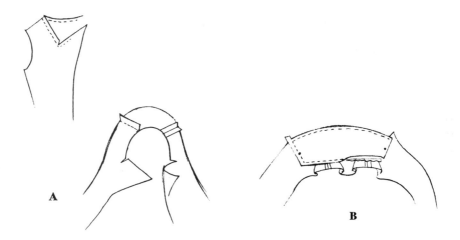

A

B

Place the facing on the jacket, with the right sides facing, and pin into place, stretching the under collar and front lapel edges slightly so that they fit exactly. Working with the upper collar and the facing toward you, sew around the seams of the collar between the large marks. Then turn up the seam allowance and sew through the same large mark, across the point of the lapel and down the front of the jacket facing. Repeat for the other side of the jacket. Be absolutely sure that the stitching at the large marks meets. If the fabric is too bulky, or if the needle won't reach the mark, leave several inches of thread before you start stitching, and sew that end of the thread to the mark by hand, threading the extra thread in a hand sewing needle.

Press the seams of the collar and the lapel points open, placing the seam over the point of the pointer and creaser or tailor's board. Trim and grade the seam in this order: above the roll line in the lapel, leave the facing seam allowance the longest (about ¼ inch), trim the jacket seam allowance narrower, and trim the backing narrower than both of the others. Below the roll line, leave the jacket seam allowance about ¼ inch and trim the other seam allowance narrower. For the collar, leave the upper collar seam allowance the widest (about ¼ inch) and trim the other seam allowances narrower.

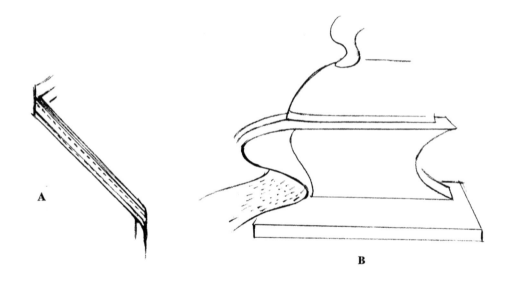

Turn the collar and facings right-side out. If you have followed the instructions and the markings carefully, the collar should be formed with the outer seam above the roll line hidden under the inside edge of the facing, and the seam below the roll line should be hidden by the outside of the jacket. The seam of the collar should be hidden by the upper collar. Press the lapels and collar so that the seams are thus hidden, and baste along the edges with silk thread to maintain these folds. Baste to within 5 inches of the bottom of the jacket. Lift up the back facing and sew the back seam allowances together with very long zigzag hand stitches, but do not force the seam allowances together if they don't meet.

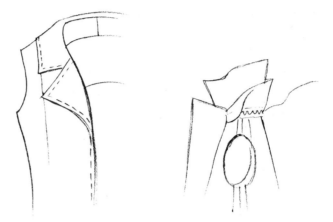

Finish the underside of the bound buttonholes, following the instructions given on page 257 in the section called Buttonholes.

Preparing the Sleeves

This pattern calls for a double-seamed set-in sleeve, which is handled like any other set-in sleeve. However, instead of having one seam under the arm, as with one-piece set-in sleeves, the two seams will fall along the sides of the arm.

Baste the seams of the sleeve, easing the seam at the elbow where indicated by the pattern. Press the seams open lightly, and make the rows of easing stitches between the notches at the sleeve cap. Draw the sleeve at the easing stitches and baste the sleeves into the armholes of the jacket, matching the markings and the notches. Try the jacket on. Pin up the bottom hem of the jacket and turn in the sleeve hems. Try the skirt on under the jacket, and decide where you want all the hems to be. Make sure that the skirt length is in proportion with the length of the jacket. Be sure the sleeves are the right length. Mark the hemlines on the sleeves and the bottom of the jacket with pins. Take the suit off and mark the pinned hemlines with rows of basting thread. Cut the basting that is holding the sleeves in the armholes of the jacket, and remove the sleeves. Stitch the seams of the sleeves permanently and press them open over the sleeve board.

Cut bias strips of the interfacing the length of the bottom of the sleeve around the hemline and 1 inch wider than the depth of the hem. Place the interfacing with one edge on the hemline and pin it to the sleeve. Overlap the ends of the interfacing and sew them to each other with a small row of running stitches. Trim off the seam allowance of the interfacing strip. Catch-stitch the top and bottom of the interfacing strip to the backing of the sleeve. Repeat for the other sleeve. To make turning up the hem of the sleeve easier, slip the sleeve, with the wrong side out, over the sleeve board. Turn the hem up along the basted hemline and pin the raw edge of the hem to the interfacing.

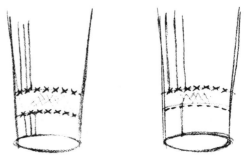

Sew the raw edge of the hem to the interfacing with running stitches. (*Note:* The raw edges of jackets and most coats are left unfinished because they will be covered permanently by the lining.) Press the hems on the sleeve board from the wrong side and then from the right side, with a pressing cloth between the sleeve and the iron.

Sewing the Sleeves into the Jacket

You have already determined how much easing the sleeve will need at the sleeve cap when you drew up the easing threads to baste the sleeves into the jacket. Place the cap of the sleeve over the end of the sleeve board and steam the ease out. Do not allow the iron to rest on the sleeve. Let the sleeve dry before you handle it. Repeat for the other sleeve.

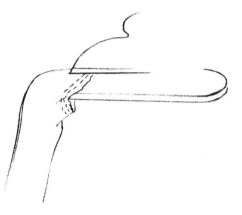

Pin the sleeve back into the armhole, matching the markings, adjust the ease as necessary, and baste around the armhole just inside the seam line. Turn the jacket right-side out and check the fit of the sleeve in the armhole. Be sure that you have not sewn any tucks into the sleeve or the jacket. Stitch around the armhole on the seam line. Make another row of stitches on top of the first row, between the notches, under the arm. Make another row of stitches ¼ inch *inside* the first row. Trim the seam allowance to ¼ inch from the second row of stitches.

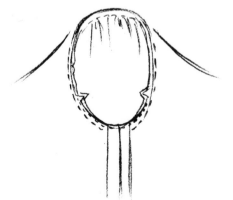

To add support to the shoulders without using shoulder pads, cut a piece of lamb's wool or heavy cotton flannel on the bias; make it 3 inches wide and 5 inches long. Fold one long edge of the rectangle in 1 inch and press. Pin the folded edge to the top of the sleeve and slip-stitch the padding to the sleeve backing.

If you are using commercial shoulder pads, pin them to the seam allowance at the top of the shoulder. Be sure that the pads are not too full, or they will distort the shape of the shoulders of the jacket. Try the jacket on to be sure that the pads are in the right place; adjust them if necessary. Slip-stitch the pad to the seam allowance.

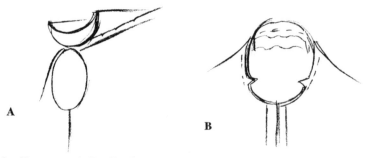

Hem the Bottom of the Jacket

Trim away the seam allowances between the hemline and the raw edge of the jacket. Cut bias strips of interfacing 1 inch wider than the depth of the hem and long enough to fit the bottom of the jacket between the front interfacings. Place the strip on the hemline. Catch-stitch the top and bottom of the interfacing to the backing.

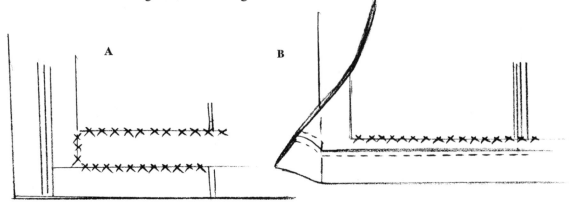

Turn up the jacket along the hemline and the facings, and press lightly. Pin the hem into place. For the front corners of the jacket, turn out the facing and trim off the fabric on the hem that will be covered by the facing, leaving ½ inch of hem fabric. Trim the hem on the facing to ⅝ inch. Clip the seam allowance on the facing and the jacket seam at a line parallel to the top of the turned-up hem, and press the seam open. Using a running stitch, sew the hem to the facing and the interfacing strips on the jacket. Turn the facing back to the inside of the jacket. Make a clip ⅝ inch deep on the facing above the line of the interfacing strip. Turn the bottom of the facing to the inside, forming a ⅝ inch fold. Using a slip-stitch, sew the corner of the facing to itself so it cannot be seen. Catch-stitch the facing to the backing of the jacket, making sure that it doesn't form any bubbles on the right side. If the fabric of the jacket ravels badly, make a row of machine stitches just inside the raw edges of the seam allowances.

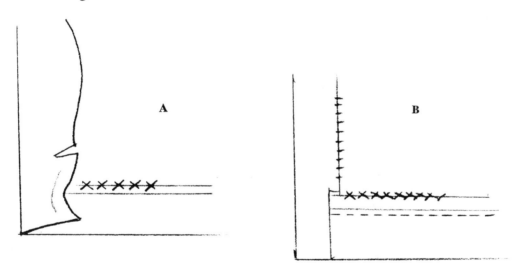

Press the jacket thoroughly and remove any basting that shows on the right side, except for the hand basting on the lapel and collar. The jacket is now ready to be lined. Hang it up on the shaped, man's coat hanger, or leave it on the dress dummy until the lining is ready to be inserted.

Prepare the Lining

Start with the back section of the lining. To form the pleat in the back of the lining (which is necessary to allow for wearing ease in the finished lining), bring the marks for the pleat together, with the right sides of the fabric facing, and pin. Baste for the entire length along the marks. Sew the darts in the back. Press the darts and the pleat, as indicated on the pattern instructions. To hold the pleat in place, make a few cross-stitches at the top of the pleat below the seam allowance. To make the cross-stitches, sew with a single strand of matching silk thread, starting from the wrong side of the lining. Knot the end of the thread and bring it up through all three layers of the pleat. Bring the thread down diagonally and make a right-angle stitch so that it comes up below the first stitch, as shown. Make another diagonal stitch, crossing the first one, and bring the needle up under the first cross-stitch and repeat for the next cross-stitch. When you have made three cross-stitches at the top of the pleat, bring the needle through to the wrong side of the lining and knot. Cut off the thread. Make two more cross-stitches through the pleat at the waistline and the bottom. Make the released darts on the front sections of the jacket, press them as indicated, and cross-stitch through all three layers of the lining, as you did for the back pleat. Sew the front sections of the lining together and sew the underarm seams. Press all the seams open. Make a row of stay-stitching at the back neckline, front sections, and underarms between the notches of the lining, just inside the seam allowances. Sew the seams of the sleeve lining sections together and press the seams open over a sleeve board. Make one row of easing stitches at the cap of the sleeve lining between the notches, just inside the seam line.

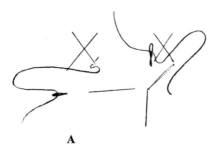

A

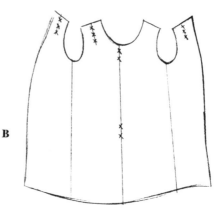

B

Insert the Lining

Press under the seam allowances of the body of the lining down the front sections, across the back shoulders and the back of the neckline, clipping along the seam allowances where necessary.

Turn the jacket inside out, but leave the sleeves right-side out. If you have a dress dummy, work with the jacket placed on it. If not, lay the jacket over the edge of the ironing board. Slip the lining over the jacket, with the wrong sides facing, and pin the lining to the jacket at the armhole and the front shoulder. Turn back the front of the lining to expose the side seam. Pin the side seam allowance of the lining to the side seam allowance of the jacket. Sew the two seam allowances together by hand with long running stitches. Stop the stitches 5 inches above the bottom edge of the jacket. Repeat for the other side. Using running stitches, sew the front shoulder of the jacket to the back shoulder seam allowance. Repeat for the other shoulder. Pin the folded front of the jacket to the front jacket facing. Pin the back neckline of the lining to the back neckline of the jacket. Lap the folded back shoulder of the lining over the front of the lining. Sew the lining to the arm-hole seam allowance with long running stitches, sewing through all layers. Slip-stitch the entire lining to the jacket, starting 5 inches above the bottom at the jacket on one side and sew up the front edge, across the back neckline, and down the other front to within 5 inches of the bottom of the jacket.

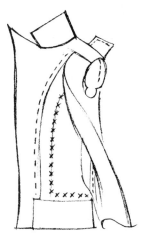

Place the jacket, right-side out on the dress dummy or the hanger, and smooth the bottom of the lining toward the hem of the jacket, being careful not to pull it too tight. Pin the lining to the jacket 2 inches above the hem, lining up the corresponding seams on the lining with those on the jacket. Fold under the lining hem (it should form a fold about an inch deep) so that the folded hem covers the raw edge of the hem by about an inch. Place a row of pins parallel to the hem of the jacket ½ inch from the fold. Remove the pins that were placed about 2 inches above the hem. Look at the jacket from the right side to be sure that the lining is not pulling at the bottom. Turn up the lining along the row of pins and slip-stitch the underneath layer of the lining to the hem of the jacket. The stitches should go through only one layer of the lining and the fabric in the hem of the jacket. Remove the pins and press the folded hem. At the corner of the lining, slip-stitch the edge of the lining for an inch along the bottom of the hem and up the front of the lining to the previous stitching.

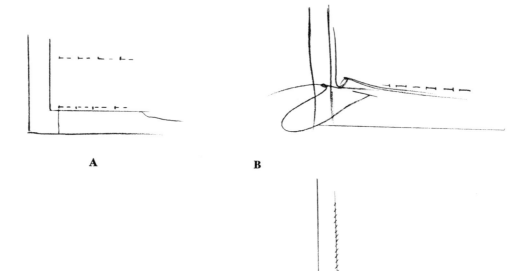

A   B

Insert the Sleeve Lining

Turn the left sleeve of the jacket to the wrong side. Turn the left sleeve lining right-side out. Once you are sure that the sleeve and the sleeve lining match (the double notch at the armhole should be at the back of the jacket), slip the lining over the sleeve. Pin the lining to the jacket at the armhole, matching the marks. Without pulling too tight, draw up the easing thread until the lining fits the armhole. Repeat for the other sleeve. Unpin the sleeve lining and remove it without disturbing the easing thread. Place the lining sleeve cap over the edge of the sleeve board and steam out the ease. Turn under the seam allowance around the armhole and press. Turn the sleeve lining inside out. Place the back seam allowance of the lining on the back seam allowance of the sleeve, having the lining aligned with any markings on the seam. Starting 4 inches above the lower edge, sew the lining seam allowance to the garment seam allowance with very loose running stitches. Stop the stitches 3 inches from the armhole. Turn the lining over the sleeve so that the wrong sides are facing. Pin the top of the folded lining sleeve cap to the jacket, matching the seams and the top of the shoulder. Slip-stitch the lining of the sleeve to the jacket body lining.

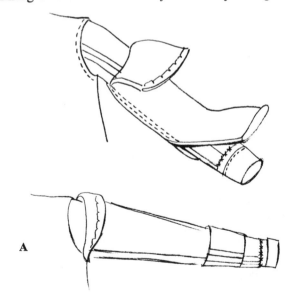

A

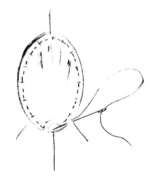

B

Fold the hem of the lining under as much as is needed to have the folded edge of the lining cover the raw edge of the sleeve hem. Place a row of pins ¼ inch above the fold. Make a row of basting stitches just above the row of pins. Repeat for the other sleeve. Remove the pins and try the jacket on. Be sure that the sleeves hang straight, without the lining pulling. If the lining does pull, remove the basting and replace the row of pins, adjusting the sleeve lining until it doesn't pull. Once you are satisfied that the lining fits the sleeve comfortably, without pulling, take the jacket off and replace the basting. With the sleeve inside out, turn up the lining along the basting and slip-stitch the underside of the lining to the jacket hem. Sew through the underside of the lining and the sleeve hem, as you did for the bottom of the jacket hem. When you have finished the slip-stitching, press the lining over the hem (it should form a ¼ inch fold).

Finishing the Jacket

Finish the jacket by sewing the buttons to the left front, following the instructions given in the section on buttons, page 249. Button the jacket and try it on. If the front of the jacket opens between the buttons or above them, sew on silk-covered snaps at the points where the jacket opens.

Coats

If you want to make a tailored coat, the instructions given in this chapter will apply—with one possible addition and one possible change.

The addition is that of an interlining, which can be added to the coat for warmth. The interlining should be cut from the same pattern pieces as the coat lining, but eliminate the pleat in the back of the interlining. Prepare the back of the lining as instructed, sewing and cross-stitching the pleat into place. Once that has been done, baste the lining to the interlining and handle the two pieces as one to complete the lining.

Most, but not all, coats are made with a free-hanging hem. Finish the bottom hem of the coat the same way as instructed for the jacket hem. Finish the bottom of the lining as best suited for the fabric (seam binding, overcast stitch, and so forth) and hem the lining to itself. Slip-stitch the bottom corner of the lining to the coat facing and make thread bar tacks at the seams to hold the lining to the coat and prevent it from twisting.

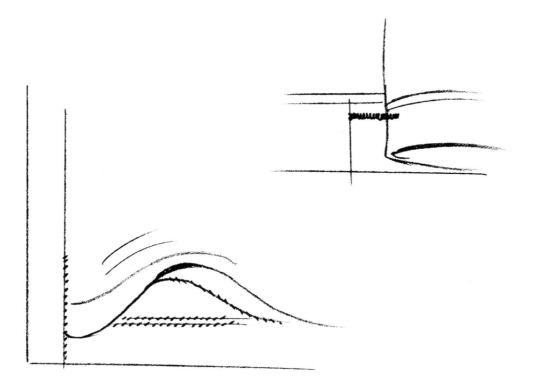

CHAPTER

ALTERING
READY-MADE
CLOTHES

Now that you have been making some of your own clothes and understand the fitting and construction of them, the knowledge you have acquired will help you to understand how ready-made clothes are made and how they should fit. While you can't remake ready-made clothes, you can make minor changes in the fit by making alterations. But before you start altering the clothes you own, or want to buy, you have to know what is possible and what is not. Except for changing hem lengths for fashion changes, all alterations are made to change the fit of the garment. From fitting the clothes you have been making, you know how clothes are supposed to fit. This will enable you to tell when trying on a ready-made garment whether the fit is correct, and if not, why not.

Apply the same rules when fitting a ready-made garment that you use when judging the fit of the clothes you sew. Refer to the chapter on altering patterns for the fitting rules that apply to all clothes. When you try on a ready-

338

made garment, check the same points: the fit of the bodice, the placement of the bust darts, the fit of the waistline seam, and the amount of fullness or tightness in general. If the garment is a full size too large or too small, you cannot remake it. However, if the changes are minor, with the help of this chapter, you will be able to make your own alterations.

The first rule to remember is that you can usually take a garment in to make it smaller, but with very few exceptions, you cannot let it out to make it larger. Except for raising and lowering hems, shortening sleeves, and moving the buttons on the garment, all the alterations described here apply to dresses and skirts. Major alterations on a tailored coat or jacket require remaking the garment which is either impossible or not worth the effort.

Ripping out Seams

Whenever you have to take out a row of stitching, use a pair of embroidery scissors and work on one side of the seam. Carefully cut every third or fourth stitch all along the seam. When you have finished clipping the stitches, pull the thread on the other side of the seam. Do not attempt to rip the seam apart, as you may cut or tear the fabric.

When you have to remove a zipper, carefully cut all the rows of stitching, working in the same manner as described above.

To take out a hem that has been chain-stitched, cut the thread and free one end of the thread, and pull (moving from left to right). The entire length of the thread will come right out.

Raising a Waistline

If you tend to be short-waisted, one of the most common problems you will encounter is a dress with a waistline seam that falls below your natural waistline. To alter such a dress, it will be necessary to take out the waistline seam and resew the skirt to the bodice, taking up the amount needed.

With the dress on, tie a piece of yarn around your waist. Place pins around the entire dress under the yarn (you may have to ask someone to help you). Take the dress off and replace the row of pins with a tailor's chalk marking. Remove the stitches that hold the waistline seam. If there is a zipper in the dress, remove it from the bottom until it is free above the chalk line. Pin the skirt to the bodice, with old seam line on the skirt matching the new seam line chalked on the bodice. Start by pinning at the center front and back. Then pin any matching darts on the skirt, the bodice, and the side seams. If you find that there is too much fabric in the bodice and it cannot be eased in to fit the skirt, you will have to take in the darts and the side seams. The bodice darts must match the skirt darts.

Machine baste the skirt to the bodice along the new bodice seam line. Try the dress on. Once the bodice fits the skirt evenly and the waistline seam fits you perfectly, sew the new seam permanently. Trim the bodice seam allowance to match that of the skirt. Sew the zipper back into place, following the instructions in Chapter 5 for applying zippers.

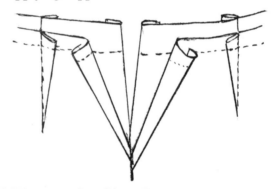

Taking in the Waist and Hips of a One-Piece Dress

If the shoulders and the armholes of a one-piece dress fit, but it is too large through the waist and hips, it can be taken in at the side seams.

Try on the dress inside out. Pin it at the side seams, taking in an even amount at both sides. Do not take it in too much, and be sure that the seams hang straight and that the dress is comfortable when you stand and sit. Take the dress off, and transfer the pin markings with tailor's chalk. Take the hem down at the sides and press the side seams together. Stitch along the markings, keeping the new seam parallel to the old one. Remove the old seam stitching and press the seam open. Resew the hem where you have let it down.

Raising a Hem

Take the hem down and press out the old hemline. Try the dress or skirt on, and mark the new hemline with tailor's chalk and pins, or use a chalk marker. If the new hem is deeper than 3 inches, measure the difference and cut it off. If you have cut off the hem, finish the raw edge in the way best suited to the fabric. Pin the new hem, making sure that the hem is even all around. Hand sew the new hem.

Taking in a Skirt

A skirt that is too large through the hips is taken in at the side seams in the same way as a dress. The only difference is that you may have to release the waistband, as shown, and remove the side zipper if there is one. When you have completed the alteration, replace the zipper and restitch the waistband and the hem if you have let it down.

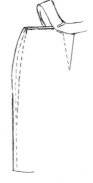

Shortening Sleeves

If you have a dress, blouse, jacket, or coat with sleeves with plain, hemmed edges (no cuffs or overlapping closings), the sleeves can be shortened easily.

For a dress or blouse, try on the garment and fold in the hem of the sleeve until the length is right. Mark at the fold with pins. Take the hem down, and with the sleeve wrong-side out, slip it over a sleeve board. Refold the hem around the sleeve at the new hemline. Pin and sew by hand. Press out the old hemline over the sleeve board.

To shorten the sleeves of a jacket or coat that has been lined, carefully cut the lining away from the sleeve. Mark and pin the new hem as for a dress. Press out the old hemline and sew the new hem. Once the outer fabric has been sewn, fold the lining in and pin it to the sleeve. Try the garment on to be sure that the sleeve lining is not pulling when you bend your arm. Slip-stitch the lining to the sleeve, leaving a ¼ inch margin on the inside.

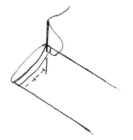

How to Tell When You Can Let out Seams

You can only let out a seam if there is enough seam allowance that has not been clipped, if the fabric has not faded, and if the old stitching will not leave marks in the fabric.

To let out the waist and hips of a one-piece dress, measure yourself where the dress is too tight and divide the measurement in half. If there is enough fabric in the seam allowance to allow for this measurement, plus ⅝ inch more, then you can let out the seam. Mark the amount to be let out on the seam allowance on the inside of the dress and press the seams together. Stitch along the markings, keeping the new seam parallel to the old stitching.

Take the hem down if the new seam extends to the hem. Cut out the old stitching and press the seam open. If the new seam extends to the hem, you will have to replace any old seam binding with a new, longer binding. Rehem the skirt.

The same alteration can be made on a skirt that is too small, as long as you don't have to alter it at the waist, which would require a new waistband. Follow the same instructions for letting out a dress that are given above.

How to Tell When You Can Let a Hem Down

You can let a hem down if there is enough fabric in the hem, or you can make a faced hem if the skirt is just long enough when the hem is let down. You can only let a hem down if the fabric has not faded, and if you are sure that you can press out the old hemline. The only way to tell if the old hemline will press out is by doing it, and for this reason, it is best not to buy a new garment that is too short.

If you want to let down the hem of something you already own, remove the old hem and press it out. Try on the garment and mark the new hem with a yardstick and pins, or use a chalk marker. Pin the new hemline and sew by hand.

If the length of the skirt is right with the hem let down, but there isn't enough fabric to make a new hem, you can make a faced hem. You can buy ready-made hem facing in taffeta or cotton, which comes 2 inches wide and with the edges turned under ¼ inch, or you can make a 2-inch strip of bias facing out of a fabric that is lighter than the garment to be hemmed. See Chapter 5, page 257 for instructions on how to make the strip of true bias. Make the strip longer than the length of the hem. Turn it under ¼ inch along one side of the length and stitch. Mark the new hem on the skirt and trim it to ½ inch below the marking line. With the right sides together, pin the bias strip to the skirt, opening out the ¼ inch fold if you are using ready-made facing, forming a fold at the beginning of the stitching, as shown. Sew the strip ¼ inch from the edge of the hem, overlapping the edge of the facing when you get to the beginning of the stitching. Press the facing down and turn the skirt up along the new hemline. Slip-stitch the opening in the facing and hem the facing to the skirt.

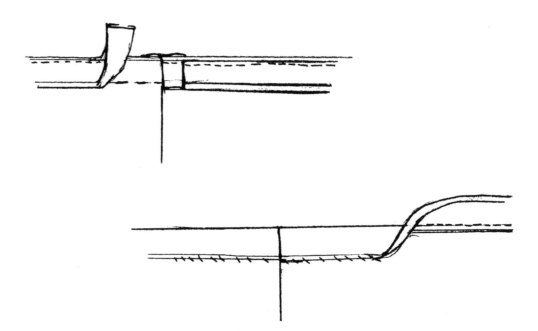

Lengthening Sleeves and Pants' Legs

Again, sleeves and pants' legs can only be lengthened if there is enough hem allowance, and if you can press out the old hemline.

For pants and unlined sleeves, let the old hem down, slip the leg or the sleeve over a sleeve board, and press the old hem out. Try the garment on and mark the new hem. Take it off, turn the sleeve or pants' leg inside out, and slip it over the sleeve board. Fold to the new hem, marking and pinning evenly all around. Hand sew the new hems.

Jacket and coat sleeves can only be lengthened if there is enough fabric, and you can't tell this until you have cut the lining away from the sleeve. Mark and pin the sleeve as directed above, then fold the lining, and pin it to the sleeve. Try the garment on. If there is enough lining fabric, it will not pull or strain when you bend your arms. If there is enough, unpin the lining and stitch the sleeve hems. Pin the lining back to the sleeve and slip-stitch in place.

Move Buttons to Make the Garment Tighter or Looser

Jackets, coats, and blouses can sometimes be made tighter or looser by moving the buttons, but you have to be careful or you can throw the hang and fit of the garment out of shape if you place the buttons too far in or too far out, or if they are not lined up evenly. To find out whether moving the buttons will work, pin the garment closed through the buttonholes to where you want the buttons to be. You must line the pins up in a straight line, keeping them parallel to the old button placement. If this does not distort the side seams or the hang of the garment, and it changes the fit sufficiently, remove the buttons and sew them where the pins are. See page 249 for instructions on how to sew on buttons.

MENDING

By mending the garments you have made or those that you have bought, you can extend the life of your wardrobe. Before you start, decide whether the garment is worth the effort needed to mend it. If the fabric is faded, or if the garment is so out of style that it spends most of its time hanging in your closet, then it is better to get rid of it and not waste the time that could be spent making something new. If it is something that is fairly new or dearly loved, then a little work will make it wearable again.

With most ready-made clothes, mending them before they need it will save you from spending extra time later. Whenever you buy something new, go over it with the following checklist in mind, and fix whatever has to be corrected before you even wear the garment.

Check the buttons and any hooks and eyes. If they are hanging by a thread, secure them before they fall off. If the buttons are already falling off, take them off and sew them back on. (See the instructions for sewing on buttons that are given on page 249.) Reinforce the stitching on hooks and eyes by going over the previous stitching with a thread of suitable weight.

If the garment has been sewn with very large stitches the seams that receive the most stress are likely to come open. These seams are the underarm seams of a sleeve, the sleeve seams, and the crotch seams of pants. Thread your machine with matching thread and stitch directly over the old seam, using a fairly small stitch (12 stitches to the inch). For pants' crotch seams, cut a piece of seam binding the length of the curved seam, pin it directly over the old seam, and sew a new seam, catching the seam binding in it.

Turn the garment wrong-side out and look at the stitching on the pockets. If it is made with very large stitches, or if the stitching is very close to the raw edge, sew a new seam with smaller stitches inside the old one. If you have a zigzag machine, overcast the pocket edges.

If the buttonholes have been made with a single row of machine stitches, go over them by hand or with your machine. (See the section called Buttonholes, page 251, for instructions.)

Seams

If the seam of a garment opens without the fabric of the garment tearing, the repair job is fairly simple.

For a seam in an unlined garment, press the seam allowances together, stitch a few inches over the old stitching before the opening, stitch the opening on the seam line, and stitch for a few inches after the opening. It is wise in cases like this to sew over the entire old seam, because if it opened in one place, it is likely to open elsewhere. When you have finished sewing the seam, press it open, or press it in the same direction that it originally faced.

For a seam in a lined garment, sew by hand from the right side of the garment. Take a stitch in the fold of the seam, then another one in the opposite side a little further on; continue taking two or three small running stitches at a time. To end off the thread, take several small running stitches in the seam itself, several inches beyond the opening, and cut the thread. See next page.

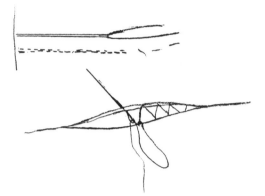

Zippers

If the thread holding the zipper breaks, use matching thread and sew the zipper back into place, using the zipper foot on your machine. If the zipper itself breaks, carefully cut it out and replace it with a zipper of the correct size, following the instructions for inserting zippers given on pages 182-194.

Hems

For all but the most casual of sportswear and housedresses, the machine-made hem should be taken out and replaced with a hand-sewn hem. If part of the hem comes down, take out the existing thread for a few inches on either side of the break, thread it through a needle, and tie it off in a knot. With new, matching thread, sew along the part of the hem that has come down. If the seam binding has unravelled or become torn, cut out the stitches holding the hem. Carefully cut the stitches holding the seam binding, and remove it. Replace the torn seam binding with new seam binding in a matching color. Resew the hem.

Turning the Collar and Cuff of a Blouse or Shirt

If a blouse or a man's shirt shows wear at the collar and cuffs, but does not show wear on the rest of the garment, it can be given new life by turning the collar and cuffs. (*Note:* You cannot turn a collar that has bones sewn into the back of it.)

With a contrasting color thread, mark the center of the collar and the cuffs. Determine the center by folding the collar and the cuffs in half. Make a basting mark at the center of the neckband and the sleeve. Mark the neck-band at the ends of the collar.

Carefully cut the thread holding the collar to the neckband, and pull out all of the loose threads. Remove the collar and reverse it. Insert it into the neckband, matching the markings at the center and the ends. Pin it place, and baste through the neckband and the collar. Machine stitch over the original stitching line with matching color thread.

Carefully cut the threads holding the cuff, and remove all the loose threads. Turn the cuff around and insert the sleeve back into it. Baste through both layers of the cuff and the sleeve. Machine stitch along the original seam line with matching color thread.

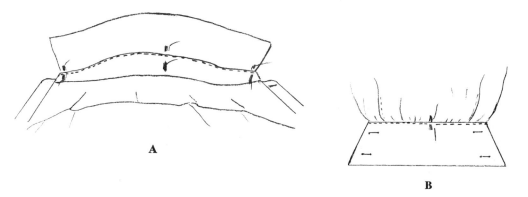

A   B

Replacing the Lining of a Jacket or Coat

If you have a jacket or a coat that still has a lot of good wear in it, but the lining is tearing and wearing through, it can be relined. This is a fairly involved job, so don't attempt it unless the jacket or coat is really worth it.

Cut the lining out of the jacket, being careful not to tear it further. Cut the lining pieces apart at the seam lines. Cut the separate lining pieces apart and press them carefully. Buy a new lining of similar weight to the one you are replacing. Use the old lining pieces as a pattern to cut out the new lining, being careful to note the width of the old seam lines. Sew the lining together and insert it into the jacket. (Follow the instructions given in Chapter 6, Tailoring, for inserting a lining into a jacket or a coat by hand.)

Tears and Holes

For casual clothes and sportswear that have been torn, the quickest way to repair them is with an iron-on patch. Iron-on patches or long strips of iron-on fabric can be found in the notions department or in the five-and-ten store. For an invisible repair, choose the color that most matches the garment, and cut a patch that will cover the tear. Round off the corners of the patch. Turn the garment wrong-side out on an ironing board and place the edges of the tear together. Place the patch over the tear, with shiny side down. Set the iron for the temperature called for in the instructions that come with the iron-on fabric—usually dry, at a cotton setting. Place the iron over the patch and allow it to rest on the patch for a minute. Do not slide the iron, as this will cause the patch to shift. Let the fabric cool, and test to see that the edges of the patch don't lift from the fabric. If they do, place the hot iron over the patch for a few more seconds.

To patch children's clothes and sportswear that have tears or holes, cut the iron-on patch in the shape of a square with rounded corners, or cut an animal or flower design out of the iron-on fabric. Choose a contrasting color, and let the patch become part of the design of the garment. Iron it on the right side of the garment, using the procedure described above.

If a garment tears or has a hole in it, and if you have some of the fabric from which it was made, you can make a fabric patch that will not be too noticeable. Trim away the fabric from around the hole along the straight and crosswise grains of the fabric, forming a square or a rectangle. Cut a patch from the original fabric in the same shape as the hole, but 1 inch larger all around. Clip the corners of the square or the rectangular hole at an angle ½-inch deep, as shown. Fold the edges of the hole to the inside. Working from the wrong side of the garment, pin the patch in place under the hole. Stitch the garment to the patch along the turned-in edges, pivoting the stitching at the corner. To make the patch extra strong, topstitch around the edges of the patch from the right side.

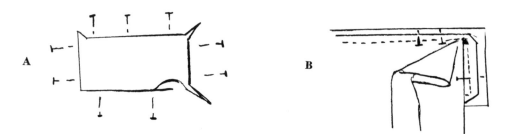

A   B

For a patch that is not as strong but less visible, prepare the hole as described, and pin the patch under the hole. Slip-baste the patch to the garment, working from the right side. For instructions on slip-basting, see page 309.

Large suede patches that are prepunched and ready to be sewn on by hand are available in notions departments and in five-and-ten stores. These are best used on the worn elbows of sports jackets and for the worn knees of casual pants and children's pants.

Darning

By Hand—Use a thread pulled from the hem edge or seam allowance of the garment, or use a darning cotton in a color that matches the fabric. In emergencies, for repairing a woolen garment, a human hair can be used instead of thread if you can find one long enough. Use a fine, sharp needle and work from the right side of the garment. Do not knot the end of the thread, and use short pieces of thread. Bring the edges of the tear together with a diagonal stitch, as shown, before you start the darning. Start by bringing the thread up from the wrong side of the fabric and work in back and forth stitches over the tear, taking up single threads of the garment as you stitch. Weave the thread in and out of the garment fabric. Make the first row of darning stitches on the crosswise grain, and then go over them, working on the lengthwise grain of the fabric.

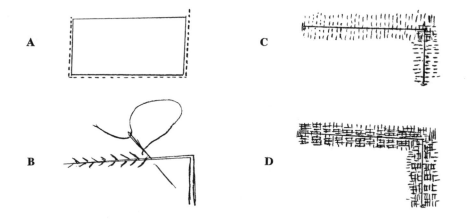

By Machine—If you have a zigzag machine that does darning, follow the instructions given in the sewing machine manual, but remember that machine darning is very visible, consequently it should only be used for sheets and clothes where it won't matter.

Braid

A tailored jacket that has become worn at the edges of the collar, the lapels, and the cuffs can be given a new look by sewing decorative braid to the edges. Buy the braid in a color and a width that will complement the jacket. Sew the braid to the collar, down the front of the lapels, and around the bottom of the sleeves. To sew the braid at the collar and lapel, it will be necessary to miter it. To form the miter, edgestitch along the inner edge of the braid to within the seam allowance of the corner. Fold the braid back along itself and press. Make a diagonal row of stitches through the garment and the braid, as shown. Press the braid over the stitching and continue edge-stitching. Once the braid is edgestitched on the inner edge, go over it again, edgestitching on the outer edge of the braid. At the bottom of the sleeve, edgestitch on the inner edge first, folding it under ½ inch when you come to the end of the braid, and then edgestitch on the outer edge.

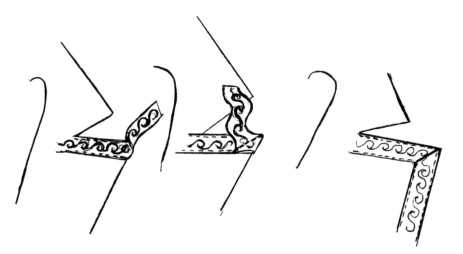

LINGERIE

Slips

Reinforce straps before they tear out. Using small running stitches, hand sew over the existing stitches, or use small machine stitches.

If the slip is worn and the area around the strap is beginning to fray, darn over the worn spot from the wrong side of the fabric. If the area is very worn, sew a small piece of ribbon over the spot, using small running stitches.

For a strap that has come loose, sew it back in the original position, using small hemming stitches, or use small machine stitches. If the slip has a facing, cut the stitches holding the facing to the slip, and insert the strap between the facing and the slip. Be sure that the strap extends down far enough so that it won't come out again. Pin the facing to the slip, enclosing the strap, and machine stitch close to the edge through the facing, the strap, and the slip.

REPLACING THE STRAPS

If the straps have become worn, replace them with a ribbon of the same width or with lingerie fabric. Cut the fabric strips the width of the strap, plus ½-inch seam allowance. Sew the strips with the right sides facing, and turn them right-side out with a loop turner. If the strap is fairly wide, cut the fabric in strips twice the width of the strap, plus ½ inch. Fold in ¼ inch on each side of the strip and press. Fold the strip in half and press. Machine stitch as close as possible to the folded edge. Make the strips as long as the original straps, and cut the old straps off. Pin the new strap in place, and sew with small running stitches or small machine stitches.

ADJUSTABLE STRAPS

Make the new strap the same width and length as the old one, using either ribbon or lingerie fabric. Remove one strap and leave the other one on the slip. Make the new strap, using the old one as a guide. These straps are usually made in one long and one short section. Place the short strap through the metal loop without a bar. Thread the long strip through the metal loop with a center bar, then through the first metal loop, and then back to the other one. Place the end of the strap over the bar and form a hem. Sew the hem in place, making the hem bulky enough to prevent the strap from slipping through the holder. Sew the strap in place, and repeat for the other strap.

SHORTENING THE STRAPS

Make the adjustment at the inside back of the slip. Make a loop in the strap, shortening the strap as much as needed. Sew the loop in place by hand or with small machine stitches. Do not cut off the loop.

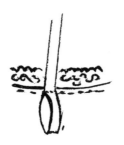

Small Tears or Runs

Small tears or runs in a knitted fabric can be repaired by hand or by machine. To fix a run by hand, work from the wrong side and make small overhand stitches past the ends of the run, catching the dropped stitch. For small tears, place the edges of the tear together, with the right sides of the fabric facing, and sew by machine in a small seam.

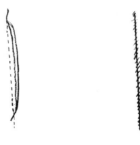

Lace

If the lace on the edge of the slip is slightly torn, sew the edges together by hand with matching thread, making the stitches as unnoticeable as possible. If the lace is torn and badly frayed, it will have to be replaced. Buy a lace that is the same width as the one you are replacing. Measure along the old lace to determine how much you will need. Before you cut off the old lace note carefully how it was sewn on. Sew the new lace on by hand in the same place as the old lace.

The worn edge of a slip without lace may be renewed by sewing a strip of lace over the edges in the same way.

Half-Slips

To Replace an Elastic Waistband

Cut off the old elastic and cut the new one the same length, plus ½ inch for the overlap. Pin the elastic to the right side of the slip, over the waist, and turn in ¼ inch of the elastic where the ends overlap. Sew by machine, using a straight stitch or a zigzag stitch. Stitch along the top edge of the elastic, stretching the elastic as it goes under the needle. Make another row along the bottom of the elastic in the same way.

To Replace an Elastic in a Casing

Make an inch-long cut into the stitching that holds the casing in place. Pull the old elastic out through the opening. Buy a new elastic the same width and length as the old one, plus 1 inch. Pin a small safety pin to one end of the elastic, and thread it through the casing. Hold the other end of the elastic to keep it from slipping into the casing. When the elastic is threaded through the casing, overlap the ends for ½ inch, and sew them together securely by hand or by machine. Let the elastic go into the casing, and sew the opening closed.

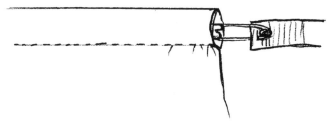

Girdles

TO REINFORCE THE GARTER JOINING

Stitch through the girdle where the garter is attached—sewing by machine or by hand—to prevent the garter from pulling out.

REPLACING THE GARTER

You can buy new garters in the notions department. Carefully cut the stitches holding the old garter, and remove it. Place the new garter in the same place, and machine stitch the elastic and the girdle.

Bras

REPLACING THE BACK CLOSURE

Buy a new back closure the same width as the one you are replacing. Cut the stitches holding the old closure, and remove it. Insert the new closure, being sure that you have the hooks facing inward and the eyes facing outward, and insert the elastic between the two layers of fabric. Sew in place by machine, following the old stitching line.

HOUSEHOLD MENDING

Repair holes and tears in sheets and bedspreads either by patching or by darning. (See pages 350-352 for instructions.)

Sheets

For a sheet that is worn in the middle, but which still has strong fabric at the outer edges, cut it lengthwise down the center, sew the selvage edges together in a seam down the center, turn in ½-inch hems on the new sides, and stitch into place.

Pillowcases

For a pillowcase that has frayed at the edges or corners, turn it inside out, and sew a new, deeper seam that will enclose the frayed edge. As long as the seam is not too deep, the pillow will still fit into the case.

Blankets

For thin or torn spots in a blanket, darn the spot with matching thread, following the instructions for darning.

Blanket Binding

The binding of a blanket usually wears thin before the rest of the blanket and must be replaced. Buy ready-made blanket binding in the notions department; it should be the same width as the old binding. If you cannot match the color, choose a color that will contrast nicely with the color of the blanket. Remove the old binding and pin the new one over the edges. Pin the corners, as shown, and stitch the binding on the edges with a long straight stitch (8 to 10 stitches to the inch) or with a wide zigzag stitch, sewing through and both layers of the binding. Slip-stitch the corners of the binding together.

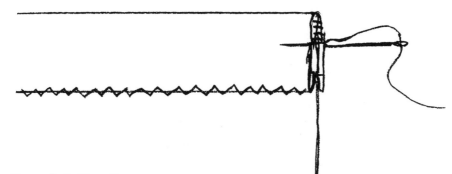

Terrycloth Towels

To give a new look to towels that have worn at the end edges, buy a 2-inch wide braid the length of both edges of the towel. Preshrink the braid by soaking it in hot water for a few minutes. Cut the frayed edge and turn under. Stitch the braid to the edges of the towel, with one row of stitching on each long edge of the braid.

Worn towels can be used to make a bathmat. Use two towels of the same size and sew them together around the edges, with the wrong sides facing. Place the towel that is most worn on the bottom. Sew braid or ball fringe around the edges of the towels.

Fine Table Linens

Holes and tears in tablecloths and napkins can be repaired so that the mending is not noticeable if you follow the instructions for darning given on pages 351-352.

For an even less noticeable repair for areas that have worn thin, you can reweave the area. Reweaving can only be done with threads pulled from the hem of the piece you are repairing. Place the worn area in an embroidery hoop. Study the structure of the woven threads, and with a long, threaded needle, duplicate the weave. Working from the right side of the fabric, weave through the lengthwise threads. After the lengthwise threads are finished, weave the crosswise threads in the same way. It may help you when doing this work to use a magnifying glass. Press the area with a steam iron after you have finished. This method also can be used to repair garments that have worn thin. It takes patience and a steady hand, but the results are well worth it.

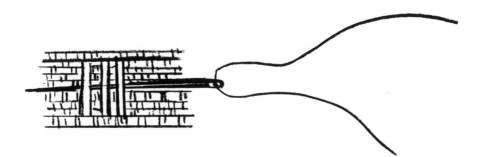

CHAPTER

9

SEWING FOR CHILDREN

When you sew for children, you will use the same sewing techniques that you use to make your own garments. Most children's clothes are simpler in design than adults' clothes, and you will soon find that you will be able to make attractive things very quickly, and save a lot of money into the bargain.

The first thing to do is determine the child's pattern size, as you did for yourself. The important thing to remember is that children's patterns are sold according to the child's measurements, and not age, as two children of the same age can vary in size. The first important measurement to take is the chest or breast size. Buy a pattern based on this measurement, and alter the rest of the pattern if necessary. Make a column, listing the child's measurements: chest, waist, hips, back waist length, and arm length. Compare them to the pattern chart sizes to determine the size you should buy. Do not buy the pattern a size larger in hopes that the child will grow into it; the result will be a garment that is just too big, and neither you nor the child will be happy with the results. By the time he or she grows into the garment, it will probably be worn out.

Measure a child for pants in the same way as you did for yourself, and make any alterations necessary on the pattern before you cut the fabric. Refer to Chapter 2 to refresh your memory about taking measurements and making pattern alterations. Measure a growing child frequently, as his or her measurements will change very quickly, and you must change the pattern size as needed.

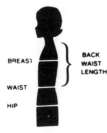

BREAST

BACK
WAIST
LENGTH

WAIST

HIP

GIRLS'

Girls' patterns are designed for the girl who has not yet begun to mature. See chart below for approximate heights without shoes.

Size	7	8	10	12	14
Breast	26	27	28½	30	32
Waist	23	23½	24½	25½	26½
Hip	27	28	30	32	34
Back Waist Length	11½	12	12¾	13½	14¼
Approx. Heights	50 "	52 "	56 "	58½"	61 "

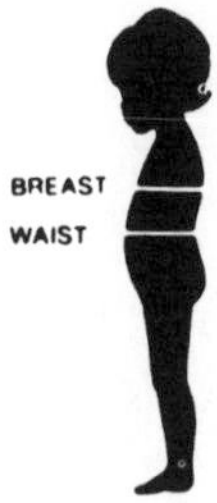

CHILDREN'S MEASUREMENTS

Measure around the breast, but not too snugly. Toddler patterns are designed for a figure between that of a baby and child.

Dress Lengths from Back Neck Base to Lower Edge

Size	½	1	2	3	4	5	6	6X
Toddler	14"	15"	16"	17"	18"			
Child		18"	19"	20"	21"	23"	25"	26"

TODDLERS'

Size	½	1	2	3	4
Breast	19	20	21	22	23
Waist	19	19½	20	20½	21

CHILDREN'S

Size	1	2	3	4	5	6	6X
Breast	20	21	22	23	24	25	25½
Waist	19½	20	20½	21	21½	22	22½
Hip				24	25	26	26½
Back Waist Length	8¼	8½	9	9½	10	10½	10¾
Approx. Heights	31"	34"	37"	40"	43"	46"	48"

BREAST

WAIST

BREAST

WAIST

Courtesy of Butterick Patterns

Growth Tucks

Growth tucks can be made along the crosswise grain of the garment and then carefully cut out to add needed length to the garment as the child grows. In order to have extra fabric to allow for these tucks, it will be necessary to alter the pattern before you cut. Once you have the pattern in the right size, draw a crosswise line on the lower bodice and/or above the hem of the skirt. Cut the pattern along these lines and spread the pattern to lengthen it. Spread the pattern 1 inch and tape the pattern to tissue paper with transparent tape. Lengthen both the back and front sections. Cut the garment according to the pattern instructions and mark the pieces of the garment along the two lines where it was lengthened.

After you have made the garment according to the pattern instructions, bring the fabric together along the two lines marked, and sew a tuck. The tuck can be made on the outside of the garment, where it will show and become part of the design of the garment. Or the tuck can be hidden by sewing it on the garment, so that just a seam will show on the outside. If you want to hide the tuck further, sew a piece of decorative braid or rickrack over the tuck. This will be removed later when you let the tuck out. If your sewing machine sews a chain-stitch, use this to sew the tuck; it will be easier to remove. Be sure that the fabric used when making growth tucks is colorfast, or the fabric inside the tuck will not match the rest of the garment if it has faded. If the sewing of the tuck shows after you have removed it, sew a couple of rows of braid or rickrack over it.

One other way of cutting children's clothes so that they can be let out later is to cut wider seam allowances at the side seams. Sew the garment along the original seam line, and sew another seam inside the wide seam allowance when needed. Taper the new seam from the old one under the arm so that you won't have to resew the armhole. Also, add a few inches to the hem of a dress or skirt so that the hem can be let down later. This can be done only with lightweight fabrics, as a too-deep hem will not hang correctly in a heavy fabric.

Choosing Fabrics for Children's Clothes

Wherever possible, avoid fabrics that have to be dry-cleaned, not only because they are less practical, but because children can develop a skin reaction to the chemicals used in cleaning. Use dry-cleanable fabrics for outer wear only.

Never buy a fabric that feels in the least bit rough or scratchy to the hand, as the child will be miserable in the garment and may even develop a skin irritation. A lot of children are sensitive to wool worn next to the skin, especially around the neck and shoulders. Unless you are sure that your child does not have this sensitivity, use woolens for skirts, pants, and outer wear only.

Children usually like clear, bright colors and interesting prints. An older girl will probably insist on helping choose the fabric she likes. To avoid a disastrous selection, like purple satin for a school dress, preselect a few fabrics that you think are suitable, and have the child choose what she likes from your selection. In general, choose sturdy, washable fabrics. In the winter, several layers of clothes (a jacket worn over a lighter blouse, for example) are more comfortable than one garment made in a heavy fabric. Avoid really expensive fabrics for all but special occasions, as they will be worn out or grown out of too quickly to warrant the expense.

For everyday clothes, choose denim, corduroy, cotton broadcloth, seersucker, piqué, gingham, lightweight woolens and blends, knits, and most combinations of cotton and synthetic fibers.

One of the most charming fabrics for dressy winter clothes is cotton velveteen, which is not expensive and is sturdy. Other good dressy fabrics for winter are taffeta, wool or synthetic challis, Viyella, which is a blend of cotton and wool, and printed pinwale corduroy. For summer dressy clothes, use cotton or synthetic voiles, cotton satin, cotton chintz from the upholstery fabric department, and cotton dotted Swiss.

If you are making a garment out of a washable fabric, be sure that it and all the trimmings, facings, or linings you use are preshrunk and colorfast.

Choosing Pattern Styles

Most pattern styles for younger children are simple and classic. For older children, the styles are usually versions of the curernt teen-age or adult fashions.

Buttons and zippers should be placed where the child can reach them, so that he or she can learn to work the fasteners without help.

Finish all seam allowances by overcasting by hand or with a zigzag stitch. For even sturdier seams, make either self-bound, French, or flat felled seams. See pages 000–000 for instructions on how to construct these seams.

Except for special occasion clothes, avoid fussy details of design, such as ruffles and other loose trims, as they are likely to be torn easily. Patch pockets are also easy victims to a child's wearing.

Appliqués, braid, rickrack, and other trims which are sewn flat to the garment are marvelous for children's clothes. Use your imagination, but don't overdo it. The best rule for children's design is keep the garment as simple and as comfortable as possible.

CHAPTER 10

SEWING FOR
THE HOME

When choosing fabrics for decorating—that is, to make curtains, draperies, slipcovers, and decorative cushions and pillows—you have to take into consideration many of the same factors that apply to selecting fabrics for clothes. The fiber content, weight, texture, and general appearance of the fabric must be suitable for the job it is going to do. A fabric suitable for delicate curtains, for example, would be completely wrong if you attempted to make slipcovers out of it.

The first thing to decide is what you want the fabric for. If you are going to make a slipcover for one or two chairs, you have to consider the colors and style of the rest of the room. If you are starting from the beginning and are redoing an entire room, you must decide whether the room will be formal or casual, and you must therefore choose the drapery, curtain, and slipcover fabrics accordingly. Decide on the main colors for the room, and coordinate the colors of the fabrics so that the overall effect will be pleasing. Determine whether you want to use a printed fabric, and if so, where the print will go. Printed draperies may match the slipcovers, or you may decide to match the print of the draperies to the printed wallpaper, in which case matching printed slipcovers would be too much.

Fabrics for decorating are roughly divided into two categories. The first category is formal, which includes satins, velvets, damasks, brocades, failles, and taffetas. These are usually used with period furniture to create a formal, elegant effect.

The second category is casual, which encompasses a large range of fabrics, including some which are usually used for making clothes. Some of these fabrics are chintz, printed fabrics which can range from light-weight lawn to heavy cottons with a linenlike appearance, polished cotton, corduroy, burlap, eyelet-embroidered cotton, which is usually white, sheers such as ninon, which can be embroidered or not, organdy, dotted Swiss, and special curtain fabrics such as Fiberglas, and synthetic blends.

When you begin a decorating project, start by looking in the special department of the store devoted to furnishing fabrics, or go to a store which sells these fabrics exclusively. Many stores will lend you large swatches of the fabrics you are interested in so that you can see how they will actually look in the room. Furnishing fabrics are usually wider than the fabrics intended for dressmaking and are therefore easier to handle, but if you are doing a casual room and cannot find what you are looking for in the usual departments, look at "dress" fabrics. If you find something there that pleases you, it can be used for curtains and decorative pillows.

Once you have decided on the color or print, there are a few other points to take into consideration. The fiber construction will determine whether the fabric is washable, and many fabrics now come with special finishes to make them stain-resistant. Be sure that the fabric is colorfast so that your beautiful draperies won't fade after only a year's wear.

The next important thing to consider is the use of the fabric. For example, slipcovers must be made of a sturdy medium- to heavyweight fabric so that they can take the wear that will be given them and also so that they won't stretch out of shape while you are making them. Curtains and café curtains can be made of any of the fabrics in the casual range, from sheer to light- or medium-weight, depending on the desired effect. Draperies are usually made of medium- to heavyweight fabrics; again the weight of the fabric will determine the finished effect of the draperies. For lined draperies, sateen in a neutral color is the most effective lining. Pillows and cushions can be made of almost any fabric except sheers.

The texture of the fabric will also determine the finished effect. If you are considering fabrics of different textures, be sure that they combine for a harmonizing effect.

Prepare the fabric in the same way as you would for dressmaking. Preshrink any washable fabric, be sure that the fabric is grain-perfect, and straighten the crosswise ends by pulling a thread and cutting along the pulled thread. Be sure to read the label for fiber content and cleaning or washing instructions.

HOW TO MAKE CURTAINS AND DRAPERIES

Curtains and Cafe Curtains

Curtains may hang straight or be tied back, and are made with a casing at the top which fits through the curtain rod. Curtains are usually made of light- to medium-weight fabrics and hang close to the window. Café curtains are made in tiers, using two or more layers to cover the window, and are attached to the rod with a casing, rings, or hooks.

Draperies

Draperies are more formal in effect and can be made of medium- to heavyweight fabrics. Hooks are used to attach the draperies to the rod.

Curtain Rods and Other Hardware

If your windows do not already have curtain rods installed, or if you want to change the type of rods, seek professional help for selecting and installing the new rods. Any expense involved will be worth it, as it will prevent your making expensive mistakes. Remember, you are already saving money by making the curtains or draperies yourself.

Always have the curtain rods installed before you take any measurements for the curtains.

The length of the curtains or draperies depends on the effect you want to create. They can reach just to the windowsill, to cover the apron of the window, or they can be one inch short of the floor. In order to measure the size of the window, you will need a steel tape measure or a wooden folding ruler.

How to Measure the Window

Measure from the curtain rod to the windowsill, or apron, or one inch from the floor, depending on how long you want the curtain to be.

Measure the width of the window from the edges of the window frame, and add the length of the two curved sides of the curtain rod to the wall.

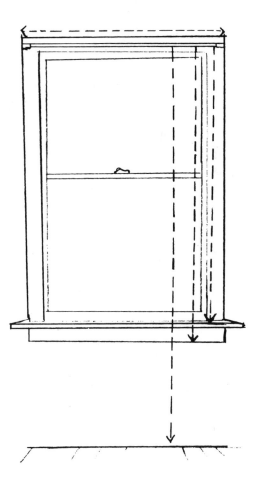

MAKING CURTAINS WITH A CASING AND HEADING

Determining the Amount of Fabric

Each window will need two panels of fabric.

To the length measurement of the window, add 4½ inches for the casing and heading, and add 6 inches for the double hems at the bottom. Add 8 inches to allow for straightening the crosswise edges. Your curtains will have a fullness double or triple the width of the window, depending on the weight of the fabric. Lightweight fabrics should be tripled; medium- and heavyweight fabrics should be double the width of the window. Divide this measurement in half for the width of each panel, and add four inches to each panel for the side hems. If the fabric is not wide enough, buy two extra panel lengths and sew them lengthwise in a French seam halfway between each panel. This will not work with printed fabrics with a repeat.

Prints with a Pattern Repeat

If you are using a printed fabric with a definite repeat, you will need extra fabric. Figure the length of each panel in inches. Divide this figure by the length of each repeat (this is usually given on the samples of furnishing fabrics, or you can determine it by measuring one full repeat along the lengthwise grain). If you get a number that is a fraction, figure in a full additional repeat. Once you have this measurement, be sure to add the extra fabric for the casing, heading, and hems.

Cut each panel carefully so that the repeat will fall in the same place on both panels of the finished curtains.

Cutting the Fabric into Panels

Before you start to cut the fabric, be sure that it is grain-perfect. Straighten the crosswise edge by pulling a thread and cutting along the pulled thread (cut, don't tear). Lay the fabric out on a large flat surface and measure the length you have determined. Cut the next panel by pulling another crosswise thread and cutting. Repeat for as many panels as you need, and be sure that all the panels are the same length.

Making the Curtains

Spread the curtain panels over the wide end of the ironing board, wrong-side up to make turning the hems easier. Work on the side hems first. Fold in 1 inch along the length of the panel and press. Fold in another inch and press again. Pin the folded edge to the panel and stitch as close to the edge of the fold as possible, using a medium-length stitch (10 to 12 stitches to the inch). Repeat for the other side of the panel and for the other panels.

At the top of the curtain, turn under ¼ inch and press. Turn the top of the curtain in a 2-inch hem and press. Pin in place. Stitch along the folded edge, sewing as close to the edge as possible. To form the casing and the heading, measure 1 inch from the folded top and mark with tailor's chalk along the width of the panel. Stitch along the chalk marks.

To make the bottom hem, turn under 3 inches and press lightly. Turn in another 3 inches and pin into place. Slide the curtain rod through the casing of both panels, and hang them to make sure that they are the same length. If not, make an adjustment in the pinned hems so that they are even, and repin. Remove the panels from the curtain rod and press the bottom hems. Stitch along the folded edge.

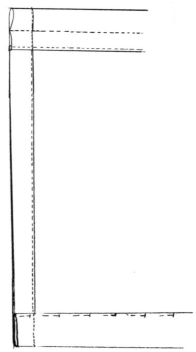

Making Curtains with a Casing

For a very informal curtain, cut the panel the same length as before, but allow only 2¼ inches at the top for the casing. Prepare the side hems as before. Turn in ¼ inch at the top and press. Fold the top hem in 1 inch and stitch as close to the edge of the fold as possible. Press the casing and prepare the bottom hem as directed. Slip the curtain rod through the panels and hem as before.

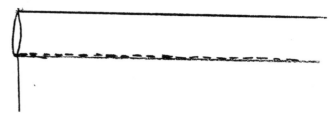

CAFE CURTAINS

Café curtains are made in tiers, usually with two tiers for each window, but they can be made with more than one tier or with only one. They are hung on straight rods which are held in place by wall brackets. The number of tiers and the length of each tier depends on the effect you want to create, and the curtain rods must be placed accordingly. Café curtains are usually made of casual and informal fabrics. For a very casual effect, the curtains can be made of felt, in which case estimate the amount of fabric needed without any allowance for hems, as felt does not have to be hemmed.

Simple Two-Paneled Cafe Curtains with Clip-on Rings

For fabrics other than felt, figure the amount needed in the following way. (In order to hang café curtains, you will need clip-on or pleater pins with rings that are attached to the top of each tier.) To determine the length, measure from the bottom of the ring (when slipped over the rod) to where you want the tier to end. To this, add 5 inches for the top and bottom hems. To determine the width, measure the curtain rod between the brackets. Double this measurement so that the curtain will be full, and add 5 inches to each panel for the side hems.

Making the Side Hems

Turn under ½ inch on the side of the panel and press. Turn in a 2-inch hem and stitch in place, sewing as close to the edge of the fold as possible. Repeat for the other side of the panel and for any other panels.

Making the Top and Bottom Hems

Turn under ½ inch and press. Turn in a 2-inch hem and stitch on the edge of the fold. Be sure that all the panels are the same length. If you are using a sheer or delicate fabric, the hems may be slip-stitched in place by hand so that the stitches are almost invisible from the right side.

Press the panels thoroughly and put the clip-on rings on the top hem, spacing them at regular intervals. Use the same number of clips for each panel. To wash or clean the curtains, remove the clips.

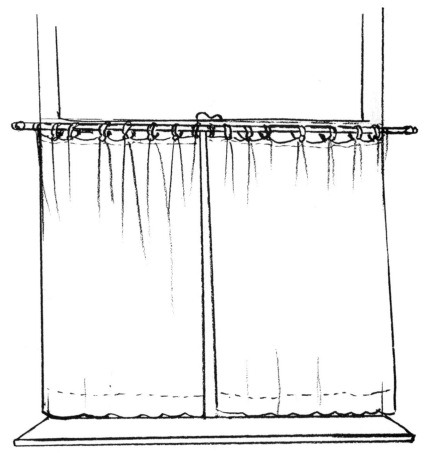

Cafe Curtains Made with a Pleater Tape

A more formal effect can be achieved by pleating the top of the curtain. This is most easily done by using pleater tape, which is sewn to the top of the curtain. The pleats are formed by using special pleater hooks, which are inserted into the pockets of the tape. Pleater tape with the scallops already in the tape are available. Special pleater hooks with rings attached to them are used for café curtains.

Determine the amount of fabric needed, as you would for regular café curtains, but don't allow for the 2-inch hem at the top—simply allow an extra ½ inch.

Place and stitch the tape before you make the side or bottom hems. With the right side of the top of the curtain panel facing you and the wrong side of the tape facing you, center the tape as follows. Place the tape so that a scallop or pleat falls in the center of the panel. Mark the side hemlines and cut the tape off, leaving ¾ inch of tape at each end. Make sure that you have a single pocket in the pleater tape at each end, and then ¾ inch after that. It may be necessary to make the side hems wider or narrower to achieve this. Cut off the extra tape on each side.

Stitch through the tape and the curtain, following the straight and scalloped guide lines on the tape. Do not stitch down the sides of the tape. Cut the curtain away from the scallops, leaving a ¼-inch allowance. Clip the seam allowance within the scallops. Turn the tape to the inside and press with the outer edge of the curtain extending above the tape. Turn in the side hems of the curtain and sew into place. Turn under ¼ inch of the tape at the sides and slip-stitch to the side hems. Stitch through the bottom of the tape, following the guide line and being careful not to sew the tape pockets closed. Using the pleater pins with rings, slip them into the pockets of the tape, as shown. Use a single end ring at each side of the panel. This will form the pleats. Make the bottom hems, and be sure that each panel is the same length. Remove the pleater pins for washing or cleaning.

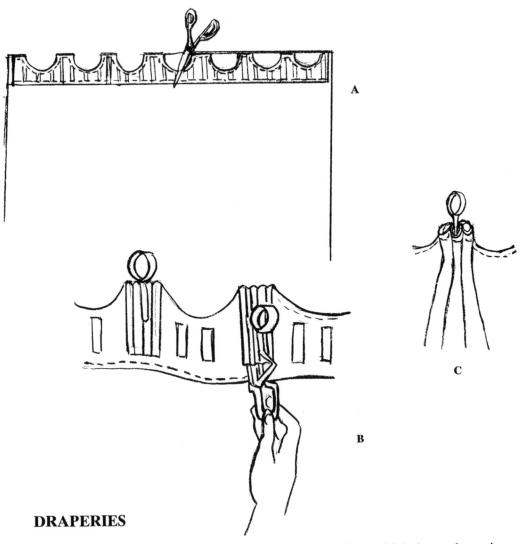

A

B

C

DRAPERIES

Draperies can be made with or without a lining, which is used to give them more body and to make them wear longer. All draperies are made with a pleated heading, and the easiest way to make this heading is with the use of pleater tape. Draperies can be window apron length or fall just short of the floor (about one inch).

The instructions given here are for lined draperies, but if you want to make them unlined, simply disregard the instructions for the lining, and turn and sew the side and bottom hems as you would for curtains.

To determine the amount of fabric needed, measure the window as you would for curtains, and add the following allowances. To the length, add 3¼ inches at the bottom for a 3-inch, double hem, making 9¼ inches in all. The width required depends on whether the draperies will hang at the side of the window or will be drawn closed on a traverse rod to cover the window. If they are to be drawn closed, allow an extra 3 inches on each panel for the overlap. Add 4 inches for the side hems. Add these allowances to the width of the window, plus the curved corners of the rod, and double the measurement to obtain the necessary fullness.

If your fabric has a repeat design in the print, see page 368 for information about how to determine the length you need.

For the lining fabric, use cotton sateen in white or a neutral color, and piece it lengthwise if it is necessary to obtain the width. The length should be 3½ inches shorter than the length of the draperies, and subtract 6 inches from the width you have figured for the draperies.

Cut the drapery panels as you would for curtains, see page 368. Clip the selvages to prevent them from puckering. If you want to add weights to bottom of the draperies to make them hang straight (these are usually used on heavyweight fabrics), sew them to the wrong side of the drapery, 6 inches from the bottom and 2 inches from the side.

Turn up the bottom hem 3 inches and press; turn up another 3 inches and press again. Stitch as close to the fold as possible. Turn up 2 inches of the bottom of the lining and press; turn up another 2 inches, press and stitch.

Place the lining on the drapery panel, right sides of the fabric facing, and pin together along the top and sides of the panel. The drapery will form folds, as it is wider than the lining. Stitch across the top and down the sides in ½-inch seam. Turn the panel right-side out. You will not have the drapery extending 1½ inches beyond the lining on each side. Miter the bottom corner of the hem and slip-stitch the lining to the drapery. In the middle of the panel, sew the lining to the drapery with a 2½-inch long thread bar tack, so that the lining does not twist away from the drapery.

Turn under the top of the drapery and the lining ¾ inch and press. Center the pleater tape over the drapery so that there is ½ inch of tape to turn under at each side, and so that the next pocket in the tape is the same distance from the side of the panel at each end. Stitch along the top of the pleater tape along the guide line, leaving ¼ inch of the drapery showing above the tape. Stitch along the bottom of the pleater tape, being careful not to sew the pockets shut. Turn under the sides of the tape and slip-stitch in place.

Place an end pin in the last pocket at each side of the panel. Then place the pleater pins at regular intervals through the pocket of the tape, as shown. Remove the pleater pins and weights for washing or cleaning.

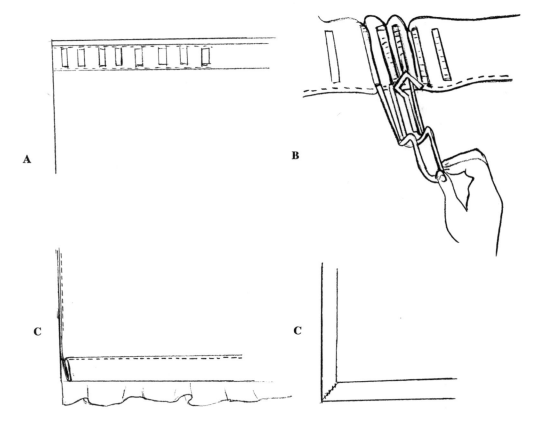

TIEBACKS

Tie backs are used to hold curtains and draperies to the side of a window to hold them open permanently. You can make tiebacks out of the same fabric as the curtain, or they can be made out of fancy braid or other trimming. Look at home furnishings magazines and in stores for ideas to use for tiebacks. The trimming department of the furnishings section of your favorite store will furnish you with a wealth of different ideas.

To make a simple fabric tieback, place your tape measure around the curtain panel and gather it in your hand to determine the length needed. Cut a strip of fabric on the crosswise grain to the width needed, plus ½ inch all around for the seam allowances. Fold the fabric in half lengthwise and pin along the edges and at the corners. Stitch, leaving a 4-inch opening on one side for turning. Trim the seam allowance at the corners and turn the strip right-side out. Slip-stitch the opening closed. Slip the tieback over the curtain panel halfway down. Attach the tieback to the wall with hooks made for the purpose.

SLIPCOVERS

Slipcovers, which are used on chairs and sofas, are a marvelous way to give a new look to old furniture. They are relatively easy to make, but they should not be attempted as a first sewing project. You should have a good knowledge of handling, cutting, and sewing different kinds of fabric before you start to make a slipcover. For your first slipcover, start with a simple chair and use a fabric that is not too expensive. Choose a tightly woven medium-weight fabric in a solid color or with a small, allover print that does not require matching.

Because every chair or sofa differs slightly in size, there are no patterns for slipcovers. Therefore, you will have to make your own by cutting the pieces for the slipcover directly on the chair. For this, you will need a few things in addition to the fabric before you start. You should have a large number of pins, tailor's chalk, a tape measure, and unbleached muslin to make the pattern.

You will also need a slipcover zipper or a nylon fastener tape, a zipper for the cushion, some cable cord to make your own cording (or as it is sometimes called, welting), or you can buy ready-made cording in a solid color to contrast with the color of your fabric.

If the chair already has a slipcover, you can make the first pattern by cutting the old slipcover apart at the seams. Before you start, label each piece of the slipcover with tailor's chalk (chair back, left arm, cushion cover, and so forth). Press the pieces of the old slipcover. Cut out the muslin pieces by pinning the old slipcover pieces to the muslin, being sure to keep the grain lines straight.

If you don't have an old slipcover to use, you will have to make the pattern out of the muslin by pinning it on the chair. Measure the chair, as shown, to determine how much fabric you will need. Write down each measurement and add up the lengthwise measurements, adding 1 inch all around each piece for the seam allowances in order to obtain the length and width of the fabric you will need. For the flounce, allow an extra 10½ inches in length and two times the circumference of the bottom of the chair. If you want to make the cording out of the same fabric, buy an extra yard.

Cut the pieces of the muslin to correspond to the measurements you have taken, and lay the pieces over the chair in this order:

1. Outside back—make the outside back in two pieces with a seam down the center. The zipper or nylon fastener tape will be inserted here.
2. Inside back
3. Seat (with the cushion removed)
4. Front piece
5. Outside arm
6. Inside arm
7. Top of the arm
8. Top and bottom of the cushion
9. Boxing width of the cushion—Cut the boxing width of the cushion in two pieces, with the back piece cut in two sections, and with a seam down the center so that you can insert the zipper. See next page.

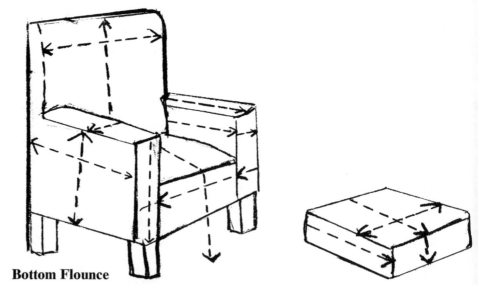

Bottom Flounce

Pin the muslin in the given order, pinning each piece to the other in a 1-inch seam allowance. So not stretch or force the fabric into place. Once the entire chair has been pinned, check it carefully to see that you have not pulled the fabric off-grain, or that there are no bubbles anywhere. Use as many pins as necessary.

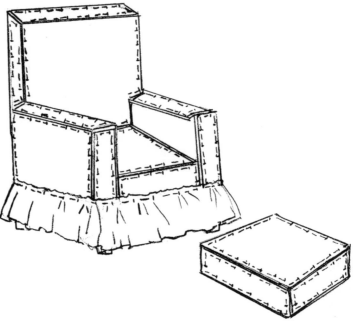

Mark the placement for the flounce 9 inches from the floor all around the bottom of the chair. This flounce will be gathered and attached in a 1-inch seam allowance, and have a 1½-inch hem. Cut the flounce on the crosswise grain double the width of the circumference around the placement mark. Sew gathering stitches 1 inch from the top of the flounce, and gather to fit the chair. Pin the flounce to the chair and adjust the gathers, placing the seams in the flounce at the sides or back of the chair so that they are not conspicuous. Pin the opening of the flounce even with the back seam of the chair.

Now that you have placed the pins on the seam lines of the pieces, mark them on the muslin with tailor's chalk. Label each piece with tailor's chalk. Cut and pin the pieces of the muslin to cover the cushion, making a seam in the back section of the boxing for the zipper.

Once you have marked the muslin pieces, be sure that all the seam allowances are an even 1 inch and then unpin the muslin. Use the muslin pieces to cut out the fabric by laying them marked-side up on the right side of the fabric, being sure to keep the grain lines straight. Pin the muslin to the fabric and cut out the fabric. Mark the seam lines on the fabric with tailor's chalk.

You will now have to repin the fabric to the chair to be sure that difference in weight between the muslin and the fabric doesn't cause it to fit differently. Pin the fabric to the chair as you did for the muslin, with the right side of the fabric facing you, and pin along the marked seam lines. Make sure that the cover fits the chair correctly and make any minor adjustments at this time. Mark any changes with tailor's chalk.

Cording

Cording is used in the seams of most slipcovers not only for the finished effect, which is very attractive, but to make the seams stronger. With the slip-cover pinned to the chair, measure the length of the seams to determine how much cording you will need. You can buy ready-made cording, or you can make your own.

To make the cording, purchase the amount of cable cord necessary in the width you prefer. Cut bias strips wide enough to cover the cord, plus 2 inches. Piece the strips where necessary. Replace the pressure foot of your machine with the adjustable zipper foot. Adjust the zipper foot to the left of the needle. With the wrong side of the bias strip facing the cord, place it over the cord and be sure that the cord is in the center of the strip. Stitch as close as possible to the cord. To sew the corded seams, place the cord on the edge of the seam, with the corded edge facing away from the seam allowance. Pin and baste into place. Stitch with the zipper foot as close to the cord as possible. Place the piece of fabric with the cord stitched to it face down on the corresponding piece, with the right sides of the fabric facing. Stitch, still using the zipper foot on top of the previous row of stitching.

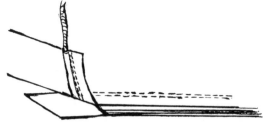

Constructing the Slipcover

Insert the zipper into the back width section of the cushion, using a center slot-seam method. (For instructions, see page 185.) Sew the back section of the cushion boxing to the front in a 1-inch seam allowance. Sew the top and bottom sections of the cushion to the boxing with a welting in the seams. Apply the welting to all the other seams, except at the bottom where the flounce will be attached, and sew the seams of the slipcover in a 1-inch seam allowance, pivoting at the corners. Join the pieces in this order:

1. Sew the inside arm to the top of the arm.

2. Sew the outside of the arm to the top; then sew the front of the arm to that.

3. Sew the front seat section to the back section; sew the top and sides of the back of the chair to that.

4. Sew the back center seam of the back section above the opening for the zipper or nylon fastener tape.

5. Hem the bottom of the flounce and sew the gathering stitches at the top.

6. Slip the entire slipcover over the chair and pin the flounce to the bottom of the chair, with the right sides of the fabric facing (the hem of the flounce will be at the top). Adjust the gathers and have the opening of the flounce corresponding to the open back seam. Smooth the flounce toward the floor, and be sure that it is the right length. If it is too long, pin it again with a deeper seam allowance.

7. Take the slipcover off the chair and sew the flounce to it without a welting in the seam.

8. Insert the zipper in the back seam allowance, using a slot-seam method, or use nylon fastener tape. (See page 265 for instructions on how to insert a nylon fastener tape.) Turn the slipcover inside out, and if the fabric ravels easily, overcast the seam allowances. Do not trim the seam allowances, but clip them where necessary to make the seams lie flat.

Skirts with different kinds of pleats can be used to finish the bottom of slipcovers. The two most usual kinds are box pleats and knife pleats. Decide how wide you want the pleat to be, and mark off the muslin first so that you can see the finished effect before you cut the fabric. The width and number of pleats will determine how much fabric you will need for the skirt.

For both box pleats and knife pleats, divide the fabric evenly, for example, make each pleat 3 inches deep. The space between the pleats will also be 3 inches. Form the pleats by folding to the marks, as shown, baste into place at the top, and sew the skirt to the bottom of the slipcover as for the gathered flounce.

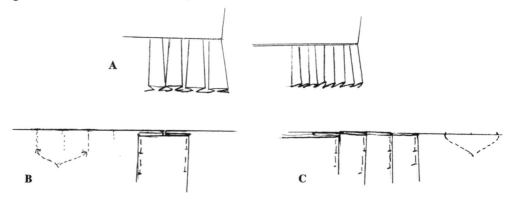

The method used here for covering a simple chair can be adapted to cover different styles of chairs and sofas, just be sure that you make a muslin pattern first and that you pin and cut evenly and carefully.

DECORATIVE CUSHIONS AND PILLOWS

Simple Square and Rectangular Pillows with a Lining Pillow

Making pillows is the simplest way of brightening up a room quickly with very little work. Except for sheer fabrics, pillows can be made out of any fabric as long as it is tightly woven. Use a loose stuffing, such as cut-up pieces of foam rubber or polyester foam, which you can buy in the five-and-ten.

Decide on the size and shape of the pillow you want, and buy twice the amount of fabric needed, adding a ¾-inch seam allowance around the edges of the two pieces.

Be sure that the fabric is grain-perfect. Cut the squares or rectangles by pulling a crosswise thread for the crosswise cutting lines, and cut along the straight grain for the lengthwise cutting lines. Center the printed motif if there is one. Make an inside lining pillow out of a lighter weight fabric, cutting it the same shape as the outside pillow, but 1 inch smaller all around.

Place the sections of the lining together and sew around the edges in a ¾-inch seam allowance, leaving 4 or 5 inches on one side open for turning. Turn the lining pillow right-side out and stuff it with the foam. Slip-stitch the opening closed.

Buy a zipper the length of one side of the pillow, minus 1 inch on each side. Sew and baste the side of the pillow you want to insert the zipper in; then insert the zipper, using a centered, or slot-seam method. Sew around the rest of the pillow in a ¾-inch seam allowance, backtracking over the previous stitching. Open the zipper and turn the pillow right-side out, and push the points out from the inside. Press the edges of the pillow lightly. Insert the lining pillow and close the zipper. This way the lining pillow can be removed for washing or cleaning. The outer pillow can also be made with a corded seam; follow the instructions on page 379 for making corded seams.

Simple Square and Rectangular Pillows without a Lining Pillow

Simple pillows can be made without an inner lining pillow and a zipper. Simply sew the squares together, with right sides of the fabric facing, and with or without a corded seam or fringe trim. Leave an opening for turning and stuffing. Turn the pillow right-side out, stuff it, and slip-stitch the opening closed.

A   B

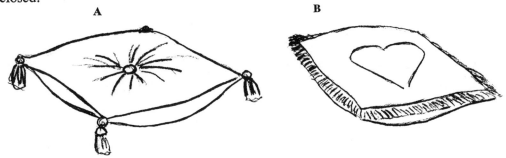

Another decorative treatment for a simple square pillow is to make two large covered buttons in a self- or contrasting fabric, and sew them to the center of the pillow after it has been turned and before it is stuffed. If you like, sew purchased tassels to the corners of the pillow.

Square Pillow with a Topstitched Trim

Cut and sew the pillow as for a simple square pillow, and leave a 5-inch opening for turning and stuffing. Turn the pillow right-side out and press the edges. Topstitch 1 inch in from the edge of the pillow, stopping the stitching the same length as the opening in the edge. Stuff the pillow so that it is nice and plump, and finish the topstitching where you have broken it off. Slip-stitch the opening closed.

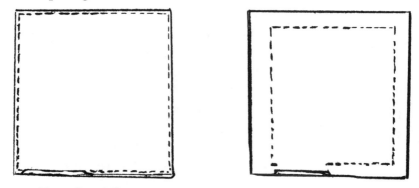

Round and Square Boxed Pillows

These pillows are made on a preshaped foam form. Buy the form first in the shape and size you want. To determine how much fabric you will need, measure the length and width of the top and bottom of the form, and also the depth and length of the boxing. The pillow can be made with corded seams or not, as you like. If you want to make a matching cording, buy extra fabric for the bias strips.

For a simple pillow without a zipper, pin the fabric on the form, leaving a ¾-inch seam allowance. Cut the fabric and pin it on the form, being careful to keep the grain line straight. Center the printed design if there is one. Mark the seam lines on the fabric with tailor's chalk and unpin the pieces. Sew the seams, leaving an opening in one seam wide enough to accommodate the form. Turn the pillow right-side out and slip the form into the pillow. Slip-stitch the opening closed.

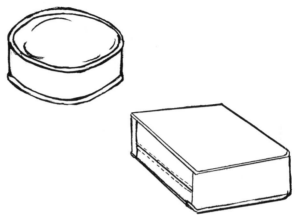

If you want to make the pillow with a zipper so that the form can be easily removed for cleaning, cut the boxing in two pieces. Make a seam allowance in the center of one section of the boxing. Insert the zipper into the boxing seam allowance, using a slot-seam application, and leave 1 inch on each side of the zipper free. Sew the other section of the boxing to the section with the zipper; then sew the rest of the pillow. To insert the form, simply open the zipper.

Bolsters

Bolsters can be covered in two ways. First buy the foam bolster form and measure it to determine how much fabric you will need.

First Method: Cut the fabric long enough to cover the entire form allowing for a ¾-inch seam allowance and enough fabric at each end to cover the end of the bolster. Turn in ¼ inch at each end of the fabric and press. Sew the fabric along the long seam, turn it right-side out, and insert the form. Make a row of gathering stitches by hand along the fold at the end of the fabric, and gather until the fabric covers the end of the bolster. Tie the gathering thread in a knot. Cover the gathers with a large covered button.

Second Method: Cut one long strip to cover the length of the bolster, plus ¾-inch seam allowances at each end. Cut two circles of fabric to cover the ends of the bolster, with a ¾-inch seam allowance around the entire circle. Insert a zipper into the long seam, using the slot-seam method, leaving a few inches of fabric free at each end before and after the zipper. Sew the circles of fabric to the long piece, using a corded seam if you wish. Clip the seam allowances of the circles. Open the zipper and slip the bolster form into the cover.

A   B

These basic pillow forms can be trimmed in a large variety of ways. Check places that sell furnishing fabrics and dress trimmings to see what is available in braids, ribbons, and decorative buttons.

BEDSPREADS

Bedspreads are easy to make and add a fresh look to the entire room. If you have a standard-size twin or full bed, there are patterns that you can use to make several different styles of spreads. Check the back section of the pattern catalogue to find these patterns. However, if your bed is not a standard size, or if you want to work on your own, you can cut the spread to fit the bed by taking the measurements of the bed accurately, and adding the necessary seam and hem allowances.

Simple throws or tailored spreads can be made of many different fabrics, including fairly heavy ones, such as sailcloth, duck, corduroy, velvet, velveteen, quilted cottons, heavy- and medium-weight cottons, denim, and synthetics and synthetic blends.

Spreads made with ruffled skirts can be made of lighter weight fabrics, such as chintz, gingham, broadcloth, poplin, and percale. They can also be made of sheers, such as dotted Swiss, synthetic sheers, and eyelet cottons if they are lined. To add a lining to any of the following instructions, cut the lining fabric to the same measurements as the bedspread, and treat it like an underlining.

Measuring the Bed

Make the bed up with the usual number of sheets, blankets, and pillows, as these will add to the size of the bed. The measurements shown here are for beds with a headboard, but if your bed has a footboard, do not allow for the bottom overhang, but allow for enough fabric to tuck in. If your bed does not have a headboard, add an overhang at the top. Measure the length of the bed down the center of the bed from the headboard. Measure the width across the top of the bed. Measure the depth of the mattress and the top of the box spring to within one inch of the floor. Add these two measurements to obtain the length from the top of the bed to the floor. The bottom of the spread should be approximately one inch from the floor.

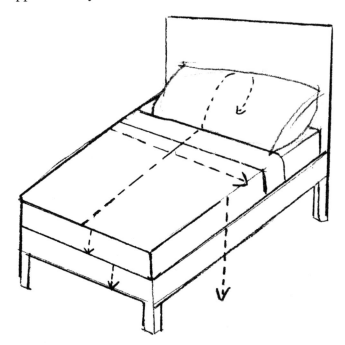

Throw Spread

This is the simplest spread you can make, but you can change the look of it by adding cording, fringe, or braids to the seams and around the edges of the spread.

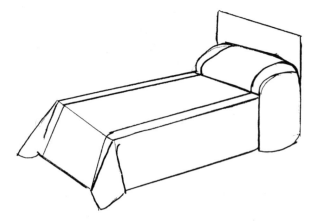

To make the throw, you will need three panels long enough to cover the bed from the headboard to the bottom of the overhang, adding 30 inches for the pillow covering and the tuck-in allowance, and 2 inches for the hems. Figure the width by adding the top width to the side overhangs, plus ½ inch for the seam allowances and 2 inches for the hems on the side panels. Add the measurements to determine how much fabric you need.

Cut the center panel, place it on the bed, and pin the two side panels to it. Sew the seams in a ½-inch seam allowance, adding cording in the seams if you wish. Turn under ¼ inch around the bottom of the spread and press. Turn in a 1¾-inch hem. Stitch the hem in place along the folded edge.

Tailored Spread

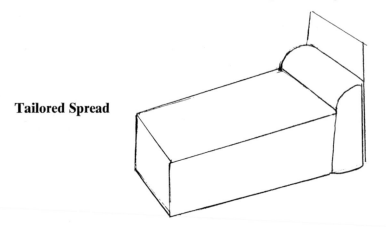

Tailored Spread

Figure the amount of fabric needed as for the throw spread, adding 11 inches to the length of each side panel for the under panel at the front overhang. Lay the center panel on the bed and pin so that the seams fall directly on the edge of the bed. Stitch the seam in a ½-inch seam allowance, pivoting the stitching at the bottom corner of the bed. Turn under the seam allowance on the center panel from the edge of the bed and stitch into place. Turn in ¼ inch around the entire edge of the spread and press. Turn up a 1¾-inch hem and stitch along the fold.

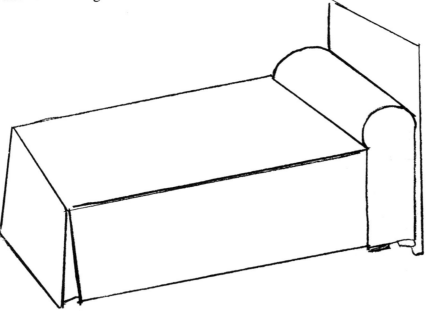

Fitted Spread with Box-Pleated Corners

Measure the top of the bed, and add 30 inches for the pillow cover and the tuck-in allowance, and for the seam allowances (½ inch) at the sides and bottom. The side panels are also measured on the lengthwise grain. To the length of the bed and pillow cover and tuck-in allowance, ½ inch for the seam allowance and 3 inches for the pleat. The width of the side panels should be the measurement from the top of the bed to within one inch of the floor, adding ½ inch for the top seam allowance and 2 inches for the bottom hem. The front overhang panel is measured on the crosswise grain. To the measurement of the foot of the bed, add 1 inch for seam allowances and 9 inches for the pleats. For the width, add ½ inch for the seam allowance and 2 inches for the hem.

Place the center section over the bed and cut to size if necessary, leaving a ½-inch seam allowance around the sides and bottom. Pin the side sections to the center panel, and at the corner of the bed, fold for the first section of the box pleat. Pin the front overhang panel to the center panel and pin the front overhang to the side panels. Form the rest of the pleat (the seam will be hidden inside the pleat). Keeping the front overhang and the side panels pinned, remove the overhang from the center panel. Sew the seams in the side panels and the front overhang. Working on the ironing board, press the box pleats. Sew the side panels and the front overhang to the center panel, using a corded seam if desired. Hem the bottom by turning under ¼ inch and pressing. Turn up a 1¾-inch hem and stitch along the folded edge.

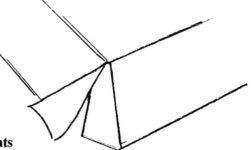

Fitted Spread with Mock Pleats

Measure as for a fitted spread with box pleats, but instead of adding an allowance for the pleats, add 4 inches to the length of the side panels and the front overhang. Cut two pieces for the back of the mock pleats; they should be 7 inches wide and as wide as the side and front overhang sections.

Pin the side and front overhang panels to the center panel, and fold back 2 inches on the side and front overhang at the corners of the bed. Prepare the backing pieces by making a ½-inch side hem on each side, and hem by first making a ¼-inch fold and then making a 1¾-inch hem. Remove the side and front overhang from the center panel. Sew the backing strips to the center panel at the corners, having an equal amount of fabric on each side of the corner. Press the turned-back folds on the front overhang and side panels, and sew them to the center panel, having the openings meet at the corners. Hem the side and front overhangs as for the backing pieces, and make sure that they are the same length.

Fitted Spread with Ruffle

Measure as for a fitted spread, but make the side and front overhangs only as wide as the depth of the mattress, and add ½-inch seam allowances around the bottom. The width of the ruffle should be the measurement from the bottom of the mattress to within one inch of the floor, plus ½ inch for seam allowances and 2 inches for the hems. To have the right amount of fullness, the ruffle should be twice the measurement around the bottom of the fitted top (piece where necessary).

Make the top of the fitted spread by pinning the side and front sections to the center section, and sew with a ½-inch seam allowance. Hem the bottom of the ruffle by turning under ¼ inch and press. Turn up in a 1¾-inch hem and stitch. Gather the ruffle so that it fits the top of the fitted spread, and sew in a ½-inch seam allowance.

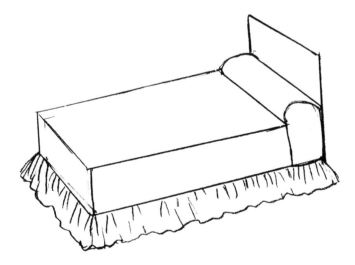

The bottom skirt of the fitted spread can also be made with knife pleats or box pleats, see the section called Slipcovers, pages 381-382, to determine the amount of fabric needed for forming the pleats.

Coverlets

A coverlet is a shortened, draped spread. Make it following the instructions given for the draped spread, but make the side overhang sections just long enough to cover the top of the box spring. A coverlet is usually used with a separate dust ruffle and can be made from a different fabric than the dust ruffle, for example, a quilted coverlet with a cotton dust ruffle.

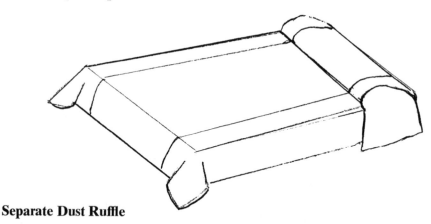

Separate Dust Ruffle

The dust ruffle is sewn to a muslin base, which is placed over the box spring under the mattress. To obtain the measurement for the muslin base,

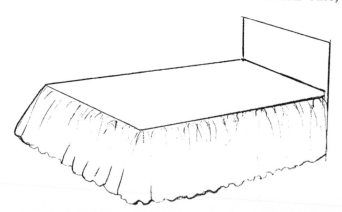

remove the mattress from the bed, and measure the width and length of the box spring. Cut the muslin to fit, piecing if necessary, and allow ½ inch all around for the seam allowances.

Measure and cut the ruffle, following the instructions given for attaching a ruffle to a fitted spread. Make the ruffle in the same manner.

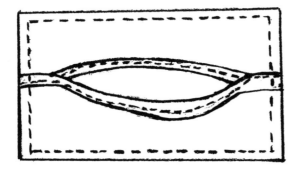

Pillow Shams

Measure the length and width of the pillow over the center of the pillow. Cut the top of the sham to those measurements, and add 1 inch all around. Cut the bottom of the sham in two sections, adding 2 inches to the width of each section and 1 inch to the length.

Hem the two sections of the underside by turning under ¼ inch and pressing. Turn in a ¾-inch hem and stitch into place. Place the two back sections over the front, with one of the back sections over the other, and with the right sides of the fabric facing. Pin into place and stitch around the sham in a 1-inch seam. Turn the sham right-side out. The back may be left open, or you can sew a few snaps to the opening.

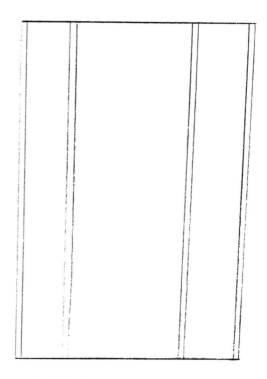

Blanket Covers

A blanket cover is used to cover the blankets when the bedspread is removed. Make up the bed with the blankets and the sheet turned back. Measure the length of the bed from the top of the turned-back sheet to the bottom of the mattress. Cut the cover in three panels, the measurement length, plus 5 inches for a tuck-in allowance if desired, and 2 inches for the hem. Determine where the side seams will fall (at each side of the top of the mattress), and cut the center panel to the appropriate width, plus 1 inch for seam allowances. Cut the side panels the same length and as wide as needed, measuring from the seam to the bottom edge of the mattress, plus 5 inches for a tuck-in and 2 inches for the hem. If you are using a sheer fabric, sew the seams in a French seam. If you are using a nonsheer, such as challis, make an ordinary seam. Hem the entire cover by turning in ¼ inch and pressing, and then turn in a ¾-inch hem and stitch. The seams may be covered with lace or ribbon, and the hem may be bound in a ribbon if desired.

INDEX

INDEX